Dancing after the Whirlwind

L. J. Tessier

Dancing after the Whirlwind

Feminist Reflections on Sex, Denial, and Spiritual Transformation

Beacon Press   Boston

Beacon Press 25 Beacon Street, Boston, Massachusetts 02108-2892

Beacon Press books are published under the auspices of
the Unitarian Universalist Association of Congregations.

Printed in the United States of America

Grateful acknowledgment is made to the following for permission to reprint: The excerpts from *Positive Women: Voices of Women Living with AIDS*, copyright 1992 by Second Story Press, Toronto, Canada, are reprinted by permission of the publisher; the poem by Tara McKibben from *Second Opinion* 13:3, copyright 1992 by The Park Ridge Center for the Study of Health, Faith, and Ethics, is reprinted by permission of the author and publisher; excerpts from *Sappho: A New Translation*, copyright 1958 by the Regents of the University of California, are reprinted by permission of the publisher; excerpts from "Little Gidding" in *Four Quartets* by T. S. Eliot, copyright 1943 by T. S. Eliot and renewed 1971 by Esme Valerie Eliot, is reprinted by permission of Harcourt Brace & Co. and Faber & Faber.

03 02 01 00 99 98   8 7 6 5 4 3 2

Text design by Julia Sedykh
Composition by Wilsted & Taylor Publishing Services

Library of Congress Cataloging-in-Publication Data

Tessier, Linda J. (Linda Jo)
      Dancing after the whirlwind : feminist reflection on sex, denial, and spiritual
transformation / L. J. Tessier.
          p.   cm.
      ISBN 0-8070-6510-2 (cloth)
      ISBN 0-8070-6511-0 (paper)
      1. Feminist theory—United States.   2. Women—United States—Sexual behavior.
3. Women—Religious life—United States.   4. Sex—United States—Religious aspects.
5. Lesbians—United States—Identity.   6. Adult child sexual abuse victims—United States.
7. Women—Diseases—United States.   8. AIDS (Disease)—United States.   I. Title.
HQ1190.T434   1997
    305.42—DC21   97-21664

What has wisdom to do with wings?

You were wise before your flying,

waiting on a wire

for the lifting of the light.   ***For Tara McKibben*** _____

Contents

Acknowledgments

Before there are books, there are conversations. My work is deeply indebted to the creative flow of talk with good people over many years. In this light, I am especially grateful to my dear friends Patrick Scott, Bill Busa, Robert McIvery, Dianne Ross, Linda Shimandle, Kim Palmore, Sharon Took-Zozaya, Amy Welch, Jackie Melvin, Kaete Elliott, Linda Filippi, Myra Gutterman, and June Peters. For more than a decade I have enjoyed an energizing friendship with Ellie Beach, and her insights grace this book in ways that neither of us could quite define.

I thank Youngstown State University for providing me with critical sabbatical time and my dean, Barbara H. Brothers, and department chair, Thomas A. Shipka, for their continued support and encouragement throughout the process. Thanks also to my colleague Christopher Bache, for listening, responding, and believing.

Several student research assistants contributed to the process of writing this book. Janice Sanguinetti and Kim Barth were helpful in the early stages, and I am extremely grateful for the very able assistance and insights of S. Zoreh Kermani and Cynthia Booher.

In addition to their writings, many colleagues have shared their knowledge and friendship with me in professional contexts. In particular, thanks to Rita Brock, Grace Burford, Emily Culpepper, Carter Heyward, Mary Hunt, Joanne Carlson Brown, Mary Daly, Patricia Reis, Susan Dunfee Nelson, Elizabeth Castelli, Maura O'Neill, Nancy Howell, Ghazala Anwar, and Thandeka. A special thanks to Catherine Keller, whose vision and compassionate mentoring have both meant more to me than I can say.

Friends and colleagues in Youngstown have also been very supportive and lent their wisdom to the work. I especially thank Dharl Chintan, Brenda McIntyre, and Saralee Greenfield. Pat Gilmartin got me moving at last and taught me so many new ways of seeing things. Many ideas in this book have been influenced by her vision. Danna Bozick has been a constant source of strength and wisdom (and taken me out dancing when enough was enough). She also read and advised me on portions of the book. Special thanks also to the students who have expanded my vision and tested my ideas, especially those in the Sex and the Sacred seminar.

Although they are now all "gone to join the roses," I thank the wondrous beings who shared with me their love and struggle, insight and anguish, while living with HIV: Don Carufo, Charles Weiss, David Susky, Krista Blake, and especially Mark Mutchnik.

It is no accident that metaphors of giving birth are often connected with writing books. Very special thanks to the midwives—to Christine Downing for midwifing this book and to Carol Fitzpatrick (because one cannot expect to write about transformation without undergoing it) for midwifing a new me.

I have been very fortunate to share this process with an editor, Susan Worst, who has contributed extraordinary skill, insight, and caring attention. Linda Howe also helped to sharpen my prose and clarify my thoughts.

I would also like to thank my parents, Rene Bird and Jesse N. Tessier and my brother, Jesse, for their unwavering faith, and especially my sister, Peggy, who has been with me in cyberspace almost daily through the process.

In acknowledgment credits of other works, I have so often read the words "without whose help I never could have ..." How inadequate these words feel now to thank my lover, Tara McKibben, who read every word and gave me so much helpful advice, and my heartson, David A. J. McKibben. Some writers stand on the shoulders of giants. I balance precariously on the fingertips of angels.

Dancing after the Whirlwind

_____

Introduction

This book is about sexual and spiritual identity and the effects of denial. Perhaps no one is entirely exempt from denial. Every culture rewards certain behaviors or characteristics and bans, punishes, or denies others. But I focus here upon a more specific question, one that has haunted me for more than a decade: What happens to a woman's spiritual identity when certain key aspects of her sexual identity—her desires, her memories, her ability to see herself and be seen as a sexual being—are routinely denied? After spending several years contemplating the devastation of denial, I began to consider another question, one that grows from my own need to move beyond pain and anger: What can we do to overcome denial and generate spiritual healing and renewal? These two questions provide the impetus for this work.

Since it is impossible to consider all forms of denial or all aspects of identity, I have chosen to focus more specifically upon the personal and cultural experiences of three groups of women: lesbians, women with histories of child sexual abuse, and women positive for HIV/AIDS. Many, if not most, cultures impose intense denial on the sexual identities of these women. I believe that this denial may have a profound effect on the development of their spiritual identity, and overcoming it may enhance the process of spiritual healing.

I chose these groups not because they are more oppressed, more denied, or more valuable than others. I focus on particular aspects of identity to illustrate, not to isolate. We are all in this together. Perhaps these illustrations can help us to struggle against cultural denial of identity wherever it exists—wherever racism, sexism, and other forms of oppression blind us to the particularities of human experience. If I fail in establishing a basis for communication among those who grieve for the losses generated by denial and struggle toward healing and thriving, then I will have accomplished very little.

Before we can fully comprehend the impact of these forms of denial on spiritual identity, we must explore more deeply the nature of the relationship between sexuality and spirituality. My own work on these questions began with metaphors—drum and dance, whirlwind and rainforest—and these provide the deep background for setting out the premises of the work in chapter 1. There also, I consider how denial separates sexuality from spirituality and the role erotic power plays in healing this dynamic. Chapter 2 then explores the interaction of sexuality and spirituality in a variety of religions and cultures. Chapter 3 takes up the consequences of denial in the lives of lesbians, women sexually abused as children, and HIV-positive women, while chapter 4 explores the process of healing and spiritual transformation. I conclude with some reflections on the heart of erotic power—a poetics of the wild. I have drawn on personal narratives, biographical accounts, research from the social sciences, and my own adventures.

As this work has developed, I have repeatedly encountered the complexities of relationality. Often, I have found that what seemed

Dancing after the Whirlwind

to be distinct categories in fact were not. Although lesbians, for example, do share experiences that differ from those of women with AIDS, there are so many connections among the experiences of women with denied identities that I could not discuss one community without the others always already being present. Likewise, I could not discuss spirituality as if it were separate from sexuality, and I could not discuss spiritual healing or renewal without repeatedly encountering spiritual crisis.

In fact, life just will not line up like language, words in a row like clothes on a clothesline. We do not first experience all the denial and chaos and crisis in our lives and then lower ourselves into the warm bath of spiritual healing, our suffering forever behind us. Even in the midst of the most chaotic storm of suffering and spiritual confusion, renewal and healing are already going on. Whether we learn to nurture it or to negate it, the spiral of new growth is already present, like the seed that opens in the earth even in the deep of the cold season, invisible but moving slowly toward the surface. Likewise, when we recognize our lives as healthy, integrated, and well ordered, worn out structures may already be in the process of coming apart.

I have therefore chosen to integrate my topics as much as possible. I hope that my points can still be made clearly, but where my alternatives have been to risk confusion or to force artificial distinctions, I have erred on the side of chaos.

Finally, I come to the question of voice, a matter about which I feel conflicted and confused. How shall I tell you what I have to say? How shall I dance through issues of inclusion and exclusion as I try to describe the process of denied identity suffered by communities of women without excluding or denying them all over again? Do I write about these women from the safe but distanced perspective of an observer, describing *them* while concealing my own vested interests? Do I write about *us*, assuming identities about which I know little, assuming solidarity of experience with women whose life experiences are very different from mine? What language is there for respectful relationality, for connection without presumption? I do not know it.

I am no longer comfortable wrapping the matter in a list of descriptive adjectives, a practice in which I have long engaged. I could provide a sentence saying that I am writing from the perspective of a (insert particular race, class, sexual orientation, spiritual persuasion, sex). This practice both clarifies and distances; it reveals my privilege and my interests, but it sets me apart in the process. It also assumes I have greater insights into the categories in which I include myself, and that may not always be true.

My employment, teaching in an urban state university in the Midwest, provides information about my class privilege and perspective. But so do the years I spent in downtown L.A., walking at night tightly gripping the "church key" can opener I kept in my pocket as a (probably useless) defensive weapon. So do all those times I had to decide between feeding myself and feeding my cat. For one thing, I know why someone who can't afford food will keep (and feed) a cat.

I have chosen to enter this puzzle by telling you about myself in the context of the narratives, theories, and perspectives I relate. I will attempt to include and reveal myself, my stories, my life, along with those of the other women in this book, letting you know about me as I would someone I meet and with whom I am developing a relationship. There are different voices in this work: me, them, and us. I cannot alter the postmodern awareness that there is no transparent communication. Since I do not wish for you to see through me (and could not do so even if I tried), I will struggle to reveal myself as I am.

When dealing with such slippery notions and difficult terms as sex, religion, spirituality, and identity, the definition dance is inevitable. We must begin with what we mean. A typical discussion would begin by acknowledging that these terms have collected many—and sometimes conflicting—definitions. Then the usual practice is to choose one, or to construct one's own, and proceed as if the matter were settled. This is unsettling.

I raise the problem of definition here because many of the significant terms I will use behave in problematic ways. Not only are their meanings multifaceted and amorphous, but their ambiguity is often critical to their meaning. The fact that the term *erotic*, for example, is used to refer to both creative and destructive power illustrates only part of the problem. It is also extremely important to note that erotic power can be creative and destructive *at the same time.*

This problem of definition is particularly complex when dealing with sexual or spiritual *identities* and their relationships. As the philosopher and theologian Joan Timmerman puts it, the ambiguity regarding sexuality and spirituality exists "not because there is no reality underlying these words, but because there is so much."[1]

Even if I *wish* to employ only careful, precise definitions—given the many dimensions of these concepts, I am not sure that I do—we cannot escape the fact that these terms are used in many different ways. And even if I create working definitions of some of these terms, and I will, my use of them will shift and change as I shift my focus. I do not consider this sloppy scholarship. I consider it honest theorizing—or at least, theorizing as honestly as I can.

I begin, then, with an exploration of the dynamics involved in *language* about sexual and spiritual identity. The philosopher of religion John Hick, following Wittgenstein, suggests that we apply the term *religion* to so many diverse examples because "each is similar in important respects to some others in the family, though not in all respects to any or in any respect to all."[2] Rather than share a set of required characteristics, religions are connected by a network of similarities like the resemblances and differences among the members of a natural family. This family-resemblance concept might also be applied to the term *sex.*

When teaching courses on ethics and religion, I have sometimes asked students in my classes to define "sex." Eventually, it becomes evident that we use this term in many, sometimes conflicting ways, and we know less about what it means than we thought. Is sex intimate, pleasureful, genital, dyadic? Does it require penetration, procreation, even touching?

In fact there are instances of sex that incorporate some or many defining characteristics, but perhaps no instance of sex incorporates them all. My use of this term acknowledges its multifaceted nature as a family relations concept. Sex may involve pleasureful genital contact; it may even connect us with the spiritual power of erotic union. And it may not.

This problem is further complicated when one seeks to define sexuality. The feminist philosopher Joyce Trebilcot effectively summarizes sexuality as "the whole range of erotic/sexual/gender phenomena which are aspects of one's actions, attitudes, thoughts, wishes, style, and so on."[3] Freud, of course, was even more expansive, including virtually all behavior and human experience as manifestations of libido.[4] While seeking a less broad and biologically based understanding than Freud, the ethicist James Nelson also takes the position that sexuality is a far more comprehensive term than sex and refers to "a very basic dimension of our personhood."[5] Definitions of sexuality may incorporate the whole range of human feelings and activities through which we express ourselves as embodied beings in relationship to ourselves and others.[6] As the theologian Andre Guindon observes, no relationship between living human beings is asexual.[7] My own approach incorporates this view of sexuality as a fundamental component of human life that deeply embodies the emotion and activity of human connection.

Like sexuality, spirituality and the spiritual require some clarification. First, I believe it necessary to distinguish between *spirituality* and *religion*, a term with which spirituality is often conflated. Spirituality must include the experience of those whose spiritual lives are conducted outside of, as well as within, particular religious organizations and structures. Far from being limited to the realm of religious institutions, spirituality is the experience of identity through connectedness, ranging from our most intimate relationships with other beings to our most expansive sense of cosmic unity. As the faculty that provides the capacity for this deep relatedness, spirituality contributes to the quest for a better society.[8]

Two illustrations may serve to illuminate this distinction between spirituality and religious belief or affiliation. Survey results published in *Out Look*,[9] a national gay and lesbian quarterly, indicate that a significant majority of gays and lesbians rate spirituality as very or somewhat important to them, while a much smaller percentage consider religion so.[10] Lacking a home in mainstream religious denominations, lesbians tend to focus on personal spirituality rather than religious affiliation, particularly that which affirms lesbian identity as a key value.

For survivors of abuse, on the other hand, spirituality is often an area of considerable ambivalence, and expanded definitions are needed to support expanded possibilities for recovery and renewal. Ellen Bass and Laura Davis, authors of a widely recognized self-help book for women survivors of child sexual abuse, define spirituality in terms of passion for life and deep feelings of connection or intimacy with other people or with nature.[11]

This distinction between spirituality and religion does not imply that the two are necessarily separate. For many, the principal context for spiritual experience, and the principal location for this deep sense of connectedness, is religious practice. Ignoring this relationship can lead to a view of spirituality and religion as unnecessarily conflicted. Although, as the lesbian example illustrates, religious structures can hinder the development of spiritual identity and growth, it is dangerous to assume this conflict where it may not exist.

I use *spirituality* to refer to our *most fundamental understanding of ourselves and our relationships and connections with others, including those with all living things, with other people, and with the cosmos* (whether or not that understanding includes a relationship with some transcendent power). Spirituality in this sense is deeply connected to identity. This definition moves us away from the disembodiment often associated with the term and emphasizes its role as part of our physical and emotional lives. It also highlights *relationality*, itself a complex term.

Discussion of relationality is now commonplace in feminist theory and incorporates a wide range of meanings. On the most personal level, relationality refers to all the relationships that we form as part of what it means to be human and that enable us to develop our self-understanding. At the metaphysical level, relationality can also refer to the interconnectedness of all things, a view of the world as an interactive web of connections in which every action or decision has far-ranging consequences. Thus, relationality also incorporates moral responsibility, mutuality, and care for others.

Considering the meanings of sexuality and spirituality leads us to the issue of their relationship. It is a central claim of this work that *there is a deep connection between sexuality and spirituality, and the renewal of this bond helps to repair the damage caused by denial.*

Although there is a strong tendency in patriarchal culture to separate sexuality from spirituality, many theorists included here have discussed the connection between these two very significant aspects of human life. My own position supports Timmerman's claim that "spiritual growth and sexuality are not only connected but causally connected, and ... one's understanding of the way they are related to each other determines one's experience."[12] However, while Timmerman interprets this relationship from a Christian perspective, I will consider their connection in terms of the broader understanding of spirituality I have set out above. Furthermore, I claim that the ways in which the surrounding culture understands and reflects the relationship between sexuality and spirituality deeply affect our lives.

The bond between sexuality and spirituality is expressed through the power of the *erotic*. In the following chapter, I will discuss the characteristics of this power, including its associations with creation and destruction, with uniting or binding together, and with love. Each of these functions serves to renew spiritual identity.

This brings us to the very problematic issue of identity itself, a concept that has by now been constructed, deconstructed, and reconstructed by so many scholars and researchers over so long a period of time, it cannot be utilized uncritically as if we really know what it means. Sociological, psychological, and philosophical theories conflict with regard to when, why, how, and even whether human identity is formed. Psychoanalytic, humanist, and cognitive theories abound. Furthermore, aspects of identity overlap and interact. Sexual identity is inseparable from bodily, personal, and relational identity. Spiritual identity is profoundly influenced by social identity. And perhaps every defining aspect of our lives is affected by our cultural place and privilege, or lack thereof (with considerations of age, race, ethnicity, gender, class, abilities, and sexual orientation). In postmodern society the pursuit of identity is so nuanced and complex, it is practically beyond comprehension.

So where do we turn? As we struggle for an answer, there are certain reference points. We identify ourselves in terms of what we do, how we feel, and how we are related to one another. Are there more fundamental levels of identity—ways to answer the question, "Who am I *really*?" This is the spiritual level of identity. However, the search for a fixed response may not be rewarded. Whoever we were this morning, we have probably changed since then.[13]

In stressing spiritual identity as an answer we create for ourselves, I am rejecting the notion that there is anything like a common human essence or a fundamental, changeless spiritual core that comprises (or determines) who or what we are. Spiritual identity is a process, always unfolding. I believe that the development of spiritual identity is enhanced by a sense of self-knowledge, personal integration, and self-affirmation, while it may be thwarted by those social forces that perpetuate, encourage, and even require denial.

Although not quite so amorphous a term as identity, denial has

also come to have many uses and meanings, from extremely techni-
cal psychological definitions to bumper sticker slogans. In the context of this work, *denial* refers to repeated and often systematic efforts to conceal, reject, or refuse to confront certain crucial aspects of
identity, whether one's own or someone else's. I will focus most specifically on denial as it relates to sexual identity. Although this understanding of denial differs somewhat from the specifically psychological definition of the term, observations from psychological
research regarding the consequences of denial are relevant and will
be incorporated into the discussion.

Our first significant explorations of identity often involve our
sexuality. As the theologian Vincent Genovesi states, "existentially it
is most frequently in the area of sexuality that an individual first un-
covers and confronts the terror and the task of establishing his or her
self-identity and integrity."[14] However, I believe that this relationship extends far beyond adolescent explorations. The forms of denial
described here, all of which at some level assault a woman's sense of
who she is and how she might grow as a sexual being, also have spiritual consequences. Where these consequences are severe, affirmation of a woman's sexual identity, and especially the sacred value of
that identity, may be critical to spiritual healing.

I make no attempt here to essentialize the experiences of these
women. If we have learned anything from our long struggle with issues of diversity, identity politics, and difference, it is that generalizations about experience are dicey at best and perhaps impossible.
Furthermore, they lead us away from the difficult but critical conversations we need to undertake in order to understand both our differences and our common bonds.

If we turn to research for guidance, we find that the study of lesbians, adult survivors of child sexual abuse, and women who are positive for HIV/AIDS as "populations" is inevitably complicated by
their cultural invisibility, a phenomenon at the heart of this discussion. There is no such thing as a representative sample of a hidden or
invisible population.[15]

I do not believe that all individuals within any of the categories I propose to discuss (or perhaps any category at all) would describe their experience of spiritual identity development (or perhaps any experience at all) in exactly the same way. But I do claim that whether or not we are aware of it, and whether or not we describe ourselves as affected by it, we all do in fact suffer some consequences of denial. More specifically, I would argue that whether or not it is acknowledged or viewed as a problem, denial of sexual identity has particular consequences for lesbians, women with histories of child sexual abuse, and women living with HIV/AIDS.

Another problem arises from focusing on particular aspects of women's lives as illustrations of denied identity. This focus may in fact participate in negating their identities by isolating one aspect of their experience as though it were definitive for their entire experience. A lesbian is more than a lesbian. A woman sexually abused as a child is far more than the total of her reactions and responses to that violation. A woman with HIV/AIDS is also a woman with many other issues in her life. These women are mothers and daughters and sisters. They are tax accountants and prostitutes and preachers. They cook, walk, climb mountains, build houses, and sneeze. In highlighting aspects of their lives that generate a response of cultural denial, I am not seeking to deny the rest of their experience or to negate the many other dynamics of their lives.

Another point that must be stressed is that many women endure multiple forms of cultural denial, including those on which I have chosen to focus here. There are, of course, lesbians who have been abused as children and survivors of child sexual abuse who are also living with AIDS. In fact, the culture sometimes exercises one form of denial to generate another. A lesbian with an abuse history, for example, may find that the surrounding culture distorts her love of women into a pathological rejection of men.

A brief additional explanation is required about the way in which I have focused my discussion. With all three groups, I have taken as my first guideline the ways in which women describe themselves. So, for example, I assume that a woman has a history of childhood sexual abuse if, and only if, she would describe herself in that way. I realize that issues such as repressed memory cause immense problems for such a definition. Research makes it abundantly clear that there are women who have had this experience and do not recall it. Further, there are women who have been sexually abused as children and yet would not describe their experience in those terms. Further complicating the matter, women may "remember" experiences that did not literally occur but nevertheless affect them deeply.[16] Acknowledging that taking self-description as a guideline will inevitably leave out the experiences of some women (and *may* include some distortion or confusion), I see no other honest way to focus my study than to rely on women's own interpretations.

It may appear that defining women with HIV/AIDS is a simpler matter—that is, a woman may or may not be infected with the HIV virus, and those infected with the virus may or may not exhibit the physical symptoms associated with a diagnosis of "full-blown" AIDS. Even this definition is problematic, however. First, as a direct result of the cultural denial I discuss here, many cases go undiagnosed, especially in women. Further, women with HIV/AIDS can also be described as women with various other physical symptoms and illnesses.[17] Again, self-definition is my principal guideline.

While the identification of women with histories of abuse and women with AIDS *may* be a factual issue, defining a lesbian is perhaps even more problematic. Marilyn Frye notes how resistant this term has been to semantic analysis,[18] demonstrating her point through the use of dictionary definitions. For example, since many dictionaries define a *lesbian* as a woman who has sex with another woman and define *sex* as "the genital union of a female and a male animal," lesbians, by definition, do not exist.[19] Frye's darkly humorous observation is important not because dictionary definitions establish or negate identity but because they reveal the cultural convolutions through which lesbian identity is rendered invisible. This denial in turn provides the justification for active discrimination.

Various definitions have been developed in an effort to expand the meaning of the term beyond the specifics of sexual activity, noting that lesbian identity incorporates many other facets of life that may be equally or more important.[20] One typical move is to describe a lesbian as one who relates primarily to women or who prefers relating with women in various aspects of life—emotionally, sexually, socially, spiritually, etc.—or whose primary "love" interest is a woman. However, women who relate primarily to other women may or may not define themselves as lesbians. Faced with this quandary, I have chosen to apply the term *lesbian* to any and all women who have adopted that term for themselves. How this term is adopted and what is subsequently done with it are some of the concerns of this work.

In the process of developing a sexual identity, lesbians confront cultural invisibility and stigmatization, which often results in personal denial. Women with histories of sexual abuse must deal with massive social denial while they struggle with their own self-doubts, shame, and dissociation. Women living with HIV/AIDS also deal continually with these issues, including invisibility, shame, and rejection as sexual beings. I wish to claim that the forces of denial so fundamental to society's oppressive attitudes toward these women may hinder not only their sense of personal identity and integrity but also the development of their most fundamental sense of self.

There is more at stake here than the validation or rejection of women's choices, experiences, and memories. We will see that denial may include rejection of a woman's sexual *identity*. The cultural failure to recognize or affirm lesbian lifestyles and relationships is also a failure to affirm the ways they have come to understand themselves. Denying the validity of a woman's memories of childhood sexual abuse also denies her own interpretation of who she is as a sexual being. Women positive for HIV/AIDS are not only denied recognition and treatment; their sexual needs, feelings, and self-understandings are also denied.

Chapter One

Eros, Denial, and the Whirlwind Within

As a whirlwind

swoops on an oak

Love shakes my heart

— SAPPHO

Now I know why Eros,

Of all the progeny of

Earth and Heaven, has

been most dearly loved

— SAPPHO

From beyond the darkness there is a sound of drumming. Not a solid or settled rhythm, but a wild and chaotic pounding like the clatter of a heart in terror or orgasm. There is the slap of skin, but no palm or fingertip beats out this cacophony. This is the sound of heels skipping and stomping up a thunder that riots in my ears, stirring my belly with a laughter that seems to come from under the earth. Someone is dancing on a drum.

This is a sound that goes everywhere with me these days. Although at first it seems to have no structure at all, to be only an erratic and thunderous percussion, a pattern begins to emerge. There is a song as well as a dance in the thunder drumming, and the song becomes more and more familiar. It is the song of tectonic plates shifting and planets spinning—the dance of wild things. This drumming lives in us.

We know this music, we human creatures. It is what newborn infants and Tibetan lamas and Yoruba shekere players and Yakima Butterfly Dancers and the crowd down at Sophie's all have in common. And I have seen it loosen the limbs and release the grins of even the most toneless and overtightened. Still, most of us now living in the world of industry and the individual have learned to fear this music, to dread the way it undoes our carefully packaged personalities. And we study how to unlearn it, to unfeel it, to tone it down. We mute the mysterious and control the chaotic, all to deny the wild within.

This denial is at the heart of many cultures. We separate ourselves from our own most natural and embodied being, and thus perpetuate alienation between spirituality and sexuality. Women learn to distrust and repress our own erotic power. If we cannot trust or accept our sexuality, we lose direction and connection; we become unable to relate what we do and how we are perceived with who we believe we are. We may temporarily ignore the inconsistencies. We may freeze, like a rabbit in headlights, unwilling to change or grow for fear that all of the structures we have established will come apart. Because what we deny will eventually rise to the surface, because the vital power of our erotic energy will find a way to express itself, pressure builds as the tension of contradiction increases. Eventually, if we can no longer be what we are not, and if there is no culturally acceptable way to be ourselves, things come apart.

Yeats reminds us that chaos eternally threatens: "Things fall apart; the centre cannot hold. . . ."[1] The central metaphor I invoke for this disintegration is the whirlwind. A more familiar image is *splitting*, which evokes a picture of a clean break—an apple or a log falling neatly into two halves. But when internal pressures build to the breaking point, the reality is not so tidy. The whirlwind shatters, explodes, scatters, blows the world to pieces. After the storm, halves are hard to find; a splintered timber here, a shingle there, many pieces broken, some vanished completely. I think *that's* what can happen

Dancing after the Whirlwind

when things come apart. But I do not think it has to happen. We can learn to listen to the rhythm of the wild, to integrate rather than isolate our own erotic power. We can learn to incorporate the chaotic dance of change into the pattern of our lives.

Our brokenness is not the result of internal conflicts alone. The pressures and confusions we experience are a response to the alienation surrounding us, and cultural denial keeps bad company. Where societies deny the erotic connection between spirituality and sexuality, the sacredness of embodied connection is also denied. Where the sacred value of this bond is denied, cultures tend to fear erotic power and to establish strict controls over sexual expression. Patriarchal dichotomies divide the world into man/culture/spirit and woman/nature/sexuality; those outside the boundaries of patriarchal control are viewed as dangerous to the established order. Sexual expression that challenges these rigid boundaries must either be brought under control or annihilated. The drums must be silenced. Enter the posse, armed to the teeth with the weapons of order: oppression of women, children, and the natural world; sexual and physical violence—atrocities perpetuated by institutionalized hatred in the name of social control.

Obviously, not every person facing these cultural pressures experiences a dramatic crisis in personal identity. We live our lives. We go on. We are more or less successful, more or less happy, more or less capable of dancing the dance through cultures that routinely make big chunks of our lives disappear. Sometimes a storm rages deep beneath the surface with no apparent outward manifestation. Sometimes we rest in the eye of the hurricane, enjoying the lull. Sometimes it seems as if the storm is very far away, happening to someone else, while our lives continue, peaceful and well ordered. Beneath the smooth surfaces of our lives, however, we can hear the wind rising.

I do not believe that we can thrive if we do not integrate those times when old structures fail. Storms will rise; they are a part of our lives. Things come apart; that, too, is inescapable (and, I think, part of the cycle of renewal upon which life depends). However, the violent disintegration of our being caused by the processes of denial and alienation is neither necessary nor natural. This is an important distinction. We can view growth, disintegration, and regeneration as a cycle through which we integrate our sexuality and our spirituality. We can also view body and spirit as enemies, turning them against one another until the tension of suppressed feeling explodes our old assumptions with the velocity of a hurricane.

The bond between sexuality and spirituality is critical because it is at the core of our identities, the place where we most deeply touch one another as human beings. It is sacred space. Sexual violence is sacrilege, not just because it attacks us at the core of who we are but because it violates the sacred ground of our living union with one another. And this violence takes many forms. Rape, sexual abuse of children, and sexual humiliation are manifest violations. So is the cultural refusal to acknowledge the possibility, let alone the reality, of genuine sexual communion between one woman and another (or one man and another). So is the massive social rejection of women who come forward to accuse their sexual violators, which exercises cultural reversals to put the victim on trial. So is responding to claims of childhood sexual abuse as a threat to the unity and sanctity of the family. So is the treatment of women with AIDS as the bearers of all manner of social sins, including diseased sexuality.

These violations are the result of a deep cultural fear that enforces order through separation and alienation. There are cultures that take no comfort in wildness, and erotic power is wild. Sexuality is so often referred to as a mystery because it takes us into wilderness, into lands uncharted and unknown. Erotic power is in itself unnamed, untamed, ecstatic, chaotic, out of control. Where this wildness is feared, denial and accompanying acts of violence and oppression may be the inevitable result of attempting to harness or suppress what cannot be tamed.

Fear, however, is not the only response to wildness. As will be seen, reverence for both the wild power of the erotic and the deep bond between that erotic power and spirituality generates many cultural expressions. When we can bring these back into harmony, we enable not only personal but also cultural healing and bring together the critical elements we need to deal with the question of identity. While these elements are in opposition, we cannot be all that we are. But when wild, erotic power is valued as sacred, we can hold our sexual and spiritual identities in deep relation; we can unfold the dynamics of identity by participating in the whole picture.

But how, given the brutal reality of cultural denial, do we overcome this alienation and incorporate erotic power into spiritual identity? How do we get there from here? This question is the central concern of this book. I believe that there are clues in the nature of the erotic bond between sexuality and spirituality itself, and that some of these clues relate to wilderness—to chaos—which takes us back into the whirlwind.

Certainly, the wild wind may be viewed as destructive—civilization tossed about and pulverized into matchsticks—but cultures all over the world have also felt in the power of nature's wildness the pulse of the divine. God speaks out of the whirlwind and asks, "Can you thunder like I can thunder?" Vayu, Hindu god of wind, moves, swift as thought, in the form of an antelope with a thousand eyes. Apache shamans transform their flesh into the whirlwind to work their curses. Pan accompanies the demon drumming with the irresistible strains of his pipe, and souls destined for the underworld respond in panic. Fire, flood, earthquake, and storm—the abyss and the maw and the unfathomable deep upon whose face is darkness—are these symbols of divine power just because they are scary, or is it that we also envision natural power as a profound and meaningful expression of divine creativity?

What have chaos and destruction to do with creativity? This I believe is the ground in which healing can grow. If the earthly/embodied/sexual is understood as antithetical to the heavenly/disembodied/spiritual, then nature must be tamed. The voice of the divine speaks from boundaries and borders built to hold back the forces of chaos. But if that which is deeply (and most uncontrollably) natural is also understood as that which is deeply (and most uncontrollably) divine, the whole process becomes one of dynamic interaction rather than opposition. Then we can hear the voice of God from the abyss, and we can acknowledge divine union in the experience of ecstatic sexual partnership. Then the destructive and creative power exemplified in all that is naturally divine becomes manifestly beautiful and good (even though it's still scary).

The power of sexuality and spirituality in our lives emerges in part from their potential to evoke significant changes in ourselves and in our surroundings. They may subvert or liberate. They may intensify our awareness of deep bonds with others, releasing the power of unconscious or irrational passions to transform the world.[2]

Bringing sexuality and spirituality into "right relation"[3] with one another means trading in dichotomy for ambiguity. While a metaphysics that disembodies the spiritual may fit neatly into all good/all bad categories, an embodied spirituality is not so well ordered. Bodies are places of pleasure and pain, of urge and gratification, of wounds and wonder. Timmerman locates this ambiguity at the center of our embodied existence:

> In our own human body is our deepest experience of ambiguity; it is both me and not me; it is our vehicle of separation as well as connection; it defines our possibilities and our limitations.... Accepting our bodiliness, not just as good rather than evil, but as the ultimate evidence of the fact that good and evil are two interpretations of the same reality, is the way we learn to accept ambiguity in larger things. It would be easier to accept our bodies as anomalies ... rather than as symbolic of the ambiguity of life. Then we could suppress one pole of

Dancing after the Whirlwind

the ambiguity and maintain the illusion that we are really of the spirit world, with the body an irrelevant nuisance.[4]

This ambiguous but lively interaction within us is a reflection of nature's organic processes. Another metaphor helps to illustrate this connection. In the rainforests of the Pacific Northwest, things rot at a wonderful rate. The seething wet of wild growth and disintegration provides a stunning illustration of the power (and strange efficiency) of chaos. When storms shake the foundations of the great trees, their roots finally loosen their hold in the soaked and spongy soil, and they fall. Immediately, they are food. A million life forms move in and take hold—fungi, rodents, insects, bacteria, vines, and seedlings. The quick disintegration and decay stimulates fecundity. As one walks through these majestic forests, one discovers occasional growths of young trees in straight rows called "colonnades." These trees have taken root directly in the trunks of the fallen logs (technically termed "mother trees"), where they have found fertile ground for growth as the old trees come apart.

This is *not* a celebration of sacrifice—a tribute to the good old mother tree who gives her life for her young. Although it is hardly my place to speak for the tree, I hold that she is impassive to her falling, continuing these deep, wet cycles of rotting and growth in just this way because she is a tree and she is there. I also hold that she is not dead but alive in a different way: she is breaking down.

Destruction and creativity are not natural enemies. They are the way things are, each always transforming into the other. Mending the rift between sexuality and spirituality must incorporate this understanding on both a cultural and a personal level. It seems to me that alienation between embodiment/sexuality and spirituality is at the core of much of the violence and cruelty that plague many cultures and lurk at the core of patriarchal oppression. If erotic passion can be understood as a central component of spiritual life rather than its enemy, healing these evils can commence. The renewal of this bond depends upon envisioning wildness not as a force to be tamed but as one profound manifestation of divine love that incorporates and integrates destruction and creativity, death and life.

On a personal level, after the whirlwind it often seems, as we sort through the damage, that everything has been lost. The pieces will not go together as they once were. Nothing will ever be the same. However, given the terrible consequences of denial and the accompanying violence in our lives, this is not necessarily bad news. If we can learn to integrate our embodied, sexual lives into our spiritual identities, we might realize creative new directions we can then describe and name for ourselves. Understanding the experience of coming apart as part of a process that also includes renewal and new growth helps us to incorporate even radical change as a component of growth.

This view is an alternative to the assumption that integration means becoming a "whole person." I am suspicious of the metaphor of wholeness. I have never heard a survivor of the terrible processes to which I refer, even after tremendous struggle and growth, state, "Now I am whole." To me the term indicates a static state, something completed, even perfected, but thereafter unchanging. I do not think that integration is the same as wholeness. There is power in the realization that after the whirlwind nothing is the same. The matter was settled for me when I heard a survivor's response to a film in which a woman survivor of childhood atrocities struggled against an unknown torturer bent upon acquiring her confession.[5] "He couldn't break her," said my friend, "because she had already been broken."

I think the feminist theologian Carter Heyward is right that we are not photographs. We can look within ourselves searching for essences or outside ourselves searching for mirrors, but the search for both identity and liberation is an "intrinsically relational adventure,"[6] developed *for* ourselves but *with* others. A living being is more like an event or a process than a completed package. Integration means that we invite all the guests to dance the dance, instead of excluding some socially inappropriate individual and then spending the evening being afraid she'll show up anyway. The party may get a little wilder when no one is left outside the doors, but oh, the intricate steps and cavorts on the floor.

Ecstasy's Bawdy Dancers

As I have explored the wilderness paths leading from denial to recovery, healing, and thriving, I have been visited by two spirits. These are not wispy, ethereal ghosts but wild, erotic, embodied beings, and they enter in a noisy tumult of laughter and drums. It was their drumming dance that resounded at the beginning of this chapter. The first appeared to me many years ago, and the second when I was already well along in writing this book. Since neither will go away, I introduce them here. They are raucous and ill-mannered, an embarrassment to cultivated society, but they serve as important guides on the path to recovered identity.

The first is Ama-no-Uzume, she of the many names, sometimes called the Dread Female of Heaven or Uzume-Ota-Fuku (she of the big breasts).[7] Known as a goddess of dance and mirth, she first appeared to me while I was researching Japanese creation mythology for my doctoral dissertation.

Her story is related to that of Amaterasu, the Japanese sun goddess. The *Kojiki* and *Nihongi*, collections of Japanese cosmology and mythology representing some of the earliest known Japanese writings, narrate their adventures.[8] Amaterasu and her brother, Susa-no-wo the storm god, both come into being when their primordial father, Izanagi, bathes in a river to purify himself after returning from the underworld. Amaterasu is born from his left eye, while Susa-no-wo emerges from his nose. From the beginning, Susa-no-wo refuses to obey the commands of his father or to rule the land appropriately. He is particularly fond of tormenting his radiant sister.

Amaterasu suffers greatly from the chaotic misdeeds of her brother. He breaks down the rice paddies, covers the ditches, and defecates and flings his feces into the halls where the first fruits are tasted. Eventually, he opens a hole in the roof of her sacred weaving hall and throws the flayed carcass of a piebald colt down among her sacred silk looms. (Some versions of the story say that she was wounded in the vagina by a flying shuttle.)[9] Amaterasu becomes so overwhelmed by his abuse that she hides away in the Cave of Heaven and refuses to come out.

With the sun in hiding, the whole world suffers in darkness. Plants wither. Life ceases to flourish. This greatly upsets the myriad deities. They gather outside the cave to try to lure her out, but they are unable to entice her from her hiding place. Finally, Ama-no-Uzume arrives on the scene. She climbs up on a large overturned tub and begins to dance her special *Kagura*, stomping resoundingly on the bottom of the bucket. As she enters an ecstatic trance, she opens her clothing and removes her undergarments. Her bawdy dance causes all the gods to laugh at once and to make such an uproar that Amaterasu peeks out to see what is going on. As she does so, Uzume calls to her, "We rejoice and dance because there is here a deity superior to you." Peeking out, Amaterasu sees her own image in a mirror the gods have hung on a nearby tree. She is amazed by the beauty of this image and gradually steps outside the cave to get a closer look. The gods immediately pull her out and seal the cave behind her, thereby restoring the sun to the world.

Years ago, a wise therapist suggested to me that when meaningful events occur in my life I might ask myself, "If I dreamed these events, what would they mean?" Turning this question to reflect on the myth, we might consider Amaterasu and Susa-no-wo, Ama-no-Uzume with her bawdy dance, and even the tub and the mirror as part of our own psyches. When we consider this story in terms of

       Dancing after the Whirlwind

shattered souls, denied identity, and spiritual recovery, we immediately recognize the fear and anger, the deep wounds to our sexual being caused by abuse, assault, and oppression. But we also recognize the whirlwind within, the internal chaos that drives us deep into the sacred cave of the unconscious. Hiding inside ourselves, we refuse the light of consciousness, preferring the dark security of unknowing. In this state, we do not recognize ourselves. We do not know who we are. Yet the cave also serves as a womb/shelter in which new life (awareness) can grow.

What draws us out? The myth reminds us of a deep source of power that is often ignored, denied, or suppressed by the surrounding culture—the energy of eros; the power of wild, exuberant, lusty women; the joy of laughter-producing dance. Like Susa-no-wo the storm god, Ama-no-Uzume is out of control, her behavior outside the boundaries of cultural norms. However, unlike the storm god, whose energy is destructive, this dancing goddess is filled to bursting with erotic joy. While all the gods laugh at her ridiculous antics, she alone has the power to lure light from hiding and restore life to the world. She calls us to a vision that reflects our true identity. She shows us who we are.

Still smiling at the rhythms of the big-breasted goddess as she pounds her feet on the wooden tub, I turn my attention to the other spirit, newly arrived and just as raucous. Here is Baubo (also called Iambe), the ancient dry nurse with whom Demeter, goddess of earth, fertility, and cultivated grain, spends a remarkable evening. Baubo first came to my attention when a friend loaned me Winifred Milius Lubell's fascinating study.[10] Several days later, I came upon her again in the work of another colleague. I had read this work before, but this time Baubo fairly leaped from the page, and I could no longer ignore her.

Demeter comes upon Baubo while wandering the earth in despair after her daughter, Persephone, has been abducted by Hades and taken to the underworld. Like Amaterasu, Demeter is so overcome with grief and rage that she has removed her life-energy from the world. Baubo alone is successful in getting Demeter to laugh: she entertains the goddess by performing a bawdy dance in which she removes her clothes and spreads her legs, revealing her vulva. As Christine Downing notes, although she is an old woman long past childbearing years, Baubo "communicates her joy in her own body, her pride in her female organs, her conviction that her sexuality is *hers*, defined neither by the men who might once have desired her nor the children she may have borne."[11]

How is it that virtually the same story emerges from both Greek and Japanese mythology? Perhaps we are having the same dream. Here again forces of death, destruction, and abuse have the power to drive life-giving energy from the world. Here again the ecstatic dance of erotic wildness evokes the healing laughter of returning life. The Japanese and the Greeks understood these bawdy dancers as deities representing the sacred reality of self-sufficient female sexuality.[12] With the ancients, we can invoke the divinely undisciplined power of laughter, of dance, and of radiant, rejoicing, sweet, sacred sex. In order to do this, however, we must join with the energies of Ama-no-Uzume and Baubo in uniting the sexual with the spiritual. Without erotic power, we cannot put body and soul together or overcome the forces of denial and destruction: we cannot really know who we are.

The Sex/Spirit Relationship

If, as many contemporary theories of identity (and many religious beliefs, both ancient and contemporary) would suggest, we are not fixed entities but ever changing combinations of identity components or moments in time, then knowing who we are is always a complex process. This complexity becomes a maze of dead ends, however, if certain significant aspects of our lives are isolated or made to conflict with one another. We are both spiritual and sexual beings. If these components of our lives are viewed as antithetical, then we must either exclude one or the other from our lives or constantly switch our focus from one to the other. We must deny our sexuality when we identify ourselves as spiritual and deny our spiritual lives when we wish to express ourselves sexually.

Historically, philosophies, religions, and cultures have long struggled with these powerful elements and their relationship. Sexuality has been viewed as deeply connected and related to the sacred, the most powerful human expression of spiritual union. It has also been viewed as the element of our lives that most powerfully alienates us from the divine, an aspect of ourselves we must suppress if we hope to achieve spiritual fulfillment.

I have claimed that restoring and renewing the connection between our sexual and spiritual lives are essential components of spiritual recovery and healing. This is not an attempt to establish a fixed relationship between sexuality and spirituality or to suggest a particular pattern of sexual/spiritual expression. Rather, our sexuality and our spirituality must be understood as dynamically interrelated, having the potential to express our most profound experience of identity and of relationship.

This is not to say that every act of sex is sacred. It *is* to claim that our sexual expression ought to be understood as a significant component of our connection to the sacred, that the ways we touch one another are related to the ways we embrace the divine. Popular culture and personal experience reinforce this connection in ways that are probably less mundane than they seem. Maybe heaven *is* in her arms. Maybe love *is* eternal. Maybe the tendency of even the most profound atheist to call upon the name of the divine during sexual experiences reveals more of the cosmic than we are typically prepared to understand.

Certainly, the union of body and soul is not a new idea. Feminist theorists, among others, have long critiqued the tendency in Western philosophical thought to view these elements dichotomously and hierarchically. Similarly, feminist theory has long incorporated analysis of an all-pervasive patriarchal logic in which man represents culture and woman nature.[13] It is evident that many cultures associate both women and nature with that which is sensual/sexual, chaotic, and out of control. Often, as I will demonstrate, cultures that separate spirituality from sexuality also use the assumption of the woman/nature connection to support oppression of women and nature as necessary to the maintenance of an ordered society. There are, however, also cultural manifestations of the woman/nature association that celebrate or express devotion toward both.

Feminist theory has occasionally become enmeshed in the contradictory tendency to celebrate the connection between woman and nature when it functions positively for women and to reject it when it serves patriarchal oppression. *If*, in fact, there is some foundational or innate connection between women and nature, it can, of course, be culturally interpreted either positively or negatively or both. Yet too often we carelessly rejoice in the goddess-worshipping affirmation of woman's special connection with nature while rejecting out-of-hand the Western patriarchal tendency to lift up that same connection in a different context.

Christine Downing takes up this issue of the relationship between women and nature in *Women's Mysteries*. Noting the obvious, that women and men are equally embodied and embedded in nature, Downing observes that certain physiological characteristics of women may make us a little less likely to disown embodiment and more likely to remember our connection to nature. The continuation of life on the planet depends upon remembering our interconnectedness with the rest of the natural world.[14] Downing calls us to attend to our own bodies; such attention may impress upon us "that as embodied humans we are finite and mortal participants in a network of embodied life."[15] Affirming our embodiment does not depend upon a view of women as more symbolically or essentially bound to na-

Dancing after the Whirlwind

ture than to culture. But it does depend upon incorporating the natural/sexual into our spiritual lives.

The dynamics of the relationship between sexuality and spirituality and its cultural unfolding obviously have important personal and social consequences. But can we really make a direct association between the way a culture understands this relationship and the way people in that culture relate to nature and to one another?

The Erotic Connection

The key to the connection between sexuality and spirituality is the *erotic*. The philosopher and psychologist Rollo May has referred to Eros as "the drive toward union with what we belong to—union with our own possibilities, union with significant other persons in our world in relation to whom we discover our own self-fulfillment."[16] I believe that this deep, wild, embodied power has an even greater reach; it is, in fact, the very heart of our desire, our awareness of and longing for interconnectedness with all things. At the most fundamental level, the erotic connects us to the sacred. This is nothing new. Prayer and ritual, art and music, even our most intense emotional relationships, emphasize this connection. But patriarchal denial of this erotic link separates our embodied being from the sacred. The tendency of contemporary culture to limit the meaning of eroticism to the physical aspects of sexual expression misses the crucial point that erotic power extends far beyond this. And limiting sexual expression to the physical techniques of need gratification or pleasure cuts us off from the erotic power of the sacred.

At the deepest level, the erotic is associated with creating and consuming, with birth and death. It is also connected to our most profound sense of bonding, union, relationality, and love. Understanding the power of the erotic gives women an access point to increased self-awareness. Audre Lorde notes that the erotic arises from "a deeply female and spiritual plane, firmly rooted in the power of our unexpressed or unrecognized feeling."[17] Because it emerges from our deepest nonrational resources, "the erotic offers a well of replenishing and provocative force to the woman who does not fear its revelation, nor succumb to the belief that sensation is enough."[18]

In Nelle Morton's famous phrase, erotic power, like liberating consciousness, comes "up from down under."[19] It stirs from the deep within, generated by our most fundamental creative energy. Joan Timmerman refers to eros as "the desire for God deep in things."[20]

This association between the erotic and unconscious power, both creative and chaotic, is reflected repeatedly in mythic depictions of the erotic. Hesiod's *Theogony* names Eros as one of the four original gods (along with Chaos, Gaea, and Tartarus).[21] Eros is "the ever-dying, ever-living god," Aphrodite's child, who later becomes Cupid, child of Venus.[22] He is credited with bringing abundance to the earth and breathing the spirit of life into the first people. In this capacity he represents the power of life over death.[23]

However, as Joseph Campbell observes, Eros is depicted not only as the sacrifice, the dying and rising god upon whom life depends, but as the dark enemy who wields the power of chaos and destruction. Though slayer and victim are seemingly in conflict, behind the scenes they are bound together, of one mind.[24]

The binding or uniting function of the erotic is also essential to understanding the link between the sacred and the sexual. Eros is the power of both human and divine union and therefore expresses the deep connection between human sexuality and divine love. Catherine Keller refers to the definition of religion to make this connection: "Religion true to its name activates connection. It 'ties together,' binding up the wounds of breaking worlds. It is the bridging, bonding process at the heart of things. There is no reason not to call this process Love: the Eros that seeks to get things together, no matter what."[25] Obviously, the uniting power of Eros may be expressed profoundly in sexual union, and many cultures ritually affirm the creative and the destructive aspects of sexuality in this context. Sexual-

Dancing after the Whirlwind

ity may be valued as an expression of the human desire for cosmic union, and sexual practices may be surrounded with taboos that confirm its dangerous power.

What, then, is the power of sex? What is its relationship to the erotic? To spirituality? Is it the intersection of life and death, the orgasmic moment when emptiness meets fullness, need meets release, time meets eternity? When we seek to suppress or manage sexuality, what are we seeking to control and why? In order to answer these questions, we must explore certain connections and distinctions more thoroughly.

One significant function of sex is communion/communication. Several theorists postulate a significant relationship between sex and language; sexuality may be viewed as that which communicates our deepest feelings of pleasure and tenderness. This communicative character has a spiritual dimension that connects us not only with ourselves and others, but with the transcendent.[26]

In *Love and Will*, Rollo May suggests that the erotic expresses our personal intentions and provides meaning to our sexual activity. However, sexual activity does not automatically generate an erotic connection. Too much emphasis on technique and neurophysiological response and too little awareness of identity and relationality are antithetical to the goals of eros. Although it seems paradoxical, given our cultural tendency to equate the erotic with sexual stimulation, contemporary views of sex may actually cut us off from the erotic.

In fact, in contemporary Western culture, sex and eros are frequently in conflict. Sex is culturally understood as a rhythm of stimulus and response, but eros is a state of being. Whereas the endpoint of sexual activity might be gratification, relaxation, and a reduction of tension, "eros is a desiring, longing, a forever reaching out, seeking to expand."[27] Mere physical sex seeks release, but Eros seeks "to cultivate, procreate, and form the world."[28] While the goal of the sex act may be said to be orgasm, "eros seeks union with the other person in delight and passion, and the procreating of new dimensions of experience which broaden and deepen the being of both persons."[29] Because the erotic longs for union and full relationality, it becomes the source of human tenderness in sexual relationships.[30]

Most important, erotic power is associated with love. In our deepest sexual awareness, when we are genuinely in touch with erotic power, we renew the union of body and soul—the sacred dimension. The erotic is expressed in the language of oneness, union, connectedness, bonding, and love. It is here that our sexuality and our spirituality most profoundly connect.

Greek Love and the Longing for Union

This understanding of the erotic as the divine power that reunites two into one is well established in human culture and emerges repeatedly as a literary and philosophical theme. One of the most notable expressions of this unifying power is Aristophanes' speech in praise of love in Plato's *Symposium*,[31] in which the connection of love and sexuality is a central theme.

During that famous drinking party and oratorical contest, the comic poet whimsically describes the original condition of humanity and, not coincidentally, the reason for our eternal quest for love. The human body, according to Aristophanes' account, was originally "a rounded whole, with double back and flanks forming a complete circle."[32] In fact, the human form was doubled in every way, with four arms and four legs, two faces, and two sets of sexual organs. There were at that time three sexes, one all male, one all female, and one partaking of both.

These humans were so strong and proud that they incurred the wrath of the gods until Zeus punished them by cutting each of them in half. Each human body then longed so passionately for its severed half that the results were disastrous. "When they met they threw their arms round one another and embraced, in their longing to grow together again, and they perished of hunger and general neglect of their concerns."[33] Zeus solved this problem by moving the sexual organs of each from their outer sides around to the front. This way, Zeus made intercourse possible, thus providing a means not only for reproduction but for satisfying desire.

This coupling of humans with one another, in Aristophanes' view, is the beginning of human love: "It is from this distant epoch, then, that we may date the innate love which human beings feel for one another, the love which restores us to our ancient state by attempting to weld two beings into one and to heal the wounds which humanity suffered."[34] Aristophanes goes on to account for diverse sexual orientations. Those humans who were originally composed of both male and female components seek partners of the opposite sex. Adulterers and promiscuous women, he notes, come from this class. Women who are halves of a female whole seek female partners. Men who are halves of a male whole "love men throughout their boyhood, and take pleasure in physical contact with men."[35] These men "are the best of their generation, because they are the most manly."[36] Plato utilizes Aristophanes' speech to acknowledge the male/female bond that provides for the continuance of the race, but clearly the superior love is that between one man and another.

In this view of human love, the strongest bonds are formed when one is fortunate enough to encounter one's actual other half. Then, affection, kinship, and love combine to inspire overwhelming emotion. Such a pair is likely to form a lifelong partnership, hating to be separated even for a moment.[37] This intense delight in the company of another goes far beyond the physical. The soul of each longs for union with its true partner, to melt into the beloved, to be one being instead of two. "The reason is that this was our primitive condition when we were wholes, and love is simply the name for the desire and pursuit of the whole."[38]

The superiority of male to female and of the spiritual to the physical are evident in the later speeches. In Aristophanes' speech, however, Plato pauses to appreciate the beauty of sexual union as a profound expression of human love. The power of this speech is in our deep response to it—the recognition of our own yearning for the wholeness of erotic union.

We may find ourselves enjoying the whimsical nature of Aristophanes' primordial description, and it is clear that Plato intends to amuse.[39] But even while we are smiling, we recognize the search for a lover who can help us feel complete, the desire for a love that "not even death can part," the inclination to cling desperately to the beloved, the sense that deep sexual communion is our most intense experience of sacred union.

It should be noted that this union, so richly experienced through our sexuality, may also take many other forms. Audre Lorde notes the function of the erotic in providing the power we feel whenever we deeply share our pursuits with another person, whatever those pursuits might be.[40] The erotic underscores our capacity for joy, so that all levels in which we sense may open "to the erotically satisfying experience, whether it is dancing, building a bookcase, writing a poem, examining an idea."[41] Still, the most obvious location of the erotic is in the yearning for and realization of profound sexual connection.

As affirmed in myriad creation stories, the two become one and together they make worlds. This is a key to the connection between relationality and identity. Keller notes the dangers of associating identity with the autonomous "separate, self-enclosed subject,"[42] a fixed essence unchanged by relations.

> However much the ego feels single and apart, this feeling may represent not truth but denial. It is less precise to call this ego separate than *separative*, implying an activity or an intention rather than any fundamental state of being. The separative self is identifiable historically, but neither essentially nor necessarily, with males and the masculine. Its sense of itself as separate, as over against the world, the Other, and even its own body, endows it with its identity.[43]

As an alternative to this separative and disconnected being, Keller posits not the soluble self of stereotypic femininity, in which one dissolves one's own identity into that of another, but a connective self.

> An ego-transcending selfhood is massively relational.... The subject encounters the world of others not just externally but also in itself, as part of its own life. Real parents, friends, foes, and trees certainly retain their status as external objects; they are freed as we retract our projections to be more exactly themselves for us. At the same time the idea of this "transpersonal psyche" arouses a sense for the delicate currents flowing from that depth where all things become part of each other.[44]

This concept of a connective self emphasizes the relational aspect of identity. Autonomy, on the other hand, implies a self that is free from external control. But without relationships, what are we free *for*? The separative self is the marooned self, and the freedom offered by this understanding of identity is the freedom offered on a deserted island. No one can tell us what to do, because there is no one there—no relations. Connective selves locate freedom relationally in the creativity of our complex interactions. We are free for one another. Our sexuality is a significant means of expression for that creative and connective identity.

In our individual sexual orientations and expressions, we locate ourselves relationally. But our sexuality is also an expression of *who we are* at a fundamental level. This is more than the social habit of establishing identity in terms of relationships—as someone's spouse, lover, fiancée, parent. It is also more than the association between sex and procreation, or pleasure, or even love. As we navigate consciousness and identity sexuality is a pole star. If spiritual identity refers to our deepest understanding of ourselves *in relation*, then we must acknowledge the key role sexuality plays in this understanding.

In considering the role of sexuality in the development of spiritual identity, we must return to denial and its consequences. If we deny or suppress the erotic level of feeling in our sexual relationships, we likewise set aside and deny the sacred dimension of our sexuality. Rollo May takes the position that the separation between sex and eros imposed by contemporary Western culture represents a "new form of puritanism" consisting of alienation from the body, separation of emotion from reason, and the use of the body as a machine.[45] In being preoccupied with sex while simultaneously defining it more and more narrowly, we repress the erotic.

The roots of this alienation between the sexual and the erotic are diverse and emerge from both philosophical and religious sources. Notwithstanding Aristophanes' fascinating account of human love, interpreters of Greek philosophy eventually put more emphasis on texts that support separating spiritual love from the body. Although Eros holds a significant place in Greek culture, this deity is increasingly detached from—and elevated over—physical love. Through the speech delivered by Socrates in the *Symposium* debate, Plato suggests the view that the highest form of love resides far beyond the limits of bodily or sexual expression.

Socrates distinguishes physical from spiritual procreation, associating only the latter with art, civilization, and social order.[46] The highest form of erotic power is evident in the "philosopher or lover of wisdom, who is capable of ascending above the sensible world altogether."[47] When one becomes capable of perceiving absolute beauty untainted by human flesh, then one may bring forth true rather than reflected goodness. Such a capacity will make one immortal and beloved of God.[48] Because women are too connected with the bodily and the physical, Plato is clear that these higher forms of love, with few exceptions, are possible only for men.[49]

Plato's view of the relationship between love and the body seems ambiguous. Although he carefully distinguishes Eros from mere physical desire, Plato continues to associate it with the human impulse to love one another. Yet he also views it as a principle that pervades all other human activities, prompting the philosopher to seek truth and the mystic to seek God.[50] For Plato, these pursuits are more refined than pursuit of physical love.

Scholars following Plato take the position that those who associate sexual with spiritual fulfillment are failing to recognize a deeper and more universal truth: the enlightened soul must eventually transcend the physical realm. What the Greeks ascribed to ignorance, Christians ascribed to sin. Although Greek philosophy certainly contributed to the alienation of the sexual and the spiritual and to the disembodiment of Eros, the principal vehicle of expression for these ideas in the West has been religion. In Nietzsche's words, "Christianity gave Eros poison to drink; he did not die of it but he degenerated into vice."[51]

Sex/Spirit Alienation

The tendency to denigrate the physical, the bodily, and the sexual is present not only in the dominant traditions of Christianity but also in the spirituality and official teaching of other dominant groups, especially those in which men rule and establish masculinist norms.[52] For Greeks and Greek-influenced Christianity, and for those in many other societies who adopted patriarchal values, the conflation of consciousness with spirituality, and the assumed transcendence of the spiritual over the physical, implied the superiority of spirit-oriented man over nature-oriented woman. Eventually, however, Christianity transformed Greek homerotic appreciation of male-male love into homophobic fear and hatred of the natural.

As we will see in chapter 2, although Christianity has been perhaps the most powerful cultural force contributing to the alienation between spirituality and sexuality in the West, many elements in Western thought have combined to cut sexuality off from spiritual life. Women were increasingly associated with the bodily, the sexual, and the physical, and devalued accordingly. Audre Lorde feels that the parallel suppression of the erotic and of women in Western culture is no accident. While men might value the erotic insofar as it serves their own needs, they also fear its power.[53] Thus, the erotic must be degraded—reduced to "the confused, the trivial, the psychotic, the plasticized sensation."[54] Women must be taught to distrust their own erotic awareness. In place of erotic connection, Western culture has substituted the pornographic.

This distinction is important for our current study. If sex is cut off from soul, then the erotic becomes the pornographic, and sexual identity is separated from spiritual identity. Susan Griffin most clearly articulates the core meaning of this alienation between the erotic and the pornographic in her landmark study *Pornography and Silence*. She argues that pornography is neither an expression of human erotic feeling and desire nor a love for the body but rather "a fear of bodily knowledge, and a desire to silence eros."[55] The pornographic mind develops when culture "has opposed itself in violence to the natural, and takes revenge on nature."[56]

The reversals that are symptomatic of denial further complicate the picture. Patriarchal culture implements its assault on eros in part by usurping and perverting the terms at issue. Thus, a culture that tolerates, and even implicitly supports, oppression and brutality against women and nature will rail against any same-sex erotic expression as "pornographic." Survivors of sexual abuse who report violations against them may be termed "evil" or "dirty-minded." Women with HIV/AIDS are often referred to as "vectors of infection" and treated as "filth."

Controlling Eros?

Anthropologists have noted what at first appears to be a contradiction in the relationship between a culture's social structures and its views of sexuality. Sex is relatively unproblematic and pollution-free in those cultures with egalitarian gender relations, *and* in those cultures in which male dominance is firmly established and sex roles are rigidly enforced. This apparent contradiction is easily resolved: concern over sexual pollution is high and taboos and regulations to control sexuality develop *when women begin to acquire some rights and power.*

Where sexuality plays a vital role in human communion with the divine and the development of spiritual identity, there is less need to consider women and nature (which represent sexual power) as enemies of enlightenment that lure seekers away from the divine. Egalitarian relationships among men and women are more likely to result. Likewise, where women have no authority and represent no threat to patriarchal culture, there is no particular concern with sexual pollution or the dangers of sexuality.

At the same time, traditions that seek to suppress the erotic often treat women and nature with horror and contempt. There is even some evidence that historical shifts from generally egalitarian to patriarchal power structures are accompanied by schisms between sexuality and spirituality.[57] Religious traditions throughout the world are among the authoritative voices calling for the control and suppression of erotic power. But there is an irony here. The very insistence on the need to maintain constant vigilance to hold the erotic at bay testifies to its continued power. Repressed erotic energy will not stay repressed.

If we acknowledge—and nurture—the presence and power of the erotic, we may incorporate the sacred into our lives through our own sexual identities and relationships. If we cut sexuality off from its rootedness in the erotic, that deep chthonic power will emerge in other ways. As May suggests, a culture that represses the erotic will experience a return of the repressed "in a primitive way precisely designed to mock our withdrawal of feelings."[58] Deny this erotic "daimon" as we might, "the earth spirits will come back to haunt us in a new guise; Gaea will be heard, and when the darkness returns the black madonna will be present if there is no white."[59]

This tendency of erotic power to return, to overcome cultural and psychological denial, explains the tendency to view sex as corrupt and as profoundly alienated from the sacred. It can also help us to understand why this view is associated with misogynistic fear of women and nature and their repression. Since erotic forces, related as they are to powerful psychic influences in the human unconscious, insistently reassert themselves, cultures that fear them must repeatedly suppress them. Thus, the assault on erotic power is continually renewed.

Karen Horney discusses the many literary and mythical depictions of "the violent force by which man feels himself drawn to the woman, and side by side with his longing, the dread that through her he might die and be undone."[60] Man strives to rid himself of this dread by objectifying it: " 'It is not,' he says, 'that I dread her; it is that she herself is malignant, capable of any crime, a beast of prey, a vampire, a witch, insatiable in her desires. She is the very personification of what is sinister.' "[61]

Men's simultaneous glorification and ostentatious disparagement of women, Horney suggests, has its roots in man's desire to conceal his dread of female power (manifested in his fear of the all-consuming vagina) and to preserve his self-esteem. What men fear in women is something "uncanny, unfamiliar, mysterious."[62]

Observing women's mysterious (that is, supernatural) gifts, man could choose either to adore woman as divine or to "Satanize" her. Many scholars have commented upon the pervasive cultural tendency to associate women with chaotic sexuality, pollution, and evil, and offer much speculation about the cause. Theories range from the anthropological (for example, a response to the threat of increasing female social rights in a patriarchal culture)[63] to the psychological (conflicts arising from the complexities of the mother-child relationship).[64] Judith Hoch-Smith and Anita Spring note the amazing predominance of reflection upon female sexuality in the male mind: "For example, it is certainly remarkable that things as *periodic* as female monthly and reproductive cycles are understood as intrusion of chaos into an otherwise orderly universe" [emphasis in the original].[65]

Projection and Denial

We need to look into the dynamics of patriarchal culture in order to comprehend this virtual obsession with the inherent dangers of female sexuality. At this point I return to Susan Griffin's distinction between the erotic and the pornographic. As I noted above, the goal of the pornographic mind according to Griffin is to silence eros by taking revenge on nature. She associates this goal with the metaphysics of Christianity, in which the spirit, associated with man, and matter, associated with woman, are viewed as separate and in conflict. Matter corrupts spirit and must therefore be controlled or destroyed. Since woman is deeply associated with nature in both pornography and Christian metaphysics, this requisite control or destruction is applied to her. The body of a woman "is culture's time-honored and conventional victim."[66]

Critical to understanding this way of thinking are the mechanisms of projection and denial. Here, the resurgent power of the erotic plays a significant role. Denial, as Griffin explains, is not a mysterious force. It is simply the mechanism through which the mind forgets a part of itself, choosing not to know what it knows. Yet through this very effort to suppress what we wish not to know, forgotten knowledge reappears in the form of projection.[67]

So it is with deep knowledge of the erotic. In the effort to suppress these forces, woman becomes a blank screen for the projections of patriarchal culture. Her real nature is erased, "and she comes to stand for all that man would deny in himself."[68] Since a woman's body evokes knowledge that the preservers of patriarchal culture are trying to forget, it becomes an object of fear and dread. In Griffin's view, the whole history of civilization can be understood "as a struggle between the force of eros in our lives and the mind's attempt to forget eros."[69]

There is another way to resolve this crisis. Fear and the suppression of erotic power, of wildness, are not only related to the negation of embodiment and sexuality but deeply bound to the dichotomies that emphasize the triumph of life over death. Regeneration, by contrast, depends on the incorporation of both life and death into cycles of renewal, on the disintegration of worn out structures and their "underworld" transformation.

When cultures fear the natural processes of sex, death, and undoing, they tend to freeze in fear, terrified of structural changes that might undermine their carefully organized hierarchies. They project their fears onto that which symbolizes these natural forces and attack the objects of their projections. When people fear these processes, they try to hold back the changes that fuel them. They try to stop coming apart. They try to stop growing. But Eros will find a way. The wildness is always the wildness. I am convinced that recognition of the relationality of life and death, and a vision of the erotic as both creation and destruction, are at the core of healing.

I used to wonder about hell, the Land of No Return. If the underworld is the ultimate metaphor for eternal, inescapable suffering, why are there all these stories of people coming back from the land of the dead? How did Inanna, the Sumerian goddess whose underworld journey was inscribed on clay tablets almost four thousand years ago, get out?[70] Or Izanagi, Persephone, Psyche, Jesus? How could they return? When I explored many stories of underworld journeys, the answer finally seemed to me almost comically simple. It's the Land of No Return because the one who emerges is not the same one who descended. Hell is transformative. If this book is in part—but only in part—an underworld journey, we can imagine this journey in many ways, and absolute dichotomies are the least productive. As Persephone turns back toward Hades, as Sisyphus slumps back down his mountain, as Izanagi locks chaos up underground only to have it

Dancing after the Whirlwind

spurt out of his nose, we may grieve for their suffering, but we must not think them lost. As women rage and weep, own their suffering and their growth, pound their feet on the skin of their pain and dance the dance, we can choose. We can turn from them in dread, dismissing them as manifestations of madness, or we can open ourselves to them and join in, dancing after the whirlwind.

Chapter Two

Sex and the Sacred

The only hope, or else despair

Lies in the choice of pyre or pyre—

To be redeemed from fire by fire.

— T. S. ELIOT,
"Little Gidding," *Four Quartets*

Every culture and every religion have varying, sometimes conflicting views of sexuality. Some may see deep connections between sex and the sacred, while others view sex as sinful and corrupt. Suppression of the erotic is not limited to any particular culture or religious view. Although some goddess-worshipping cultures celebrate sexual/spiritual union, for example, reverence for female images of the divine has certainly not prevented violence against women, children, and nature. Christianity has been a major contributor to the alienation of sexuality from spirituality, but Christian theologians have also expressed deeply relational views of body and soul. Eastern religious traditions may reject the radical dichotomies of Western monotheism, but they may also reinforce hierarchies of spirit over nature and of man over woman.

Neither is it helpful to adopt, as some revisionist historians have done, a simplistic (de)evolutionary view, which assumes that earlier cultures valued the erotic connection between sex and the sacred while later cultures drove them apart. It is tempting to embrace the view that wounds could be healed and identities restored simply by reconstructing the mutuality of an idealized past. However, it is also irresponsible to ignore the factual and theoretical problems with this approach.

Even *if*, as some theorists of matriarchal prehistory claim, there once were egalitarian, nonhierarchical, nonmilitaristic, economically thriving communities, they were not a universal phenomenon. (Otherwise we are left with the problem of determining an origin for the militaristic hordes that conquered them.) Even *if* goddess worship once constituted the ritual focus of nonpatriarchal cultures, goddess worship does not, in itself, preclude patriarchy; there are contemporary cultures in which goddess worship and misogyny coexist. Even *if* things were better for women and nature somewhere some time in the past, we are not there now. We are where we are. And we need ways to heal the alienation between sexuality and spirituality here and now. Locating sexual/spiritual relationality in the past also blinds us to contemporary cultural resources for restoring this union.

Some specific examples may help to illuminate how the erotic connection between sex and the sacred has sometimes been maintained and why at other times it has been broken. A sense of the deep connection between sexuality and spirituality may be found in many historical periods and geographical areas: among Samoans, Melanesians, and Inuit, in texts as diverse as the *Kama Sutra*, the Hebrew *Song of Songs*, and Islamic erotic literature, in rituals of phallus worship and tantric devotion to the lingam and yoni, in kundalini yoga and the erotic sculptures at Khujarao, and in the lusty gyrations of bawdy goddesses. Likewise, taboos and law codes throughout the world underscore sexuality's sacred power while also illustrating human attempts to suppress, harness, or control it. Examples of connection and alienation, freedom and fear, are abundant in both Western and Eastern traditions.

My caution against idealizing the past or adopting too simplified an evolutionary theory is not meant to dismiss possible insights from ancient goddess-worshipping traditions or from cultures such as Hinduism and Buddhism, which practice contemporary goddess reverence. Our cultural scars are deep, and some of the most effective healing arts have ancient roots. Some scholars have presented goddess traditions very effectively as a rich resource for renewing and sustaining the bond between sex and the sacred.[1] These theories can be—and *are* being—developed on a sound foundation of research without recourse to overgeneralizations about the past or false optimism about the future. Where this work brings the value of goddess-worshipping traditions to the surface, it often does so without oversimplifying the complexities involved.

Experiencing the power of goddess images in art, literature, and ritual, including imagery depicting sacred sex, may be useful in healing the damage of denial and restoring women's creative energy.[2] In fact, an appreciation of goddess imagery may be valuable even for women who do not participate in wiccan, pagan, or other goddess-worshipping rituals and traditions. Goddess imagery serves as counterpoint to the ubiquitous symbolism of the father god, making it possible for women to find the goddess in themselves.[3]

One stirring view of the contribution goddess imagery can make is set out in Nelle Morton's essay, "The Goddess as Metaphoric Image." Writing as a feminist theologian, Morton describes herself as a "Goddess woman" but not as one who views the Goddess as an object of worship. She stresses the various ways in which the Goddess image has enabled her to break through old barriers and make way for a new vision. To substitute the image of the Goddess for the traditional view of God "immediately confronts the maleness in God, which produces a shock, a shattering, and opens the way for exorcising the old image."[4]

In Morton's personal stories of encounters with Goddess imagery, many possibilities for new visions of female power unfold. Unlike the male God who requires continuous gratitude and praise, the Goddess "works herself out of business. She doesn't hang around to receive thanks." When we no longer need to focus on praising the divine, we can instead reflect upon the transformation that Goddess imagery evokes within us. This insight brings us to see the connection between the beauty of the Goddess and our own embodied beauty as women.[5]

> Since the Goddess works herself out of the picture, we are better able to come into our full and whole inheritance that would make us one in our bodies, minds, and spirits. We can claim our sexuality as pervasive and as ourselves. We can claim our bodies as ours and as ourselves and our minds as our own and ourselves. This sense of oneness within and with one another has brought us into more erotic relationship with one another as women.[6]

In this view, goddess imagery renews connections between sexuality and spirituality, body and mind, by bringing women back into contact with the sacred value of their own female power. The erotic power of the goddess is healing power. By restoring eros to sexuality, She counteracts the projection, alienation, and denial of patriarchal culture. By offering women female images of the divine, She holds a mirror to the sacred power within us.

In her description of her own journey to the Goddess, Carol Christ links her encounter with divine female power to the discovery of her own power as a woman and to the realization of sacredness in nature: "Not until I said *Goddess* did I realize that I had never felt fully included in the fullness of my being as *woman* in masculine or neuterized imagery for divinity. Moreover, I found in Goddess spirituality an image that affirmed my own experience of the holiness of nature as a significant element in the divine reality."[7]

For women, one obvious connection with goddess imagery

emerges from the female capacity to bring forth life. In goddess cultures, this generative capacity is often, though not always, associated with sexuality. The connection between the goddess and sexuality may be manifested in the generative power of the goddess, including the creation and nourishment of plants, animals, and people. Christine Downing notes that the Great Mother worshipped in many cultures, including those of the Fertile Crescent, the Indus Valley, and the area around the Aegean Sea, is first and foremost associated with the provision of food, and that certain goddesses were believed to have taught humans how to grow grain.[8] Often in these cultures, human sexuality and agricultural cycles are closely connected, so that human sexual activity in the fields is viewed as auspicious or even vital, especially during planting and harvest.[9]

The voluptuous shape of ancient goddess figurines demonstrates the interaction between being and function in the ancient myth-making imagination. As Downing puts it, "What a goddess does she also is. So the giver of food is herself food." The generous goddess shapes were meant not so much to convey sexual attractiveness as to demonstrate "the prodigality of the milk-giving mother and her procreative potency." Goddesses associated with vegetal fertility were also linked to human fertility: "Ancient agricultural rituals were shaped by an intuition of the analogies between planting and sexual intercourse, between harvesting and childbirth."[10]

Rituals of goddess worship may also include human sexual activity as an expression of appreciation for the goddess's generative aspect and as a form of participation in it. The goddess Durga in Hindu worship is said to enjoy sexually explicit gestures and comments during Durga Puja, the autumnal harvest festival.[11] Sita, a Hindu goddess whose name means "furrow," is associated with the fertility of ploughed earth. Hindu texts depict her as married to gods associated with rain and fertility, probably illustrating the perception that the fertility of the cosmos results from interaction between sky and the earth, male and female.[12] This sky/earth creative generativity is also evident in the marital union between Indra, a sky/rain god, and Sri-Laksmi, an extremely popular Hindu goddess associated with prosperity, abundance, and good fortune.

In the course of her history as told in various Hindu myths, Sri-Laksmi has been associated with a number of other male deities (earning her a reputation as fickle), but by the late epic period she is almost exclusively depicted as consort of Visnu.[13] In these myths, their connection comes about in the context of the churning of the cosmic milk ocean by gods and demons. Here, Sri-Laksmi "herself represents the miraculous transformation of the formless waters into organic life."[14]

This generative activity of churning the waters is closely paralleled in the Japanese creation story. Izanami and Izanagi, the primordial parents, begin creating the world by churning the cosmic waters with a divine spear and then letting the congealed substance drip from the tip of the spear into the cosmic brine. Descending from heaven to the island thus formed, they carry on creation through erotic union. The cosmogonic account in the *Kojiki* is quite explicit:

> At this time [Izanagi] asked his spouse [Izanami], saying:
>
> "How is your body formed?"
>
> She replied saying:
>
> "My body, formed though it be formed, has one place which is formed insufficiently."
>
> Then Izanagi-nö-mikoto said:
>
> "My body, formed though it be formed, has one place which is formed to excess. Therefore, I would like to take that place in my body which is formed to excess and insert it into that place in your body which is formed insufficiently, and [thus] give birth to the land. How would this be?"
>
> Izanami-nö-mikoto replied, saying:
>
> "That will be good."

Then Izanagi-nö-mikoto said:

"Then let us, you and me, walk in a circle around this heavenly pillar and meet and have conjugal intercourse."[15]

Connections between the sexuality of the goddess and generativity are not limited to the cultures of the East. The goddess Inanna was worshipped in Sumer from the early part of the third millenium B.C.E. to the beginning of the first millenium B.C.E., and in the form of the Babylonian goddess Ishtar until near the end of the first millenium B.C.E. During this period, she played a central role in Sumerian ritual, including a royal marriage ceremony through which the king united with the goddess to ensure the fertility of the land.[16] Inanna herself is depicted as sexually eager and active, as is evident in a hymn dating back to approximately 2000 B.C.E. Here, the courtship between Inanna and her consort, Dumuzi, god of the date palm, is vividly described:

My vulva, the horn,
The Boat of Heaven,
Is full of eagerness like the young moon.
My untilled land lies fallow.

As for me, Inanna,
Who will plow my vulva?
Who will plow my high field?
Who will plow my wet ground?[17]

Another hymn emphasizes the sexual passion and pleasure Inanna enjoys with her consort:

He shaped my loins with his fair hands,
The shepherd Dumuzi filled my lap with cream and milk,
He stroked my pubic hair,

He watered my womb.

He laid his hands on my holy vulva,

He smoothed my black boat with cream,

He quickened my narrow boat with milk,

He caressed me on the bed.[18]

This is no allegory. This is the shaping, smoothing, stroking wonder of divine sex. As these poems demonstrate, the sexual power of the goddess is centered not only on her generative capacity but also on the great pleasure and energy she derives from sexual union.

In ancient Egypt, the incarnation of generative sexuality is Isis. Her love for her twin brother, Osiris, is so great that they embrace sexually in their mother's womb.[19] After Osiris is slain by his wicked brother, Seth, Isis demonstrates her powerful magic and great devotion by recovering his body, reviving and copulating with his penis, and conceiving the god Horus. In the Greco-Roman world, Isis is associated with the Greek goddesses Demeter and Aphrodite as a manifestation of irresistible sexual attraction.[20]

In these examples, the sexuality of the goddess is overwhelmingly heterosexual and procreative. However, the erotic generativity of the Great Goddess worshipped in Old Europe (between 6500 and 3500 B.C.E.) may originally have been contained within herself, without need for another. In her study of the goddesses of Old Europe, Marija Gimbutas specifically separates imagery of life creation, generativity, and multiplicity from heterosexual coitus. These goddesses, she notes, were "not Venuses or beauties, and most definitely not wives of male gods."[21] The Great Goddess of the Paleolithic period contained all power of life, death, and regeneration within her—there is no trace of a Father God.[22] Gimbutas holds that later descriptions of these goddesses as brides, wives, and daughters were a response to the development of patriarchal and patrilinear systems. As these systems became well established, the Earth Mother of Old Europe no longer had the ability to bring life to plants without intercourse.[23]

Although the life-creating power of these ancient goddesses is not dependent on heterosexual intercourse, it seems a mistake to assume that their generative activity is therefore devoid of erotic aspects. Similarly, the vulva, buttocks, and breasts of the goddess depicted in numerous sculptures and other objects represent generativity, multiplicity, and abundance, not enticements for the penetrative power of male deities, but She is not therefore deprived of sexual power. Her generative power *is* erotic—contained within her own being.

In a contemporary vision of this self-generative cosmogony, Starhawk imagines the goddess as she gazes into "the curved mirror of black space," beholds her own reflection, and falls in love with it:[24]

> She drew it forth by the power that was in Her and made love to Herself, and called Her "Miria, the Wonderful."
>
> Their ecstasy burst forth in the single song of all that is, was, or ever shall be, and with the song came motion, waves that poured outward and became all the spheres and circles of the worlds. The Goddess became filled with love, swollen with love, and She gave birth to a rain of bright spirits that filled the worlds and became all beings.[25]

Along with self-contained sexuality, goddess traditions also include same-sex erotic themes. Christine Downing has illustrated the presence of same-sex love as a significant component of goddess sexuality in Greek myth. No goddess in this tradition, she notes, is depicted merely as a contented wife. And given that subservience is not a characteristic typical of divinity, heterosexual relationships among divinities are often problematic. Although overt same-sex sexual relationships are rarely depicted in the goddess traditions, there is ample material demonstrating female erotic connection. Downing notes, for example, Demeter's function as "a woman-identified goddess," Athene's close association with women, and Hera's role at the center of women's devotional cults.[26] The goddess who most clearly represents women's love for women, however, is

Artemis. Her commitment to women and her love for them are major components of her nature, and she prefers the company of her nymphs and the wild things of the forest to that of men. Although this love for women has a sexual dimension, Downing holds that it is a mistake to understand it in primarily erotic terms. The essential character of this wild goddess is chaste, virginal, and solitary. This chastity is not, however, to be confused with frigidity. Rather, it is an expression of her passion: "She gives herself to her own passion, her own wildness—not to another."[27]

In contrast, as Downing notes, "What Artemis refuses to give, Aphrodite gives freely."[28] Aphrodite epitomizes not only generative sexuality but also the deep, sensual pleasure of lovemaking. Downing exuberantly describes Aphrodite's passion for passion:

> For Aphrodite is the goddess of all erotic love, all sensual pleasure, all delight in beauty. Though far more than a goddess of sexuality, she is that.... She blesses all lovemaking that is dedicated to mutual enjoyment (rather than to domination of another or to procreation)—whether marital or adulterous, heterosexual or homosexual, between men or between women. She is the goddess of poet and philosopher, as well as of courtesan and whore.[29]

Aphrodite is also associated with growth, vigor, and fertility, including the power that causes seeds to grow, flower, and reproduce; the fragrances that arouse sexual yearning; and the mating of animals.[30] Her powerful sexuality is her dominant characteristic: in fact, the Greek term *aphrodite* means sexual desire or sexual intercourse. She is, however, far more than a goddess of genital sexuality: "her love had a cosmic dimension, was the source of all life, all renewal."[31] Priestesses dedicated to Aphrodite functioned as her representatives in some temples, providing renewal through sexual union.[32] To experience a state of intense sexual desire was to be infused with the power of the goddess.

The feminist scholar Carol Christ, who views herself as a contemporary priestess of Aphrodite, links her dedication to the goddess to the recognition "that the transforming power of sexuality is a mystery, never to be understood or rationally controlled, only to be experienced again and again in its cycles of joyous communion and separation."[33]

Thus far, I have focused on the erotic power of the goddess as a force of generation and creativity. However, the goddess's sacred sexuality also has a chaotic or destructive aspect that is connected to, rather than separated from, her creative power. Gimbutas observes that Old European goddess symbolism is "lunar and chthonic, built around the understanding that life on earth is in eternal transformation, in constant and rhythmic change between creation and destruction, birth and death."[34] Goddess-worshipping cultures draw on myths and rituals to incorporate the chaotic or destructive aspect of divine sexuality into cycles of renewal.

In the Japanese cosmogony described above, the destructive aspect is introduced when Izanami gives birth to the god of fire. As the flaming heat of her offspring consumes her womb, Izanami dies and descends to the underworld. When Izanagi follows her, seeking to return her to the upper world in order to continue the process of creation, she is moved by his devotion but must ask permission to leave. She instructs him to wait for her and cautions him not to strike a light. But he is unable to bear the dark and lights the end tooth of his comb. In the dim light, he beholds the body of his spouse in an advanced state of decay. Unable to bear the sight, he flees back to the upper world and rolls a large stone over the opening. Yet he is not successful in keeping the power of death and destruction underground: in the very process of cleansing himself after this underworld journey, he brings into being not only the deities of sun and moon but also Susa-no-wo, the storm god (right out of his nose).

This story reminds us that the forces of chaos and destruction cannot be conquered. Creativity and degeneration are both essential components of erotic power. Furthermore, creativity is not neatly separated from destruction, nor life from death, male from female.

The later adventures of the Japanese ancestral sun goddess Amaterasu continue to manifest a violent sexual aspect, especially her encounters with her chaotic storm-god brother.[35]

Goddesses of other cultures also demonstrate this destructive power. In her unmarried state, the Hindu goddess Durga "is portrayed as possessing untamed sexual energy that is dangerous, indeed, deadly, to any male who dares to approach her."[36] Likewise, in the Babylonian *Epic of Gilgamesh*, Ishtar's sexuality is dangerous, disruptive, and possibly excessive. This overwhelming sexual energy threatens to consume those with whom these goddesses consort, as when Aphrodite incites uncontrollable sexual desire.

> When she infuses a devotee/victim with her power or presence, his or her world becomes greatly intensified. Obsessive preoccupation with a lover is common, a preoccupation that is often incapacitating, ruinous, disruptive, and tragic. But under her influence—absorbed, overpowered, drugged, maddened by her—nothing else matters.[37]

In spite of myriad examples depicting the female divine as sexually active and powerful, and associating creation with sexuality, the power of the goddess's sexuality is sometimes manifest in its restraint. Several goddesses are specifically associated with virginity, including the Buddhist Kwan-Yin, and the Greek Hestia, Athene, and Artemis. Even such overtly sexual goddesses as Inanna and Aphrodite are referred to in some texts as virginal or sexually innocent.[38]

Even where the goddess ruled, the overwhelming energy of sexuality was sometimes viewed as too dangerous, requiring restraint or control in order for human culture to be sustained. Although goddess traditions can serve as a resource for themes and images that value the connection between sexuality and spirituality, these ancient cultures also contained seeds of sexual fear, which may eventually have generated a view of sexuality as a threat to cultural (and spiritual) stability.

Monotheism and Dichotomies

Monotheism eventually magnified the ancient view of female power and nature as dangerous by elevating the spiritual over the natural realm. In Western religious traditions, a vast alienation between sex and the sacred developed, one repeatedly reinforced through the myths, traditions, and theologies of monotheism. Sexuality was often viewed as a temptation generated by the body (and the powers of evil) toward the corruption and destruction of the soul (and humanity's obedience to God). Boundaries must therefore be erected and repeatedly reinforced in order to keep the wild power of sexuality from obliterating the carefully marked trails demarcating our souls' journey toward salvation and leading the soul to stray from them.

The profound alienation between sexuality and spirituality, between body and soul, is rooted metaphorically in Eden. In her extensive study of the Genesis creation story, Elaine Pagels describes its enormous influence on Western culture. Commencing about 200 B.C.E., certain Jews, and later Christians, used the creation story to reveal and defend prevailing values, including those regarding sexual behavior. They interpreted the encounter between Adam, Eve, and the serpent with an emphasis on the distance between God and humanity and the grave dangers inherent in passionate sexual desire.[39] By the fifth century, these attitudes had culminated in Augustine's declaration "that spontaneous sexual desire is the proof of—and penalty for—universal original sin."[40]

By linking carnal desire with original sin, Augustine most thoroughly expresses alienation between sexuality and spirituality. But the seeds of this alienation were planted centuries before his time. Pagels convincingly demonstrates that Jews had for centuries taught that the sole purpose of marriage and the sexual relationship was procreation. Practices that threatened or did not contribute to this goal—prostitution, homosexuality, abortion, and infanticide—inhibited population growth and thus threatened the stability and survival of the Jewish people. Such activities were opposed by Jewish law and custom, although tolerated by their pagan neighbors. The impurity laws banned even marital intercourse unless it took place at times most likely to result in conception.[41] Jewish teachers likewise supported polygamy, the divorce of infertile wives, and other practices that facilitated procreation. These codes and proscriptions reinforced population growth and cultural stability, but they also further alienated the sexual from the spiritual. Only procreative sexuality remained within the realm of the sacred.

Andre Guindon points out that Jewish sexual ethics were strongly influenced by monotheism's rejection of any possible association between Yahweh and any other divine being. Myths of divine union and related sexual rites accordingly disappeared.[42] The passionate sexual displays enjoyed by Sumerian and Canaanite deities became anathema. And, unlike the Great Goddess, the disembodied God of monotheism does not make love to himself.

Christianity: "Rebellion in the Flesh"

The teachings of Jesus radically challenged some of the views of sexuality common among his Jewish contemporaries. He adamantly insisted that no legitimate grounds existed for divorce and emphasized celibacy as a state higher than marriage.[43] Yet, while challenging the status quo, Jesus' ideas did not necessarily enhance the role of sexuality in spiritual life. Rather, his early followers tended to reinforce alienation between the sexual and the spiritual. Paul took Jesus' understanding of the importance of celibacy even further by encouraging married couples to live as if they were not married. Pagels stresses that this teaching was based not on a revulsion against sexuality but on a belief in "the necessity to prepare for the end of the world and to free oneself [from social commitments] for the 'age to come.' "[44] Yet a negative response to sexuality took root from these early views.

Over time, Christian leaders reshaped these radical gospel teach-

Dancing after the Whirlwind

ings to serve the purposes of first- and second-century churches seeking stable models for family life and communities of worship. Eventually, a "durable double standard" developed endorsing marriage "but only as second best to celibacy."[45] Christians also retained the position, clearly established in Jewish law, that the sole legitimate purpose of marriage, and the only rationale for sexual intercourse, was procreation.[46] Interpretations of the Genesis story provided justification.

Pagels argues that the value placed on celibacy in early Christianity was linked not only with purity but with freedom:

> Those Christians who proclaimed freedom from social and political entanglements defied those who valued human life according to its social contribution, and in the process, ... envisioned a new society based on free and voluntary choice. The majority of Christians married but continued nonetheless to assert the primacy of renunciation. In their resistance to conventional definitions of human worth based upon social contribution, I suggest, we can see the source of the later western idea of the absolute value of the individual.[47]

The association of chastity with freedom did not remain the predominant view. After Christianity gained imperial favor and became the official religion of the empire, church leaders came to read the story of Adam and Eve in terms of sexual corruption, human moral impotence, and a "sexualized interpretation of sin,"[48] The spokesman for this view was Augustine, the influential bishop of Hippo, whose view of human nature "became, for better and worse, the heritage of all subsequent generations of western Christians and the major influence on their psychological and political thinking."[49]

In his pictorial essay *The Axis of Eros*, Walter Spink notes that the descendants of monotheistic tradition in the West tend to explain their fate in terms of their guilt and sense of sin. They adopt beliefs in such doctrines as original sin and the fundamentally corrupt nature of humanity in order to explain their sense of doom and create doom in response to their beliefs.[50] The connection between sin (with its associated doom) and sexuality is evident in writings of the early church.[51] Among its proponents, Augustine has been particularly influential.

The story of Adam and Eve leads Augustine to a number of conclusions: sexual desire is sinful; every human being, from the moment of conception, is profoundly corrupt; and Adam's sin extends to all of nature.[52] The effects of these interpretations are felt by those who live in cultures they have influenced, whether Christian or non-Christian.

The Bishop of Hippo heartily located the relationship between sin and sexuality in the transgressions of the first parents—a disobedience that forever condemns all humanity to the perilous struggle between soul and flesh. Although their souls and bodies were created to be under the authority of their rational will, Adam and Eve undertook an internal "rebellion" against God's rule, and flesh triumphed over spirit.[53]

Augustine, in fact, affirms the diametrical opposition between flesh and spirit and between sin and chastity. Lust of the flesh is a very powerful craving.[54] Though there are other lusts, such as those for revenge, money, conquest, and applause, he is particularly awed by the power of this human condition, which

> not only takes possession of the whole body and outward members, but also makes itself felt within, and moves the whole man with a passion in which mental emotion is mingled with bodily appetite, so that the pleasure which results is the greatest of all bodily pleasures. So possessing indeed is this pleasure, that at the moment of time in which it is consummated, all mental activity is suspended.[55]

Augustine is evidently anxious regarding the power of lust to overwhelm the will. Human procreative members seem to have a mind of their own, being ruled not by our will "but by a certain independent autocracy."[56] In fact, Augustine's view of sexual desire as a

Dancing after the Whirlwind

tormenting and insatiable appetite has caused some scholars to characterize him as a sexual addict.[57]

Although Augustine associates lust with sinful craving, he does not necessarily rule out intercourse in Eden. Our first parents in paradise did not initially feel "that lust which caused them afterwards to blush and hide their nakedness."[58] Lust commenced only after sin entered the picture. In fact, since humans were charged with the duty to increase and multiply and replenish the earth before human disobedience and sin, the begetting of children must have been possible without sin. Augustine, although concerned that unchaste minds may find his discourse obscene, undertakes to explain how this might be accomplished: "The man, then, would have sown the seed, and the woman received it, as need required, the generative organs being moved by the will, not excited by lust."[59]

His discourse on the human capacity to exercise will over the body draws Augustine to very earthy matters. He discusses the capacity of some people to maintain control over bodily functions such as wiggling their ears and even regurgitating previously swallowed items whole.[60] Of some note is the ability of those "with such command of their bowels, that they can break wind continuously at pleasure, so as to produce the effect of singing."[61] Command, it seems, is the issue, but human sin has robbed us of that capacity where sexual matters are concerned.

In paradise, offspring may have been begotten at the command of the will, the husband lying upon the bosom of his wife "with calmness of mind and with no corrupting of the integrity of the body."[62] Just as menstrual blood is emitted from a virgin's womb, male semen might enter the womb without disturbing the integrity of the female organ. Augustine refrains from further discussion of specific methods, stating that "modesty shuts my mouth, although my mind conceives the matter clearly."[63] The mortal sin of the flesh, it seems, is not the physical act of intercourse but the lack of will to command it without lust, a failure deeply embedded in every person for all time as a direct effect of original sin. The capacity to procreate without uncontrollable desire is now forever lost, because Adam succumbed to "the seductive lure of liberty."[64]

If command is the issue, then the power of the erotic, always carrying us beyond the realm of will and reason, threatens our very souls. Augustine's belief that lust is "universal, infinite, and all-consuming"[65] derives from his own personal experience. Confronted by the wild power of his own sexual desires, Augustine interprets lust as the signal indicator of damnation. Without a way to incorporate erotic power into the soul's spiritual journey, he must relegate it to the devil's work.

Later Christian doctrine takes up Augustine's association of sexuality, sin, and uncontrollable desire but insists that we *do* have the ability to control or suppress it. Guindon observes:

> This conception is everywhere present in popular presentation of the Christian view of sex. What "you feel like doing" is opposed to effort, control, discipline. The reader is never told exactly either how this is done or what the outcome will be for the "sexual feelings." But the program sounds like the tyrannical regime of will-power ruling over messy genitality. The proper place of sensuality is bondage.[66]

Over the centuries, Christianity has come to support the view that physical sexuality is only permissible if kept within very specific parameters. Otherwise, it will drag us down into animalistic, even demonic realms. Vincent Genovesi demonstrates how powerfully this view has been incorporated into the culture by noting that the expression "living in sin" typically refers to sexual activity rather than pride, greed, or social injustice.[67] This ethical formulation lives on in the teaching of the Christian church: "Sex is dirty, save it for someone you love."[68]

Augustine's view prevailed, and sexuality became the central taboo in Western monotheism, the principal paradigm for that which is out of control, that which must be purged. Such a view denies that it is possible to incorporate sexuality into spiritual life. The threat

Dancing after the Whirlwind

posed by erotic power must be resisted by imposing strict controls on sexual expression. But given the obvious joys of sexual ecstasy and love, given the alternative possibility of incorporating embodied sensuous life into spirituality, why would a culture choose a path of suppression and control? Part of the explanation may be the tendency I have noted to associate doom with sin; suffering comes about as a consequence of humanity's fallen nature.

But why would Augustine's paradoxical, perhaps even preposterous, association of sexuality with sin prevail in Catholic Christianity? Pagels postulates that people tend to accept blame for misfortune because they often "*would rather feel guilty than helpless*" [emphasis in the original].[69] Her observation is crucial. Our guilt, though painful, reassures us: events that appear to be random are actually the result of specific laws of causation. Since many of these causes lie within the moral sphere, they must be subject to human control.[70] Because we fear that which is beyond our control, we seek explanations, even painful ones, for what befalls us.

Sex-Positive Christian Theologies

The suppression of sexuality within Christianity has undoubtedly contributed to many of our social ills. However, some Christian theologians contend that alienation does not derive from the heart and source of Christian teaching and belief. In fact, they take the position that a separation between sexuality and spirituality is fundamentally un-Christian.

These Christian thinkers suggest that sexuality and spirituality should be viewed as two deeply related aspects of human nature. A fully integrated spiritual identity requires the incorporation of embodied relationality, including sexuality. Do these alternative Christian views offer possibilities for overcoming denial and affirming that the resounding rhythms of the natural body are crucial to our spiritual identities?

Among the best-known Christian proponents of the view that sexuality and spirituality are deeply connected is James Nelson. In developing his sexual theology, Nelson highlights the communal connection between sexuality and language (see chapter 1). The mystery of sexuality is the mystery of our need for the physical and spiritual embrace of others. According to Nelson, human nature is profoundly social—we realize our true selves in a "communion of love."[71] Through our sexual being, God calls us into communion, reaching out to touch and embrace, emotionally, intellectually, and physically. Sexuality is neither accidental nor peripheral to our becoming ourselves; rather, it grounds our capacity to love, both physiologically and psychologically, and is thus at the center of our relatedness. This communion of human love also provides the basis for our encounter with divine love. If God is met as "the One whose continuing incarnation is expressed through creaturely relationships, then our sexuality is a sacramental means for the love of God."[72]

Other Christian voices—among them, Andre Guindon, John Dwyer, Vincent Genovesi, and Evelyn Eaton and John Whitehead—affirm the deep connection between sexuality and spirituality as authentic, practical, and traditional.[73] These theorists often base their view on faith in the immeasurable goodness of the creator and the related belief that nothing could be created that is evil in itself.[74] Others stress combining a Christian ethic of love for humanity with the acknowledgment of the fundamental role of the Incarnation—the union of divinity and humanity in Jesus—in affirming our embodied relationality.

In this view, sexuality is—or should be—a way to translate love into action. By living the miracle of the Incarnation, Christians should affirm their commitment to realizing God's revelation in the form of Christ: love becomes flesh.[75] In this call to love, sexuality plays a crucial role that is related to its communicative nature. Our most deeply embodied relationships should reflect the divine love manifested in the form of Jesus. "God becomes not a human being nor a moral agent nor a thinking person but *flesh*. God enters into a

Dancing after the Whirlwind

life like ours—bodily, sexual, emotional. The Incarnation is good news for the flesh."[76]

Incarnation is an erotic idea. The embodied divine is one who touches, who loves, who drinks and dances. If God has a body, God can suffer, and we can relate. And if God has a body, then God can die and be reborn. This living God, this union of human and divine, reflects the power of Eros at its best. But divine Incarnation is not enough to redeem erotic connection in Christianity, especially when it is understood to have taken place just once, for one human/divine being, in one time and place. As long as our bodies remind us that we are not divine, it becomes difficult to bless sex. And many Christians continue to cringe at the notion of a sexual Jesus, while pornography capitalizes on the suppression of eros to exploit sexualized images of the crucifixion.

Andre Guindon takes sex-positive Christian theology a step farther. Resisting the body-soul dichotomy and drawing on associations between God and embodied love and between sex and language, Guindon argues for a sexual ethics that integrates tenderness (spirituality) and sensuality (sexuality). Tenderness, which refers to the spiritual side of the self, involves our sense of meaning and the emergence of emotional states such as love, attention, care, delight, and amazement.[77] Sensuality is linked with our embodiment and an affective life that gives rise to erotic sensations, desires, and pleasures.[78] These two—tenderness and sensuality—never exist separately but live "in a tensional and dynamic unity."[79] As they blend more and more into one another in mutually respectful and loving relationships, they become more mutually energizing, eventually achieving sexual integration. Through this integrative work we may become selves "whose spirits are enfleshed, perfectly at home in their sexual bodies, and whose bodies are spiritualized, expressive of their sexual selves' genuine identity."[80] Sexual *dis*integration comes about when tenderness and sensuality fail to merge "into an integrated human wholeness."[81]

Guindon's view strongly emphasizes the interplay of body and soul, the dynamics of the dance. Though he speaks of wholeness, his concept of sexual/spiritual integration emphasizes the dynamism and energy inherent in the relationship. If he sometimes tends to equate sexual/spiritual harmony with a perfected state rather than with the ongoing interaction between the two in the dynamics of our most intimate relationships, his idea of an integrated identity certainly challenges rigid dichotomies.

Guindon's approach emerges directly from his use of a language model to understand sexuality. Sex is "the very condition of our being-in-the-world as enfleshed spirits," and thus it affects and symbolizes our whole personality.[82] Sexual language tends, therefore, "towards the establishment of a relationship based on the totality of who we are."[83] In fact, it is the only language capable of adequately expressing our most fundamental being: "How, indeed, will a carrier of enfleshed meaning express his or her unutterable experience of personal uniqueness to others without the sensually tender connotations of sexual expression."[84] If the meaning of sexual activity finds expression in truthful communication between intimate selves,[85] it is also the capacity through which we recognize a relational God.[86] For Guindon, "the word that does not take flesh does not live among us. This is the only way that anything spiritual can pitch its tent among us: through embodiment."[87]

One of Guindon's most significant contributions to sex-positive theology is his association of sexuality with freedom and love, a view very different from Augustine's: "As a generator of intimate interpersonal relationships, human sexuality opens up a space for personal freedom to enhance the personality of others through love and, indivisibly, to be created anew by love."[88] This view also points to an understanding of sexual perversion that avoids the typical association with particular types of behavior. The literal meaning of perversion is "to cause to turn from what is good to what is evil, to overturn, to distort, to corrupt."[89] If sexual language is a particularly human means of conveying love, then *corruption of sexuality comes about when we use it to express hatred.* When sexual language lacks "the generosity of love," it becomes a perversion, "an ugly corruption" of God's language. In this category Guindon includes all forms of sexual violence and exploitation, from disguised manifestations such as attitudes of dominance to overt sexual assault.[90]

Guindon's interpretation of perversion seems to me an effective theoretical basis for understanding sexual abuse and denial of sexual identity as sacrilege. Sexuality as sacred erotic connection expresses our freedom for one another; it speaks the divine language of love. When it is perverted, violence, abuse, and sexual oppression and humiliation are the consequence. This understanding of sexual perversion is, in my view, critical in formulating a liberating approach to the sexuality/spirituality bond. Where the communion of love is present, sexuality becomes a means to express the generative power of the divine. "Pregnant with love's generosity, human sexuality discloses, for those who have the experience of truly being cared for or of actively caring for another, the fecundity of a God who is love."[91]

Sexuality thus serves as a powerful vehicle for communication and self-understanding, but it is also a means of reaching beyond ourselves. The theologian John Dwyer notes the possible role of sex in "liberation from egoism," which can lead to deeper spiritual communion: "Sexual love awakens the feeling of wanting to give and wanting to please, of wanting to give of oneself wholly and entirely."[92]

It is in this generously relational sense that I view sexuality as a critical component of identity, remembering that identity is formed in a relational context. Of course, Dwyer's emphasis on the giving aspects of sexuality can also be interpreted to encourage the kind of "selfless" approach to sexual relationships that is very dangerous to women. Sexual exploitation thrives on the belief that certain individuals in society (those without power) are supposed to give of themselves "wholly and entirely." Such exploitation has a signficant history within Christianity. To give of ourselves to a beloved can be ecstatic, but self-sacrifice is not, in itself, a good. Sacrificing our own desires for the benefit of others through acts of love may express the essence of Christian piety—but Christianity has historically assigned the martyr role in a fairly biased fashion. And too many women die inside, because they unconsciously believe that religion requires it.

The preceding theorists hold that deep spiritual communion in relation to sexual bonding depends entirely on mutual desire and pleasure, on a *balance* of giving and receiving. Christian theologians who affirm the value of sexuality in spiritual development also tend to resist patriarchal assumptions of female inferiority and the right of human beings (read males) to dominate nature. Sometimes utilizing the same mythologies that have traditionally been interpreted to support oppression, these theorists lift up a different vision.

Feminist and Womanist Theologies: Relationality and Justice-Making

Given the dynamics of alienation between sexuality and spirituality, and the associated suppression of women and nature, it is not surprising that the most powerful and articulate voices in defining a sex-positive theology (or thealogy) are those of feminist and womanist theorists. Christian and post-Christian feminist and womanist approaches are challenging the well-established theological traditions of alienation.[93]

Carter Heyward raises the provocative questions implied by a new sexual ethics:

> Are our bodies really good? naturally good? precious gifts of God? If so, is the erotic energy that moves between us a fundamentally good energy? ... What distorts this goodness? Could it be that the burden of ethical proof is really upon us to discover under what circumstances sex is wrong (abusive, violent, degrading, compulsive) rather than, as has been historically the case among Christians, under what circumstances sex is right?[94]

Dancing after the Whirlwind

Feminist biblical scholars have also challenged widely held assumptions about the role and place of women in the early church, applying a "hermeneutics of suspicion" to patriarchal biblical interpretations and bringing fresh insight to textual meaning.[95] Instead of accepting a literal interpretation of Christian scripture as absolute truth, these scholars interpret Scripture in light of its social and political context and its likely impact on the lives of women.[96] This change of focus often leads to new insights.

Phyllis Trible, for example, sheds new light on the creation story. Her analysis of the grammatical structure and rhetorical style of the text suggests that the relationship of the first couple is one of mutuality and equality rather than male dominance and female subordination.[97] It also emphasizes woman's sexuality as a significant aspect of her being. At the same time, Trible considers the story an expression of the ongoing conflict between life and death. The woman created by Yahweh God is the culmination of creation, the fulfillment of Eros:

> She is unique. Unlike all the rest of creation, she does not come from the earth; rather Yahweh God builds the rib into woman. . . . Hence, woman is no weak, dainty, ephemeral creature. No opposite sex, no second sex, no derived sex—in short, no "Adam's rib." Instead, woman is the culmination of creation, fulfilling humanity in sexuality. . . . With her creation eros reigns.[98]

For Trible, the text of Genesis 2–3 is the story of Life (Eros) and Death (Thanatos). Eros is created in joy, unity, and delight, but an act of disobedience results in disintegration and decay. "Truly," as Trible tells it, "a love story has gone awry."[99] Alienation disrupts the erotic connection between God and humanity. In Trible's retelling, Eros and Thanatos are at odds. Unlike the goddess traditions, which celebrate both the creative and the destructive aspects of erotic power, here the dichotomy between life and death and between good and evil is preserved. Death is not part of the natural cycle of regeneration and renewal. Death is punishment.

Trible adopts Freud's interpretation of Eros as the life force that struggles against death. Other feminist theologians, however, and feminist writers such as Audre Lorde, Susan Griffin, and Adrienne Rich, view erotic power from a different perspective. Most focus on the function of Eros in combating oppression and injustice.

The value of Christian tradition in terms of justice-making for women is most succinctly expressed by Rosemary Ruether's "critical principle of feminist theology." Ruether asserts that whatever succeeds in *promoting women's full humanity* "is of the Holy, it does reflect true relation to the divine, it is the true nature of things, the authentic message of redemption and the mission of redemptive community."[100]

For more than a decade, feminist theologians have applied this principle through various theologies and experiences to highlight the power of relationships, especially those between and among women, and to promote the full humanity of women. In feminist theology this relational focus is connected to the notion of embodiment. Beverly Harrison establishes the ethical framework. Beginning with our bodies, we come to realize that everything we know and value comes to us through our sensuous connection to the world.[101] Since relationship is central to the process of developing embodied knowledge and values, moral agency means putting those values into practice and recognizing that sensuality is fundamental to the ways in which we live and love.[102]

It is a basic feminist assumption that embodiment connects us with connection. Living in and through our bodies, we are constantly reminded that we are relational beings. Why is this so? What is it about having bodies that emphasizes relationships rather than autonomy or isolation? After all, bodily parameters might just as logically represent boundaries separating one being from another. Were it not for all the wonders of sensuous stimulation, this might be our focus. But our bodies are first and foremost the place where we expe-

Dancing after the Whirlwind

rience interaction with all and every—the place where we touch. That is the erotic key to the relational nature of embodiment: We touch. We move through life rubbing our skins on the world.

This sensuous contact in turn enlivens our interconnectedness with one another. To explore the full implications of this interconnected relationality, I will focus on the work of three women whose insights into the transformative nature of erotic power have helped redefine the sex/spirit relationship: Carter Heyward, Mary Hunt, and Rita Nakashima Brock.

Carter Heyward incorporates Harrison's ethical framework into a sexual theology based on an understanding of the erotic as sacred power. Interconnectedness implies responsibility. Building her view of the erotic on foundations established by Audre Lorde, Heyward associates lovemaking with justice-making—"right, mutual, relation."[103] But it is also about love: the erotic is "our most fully embodied experience of the love of God."[104]

Augustine equates sin with lust, the inability to control ourselves. Heyward also believes that control is a critical issue, but she turns Augustine inside out: sin is the violation of the sacred bond between sexuality and the sacred, whether that violation is enacted through sexual violence or through structures of global domination and subjugation. It is the failure to achieve right relation. Power used in other than mutually empowering ways is abusive. Like Guindon, Heyward understands perversion in terms of its literal meaning, to be turned around completely. Out of this understanding, she posits a stance of resistance to the forces of social evil. Even scripture is perverse when it is used in service of "racial hatred and discrimination, economic exploitation, sexual, gender, and other forms of injustice, christian imperialism and other forms of domination," because it is "turned around completely from the possibility of being shared as a resource of love and liberation."[105]

Right relation begins, of course, on a personal level. We experience the sacred value of erotic relatedness when we actively seek to liberate one another from the damage of denial, the "brokenness and despair wrought by abusive power relations in the great and small places of our lives."[106]

Heyward develops her understanding of mutual relatedness directly from her understanding of friendship as a sacred act of soul-touching.[107] Within the framework of this communion, drawing on the awareness our senses bring us, we develop our own sense of values and obligations, our own vision, which then becomes our principal resource for spiritual and theological authority.[108] "With my people—friends, *compañeras*, sisters and brothers, known and unknown—I realize that our creative power in relation, the power of our godding, is the wellspring of our sexualities; our yearnings to embody mutually empowering relations, our desire to live into our YES."[109]

Mary Hunt picks up Heyward's understanding of justice-making as "right relation," basing her relational theology on the "fierce tenderness" of female-female friendships.[110] Friendship, a "central relational experience" for women, has the power to transform relationships and change social structures.[111] Hunt's woman friends, then, are "justice-seeking" friends. "Justice involves making friends, lots of friends, many kinds of friends. . . . [J]ustice is the fundamental relational goal that issues from communities of accountability where change takes place. Justice is the reason for personal nurture. Justice-seeking friends empower one another to keep making change when the work is hard."[112]

Hunt's model of friendship depicts four elements, love, power, embodiment, and spirituality, in dynamic interaction. When these four elements are all present and functioning in harmony with one another, the friendship not only thrives, but it also transforms: "It generates something new for both persons and for the larger community of which they are a part."[113]

In her discussion of embodiment, which specifically includes sexuality, Hunt stresses that all our activities and interactions are bodily mediated. Therefore, "virtually every relational act is a physi-

Dancing after the Whirlwind

cal event."[114] Her understanding of spirituality emphasizes the choices we make and their impact on our physical surroundings as well as our personal, social, and political relationships. Embodiment and spirituality also interact with love, which represents not separation, but our unity with others and our power to make choices, individually and communally.[115]

Rita Nakashima Brock sets out another full-bodied theology that incorporates the value of love, erotic power, and relationality in *Journeys by Heart.* Contemporary culture, she postulates, suffers from a "brokenheartedness" brought about by sin. In this reading, sin is equated with the damage to the self and the heart caused by patriarchal oppression.[116] Fear of our own deep passions, including our anger and our sexual and sensual feelings, is passed from one generation to another.[117] Because this false self learns to hate and fear sensuality and the body, reclaiming our bodies and our deeply embodied feelings allows us to reclaim ourselves. Loving touch reassures us that we share the world with caring others.[118] The power that heals brokenheartedness and empowers the faint of heart is the power of the erotic: "The fundamental power of life, born into us, heals, makes whole, empowers, liberates. Its manifold forms create and emerge from heart, that graceful, passionate mystery at the center of ourselves and each other."[119]

Christ, "the revelatory and redemptive witness of God/dess's work in history," is, for Brock, also "Christa/Community." Eros represents the power of connectedness in community that brings this witness into being and acknowledges Christianity's experiences of brokenness and the "sacredness of erotic power in human existence."[120]

Justice-seeking friends, fierce tenderness, healing the heart—all three views enliven the spiritual journey by incorporating the erotic. But perhaps they do not take the untamed nature of this power—the out-of-control wildness that so distressed Augustine—seriously enough. Perhaps they do not see the threat implicit in embodied power. Is feminist eros too nice? Does it fail to acknowledge the dangers along this path, claiming justice, love, mutuality, and harmony for the erotic and attributing all fear, grief, and pain to patriarchal causes? Perhaps the feminist view forgets the hurt in love and the fear in sex, the potential for damage when passions collide. K. Roberts Skerrett cautions feminists not to forget the tragic within the erotic.[121]

Feminist eros, however, is not unilaterally blithe. Carter Heyward, for example, acknowledges that erotic ambiguity is fundamental to our lives: "I was coming to believe that the capacity to live in ambiguity, to accept it, to make ethical decisions in it and act on these decisions . . . is a capacity born of wisdom and seasoned in courage."[122] She describes certain of her relationships as "chaotic, embodying the sort of psychospiritual raw material out of which real love is born, but not without struggle."[123] As a response to this chaotic ambiguity, Heyward recommends community: "We need to be spinning webs of honest, intimate friendship and support, expanding circles of companions with whom to touch our strength. . . . These God-bearing wombs of compassion are what will enable us to tolerate ambiguity and learn to sift chaos as lightly as a bakerwoman does her flour."[124]

All three theologians also agree that justice will not be achieved or hearts healed until embodied eros engages oppression, including the bitter dichotomies of race and class. Writing as a Japanese-Puerto Rican immigrant American, Brock observes that Christianity has sometimes been able to loosen patriarchy's stranglehold when it has moved into other cultural contexts, such as Asia.[125] She also notes its contribution, as "an iconoclastic tool of liberation and life-giving power," to the people of Latin America and the African American community.[126] These contributions do not nullify the patriarchal oppression of Christian institutions, but Brock holds that one cannot simply dismiss Christianity as hopelessly patriarchal and oppressive "unless all women are regarded as middle class and white."[127]

Dancing after the Whirlwind

Although Brock's Christian theology celebrates the power of women's sexuality, Kwok Pui-lan points out that African American and third world women rarely discuss the power of female sexuality.[128] She attributes this rejection of the language of the erotic to a history in which their sexuality has been institutionally controlled and degraded, their bodies sold into slavery and prostitution.[129] As these women, who are doubly disenfranchised, develop their own spiritual response to oppression, suffering, and humiliation, they have interwoven scriptural reflection with themes of liberation, activism, creativity, strength, and community.[130] A critical aspect of this spirituality continues to be what Cheryl Gilkes calls the nurturing of "a healthy self-love," including love and respect for one's own body.[131]

The feminist contribution to reconnecting sexuality and spirituality is by no means limited to Christian theological reflection. Feminist authors writing from Jewish and Muslim perspectives, for example, have also made important contributions to a relational sex-positive view.[132] Other powerful feminist voices speak from outside (in some cases, far outside) the structures of organized religion. In keeping with my position that spirituality is not limited to religious expression, I invoke the power of feminist thinkers who have flown the coop.

Mary Daly continues to evoke frustration and anger as well as admiration and sustained, raucous humor. Her early works, especially *Beyond God the Father*,[133] have forever altered the course of Christian theology. Yet Daly chose long ago to depart from the ranks not only of Christians but of theologians. Daly often reminds me of that kid on the home block of my childhood who always pushed us further than we wanted to go. She was always up ahead yelling, "Come on, sissies," and we were always scandalized, envious, disapproving, admiring—never willing to go that fast or that far. From Daly's earliest call to realize the promises made at Vatican II (*The Church and the Second Sex*),[134] through the Harvard Memorial Church Exodus (*Outercourse*),[135] to her recent call to join her on the other side of the moon (*Outercourse*, especially the "Fourth Spiral Galaxy"), Daly has always wanted more from feminism than feminism has been willing to give. Still, her call continues to be heard. As in the old neighborhood, after running along for some time, we often find ourselves in a place we recognize—a place Daly has already been.

In terms of erotic power, Daly's guiding principle is Pure Lust— "the high humor, hope, and cosmic accord/harmony of those women who choose to escape, to follow our hearts' deepest desire and bound out of the State of Bondage, Wanderlusting and Wonderlusting with the elements."[136] One of the most intriguing (and, for many, frustrating) aspects of Daly's approach to Eros is her insistence that women can simply choose to leave patriarchal bondage behind and proceed by leaps and bounds into the spinning and spiraling consciousness that connects us "with auras of animals and plants, moving in planetary communion with the farthest stars."[137] Pure Lust is "pure Passion; unadulterated, absolute, simple, sheer striving for abundance of be-ing; unlimited, unlimiting desire/fire."[138] This sense of totality, of unlimited power, has caused many to view Daly's approach as unrealistic. It is also what has made her work so compelling for so many wild women.

Daly acknowledges the power of patriarchal oppression, contrasting her principle of Pure Lust with the pure lust of the patriarchy, "a deadly dis-passion" associated with "the life-hating lechery that rapes and kills the objects of its obsession/aggression."[139] This "violent, self-indulgent desire" seeks to "level all life, dismember spirit/matter, attempt annihilation."[140] Again, where spirituality is separated from erotic power, the result is alienation, violence, and oppression. As for hope of a Christian feminist reformation, Daly summarized succinctly: "If God is male, then the male is God."[141] And she knocked the dust from her sandals.

In describing her own "spiritual, political" journey, Emily Culpepper counts herself among those women who "do not join or name ourselves after any specific religious tradition."[142] Noting that an increasing number of women are choosing to "create more eccentric pathways that aid and encourage others to deviate as widely as possible from patriarchal centers of meaning,"[143] Culpepper describes another way. Like many of the women whose experiences I am considering here, Culpepper's approach to spirituality rejects not only the confines of orthodox patriarchal religious tradition but also the limit-setting boundaries of all institutionalized paths. At the same time, it leads from the feminist insight that "the personal is political" to a wider understanding that "the personal is political is spiritual."[144] Such an insight makes way for Culpepper's vision that the whole world is sacred text. With her, we have our lifetimes to learn to read.[145]

Feminist and womanist voices on a global level converge in emphasizing the union of sexual and spiritual power and the sacred value of eros. Although certain themes reappear in their work, these theorists do not belong to a particular "school" of thought or affiliate themselves with a common academic or religious institution. The coherence among their varied perspectives seems to me to be directly related to the power of eros at work.

Throughout the world, women working in libraries and studies and gardens, in hospitals and kitchens, have become aware of the fierce spiritual joy and power of erotic connectedness—and of the need to resist the oppression and injustice striving to turn that joy into fear. And then these women write. For decades, their thoughts and words took form individually; eventually they were "heard into speech" by feminist and womanist communities as women began to share their work with one another.[146] What we eventually discover is that each voice represents a thread in the quilt, a piece in the puzzle, a theme in the composition—though there are patterns of similarity, each contribution is unique and essential. If there is a commonality among the women who have contributed to this body of spiritual work, it emerges not because their words are derivative but because they are inspired.

Eastern Religious Traditions:
The Dance of Divine Union

As we have seen, some Western religious traditions alienated human sexuality from spirituality. I have also explored alternative views in which the two are deeply connected. Do certain Eastern religious views provide help in affirming erotic power, thus restoring sexual identity and sexual expression to the realm of the sacred? Lacking the absolute dichotomies of certain Western theologies, do they place less emphasis on control, suppression, and judgment?

Clearly, the array of images, rituals, and works of art and literature emerging from Eastern spiritual traditions is far too vast and varied to provide a basis for generalization. And if the range of possibilities in a historical religious tradition like Christianity is immense, it is quite beyond comprehension in those religious traditions whose roots are hidden in the shadows of prehistory. One can only consider a few particular ideas and examples. One might turn, for example, to certain religious expressions in Indian culture. Agrarian and pastoral, Indian civilization celebrated spiritual and sexual love. The noble cults worshipped the life-principle through their doctrines and through magical rituals and practices that used sex to release the unconscious.[147] Here, sexual and spiritual are intentionally and functionally merged.

This merging is rooted in the nature of the divine: the force that causes Brahman, the absolute and undivided divine reality, to divide into the many, and leads the many to seek oneness, is desire.[148] Unlike the Greeks, for whom the mythological theme of splitting and striving for union is a curse borne by humanity, in Indian religion it is seen as a gift of the divine: "The union of male and female thus became the symbol, from the earliest times, for the union of all forces, and the pleasure of the body in mating became, under accepted religious and social forms, linked with the sanctity of procreation *and an end in itself* [emphasis mine]."[149]

In India, divine nature still invites union. Walter Spink contrasts the "upraised hand (*abhaya mudra*)—the gesture of invitation and protection, the paradigmatic gesture of the Indian world,"[150] with the pointing and accusing finger of the Western God. In the West, under the judgment of a transcendent God, humanity struggles to overcome its profound corruption. The Indian mind, in contrast, "asserts that assurance of identity with the ultimate power."[151]

The contrast between Western and Eastern visions of earthly and heavenly paradise echoes the contrast in understanding of divinity. Eastern deities are dancers, whose sensuous interactions reflect the creative and destructive play of the cosmos: "How different an earth is that wherein the moon is always full—that earthly Eden (the phenomenal world) where Krishna still pursues and is pursued, plays in delight forever, and is played upon."[152] While the God of Western monotheism abstains from all bodily indulgences, this Indian god is "subject neither to such compulsions of morality, nor to moral censure."[153]

There are many Indian manifestations of this divine embodied freedom. Hindu devotion to Krishna may, for example, be expressed through an overt celebration of ritual sexual union as a sacred display of erotic power. Unlike European romances, such as the story of Tristan and Iseult, which focus on singular devotion, Lord Krishna has the capacity to multiply himself boundlessly, achieving over the centuries "an ecstasy of wanton rapture of the most prodigious spread."[154]

When Krishna calls the cowmaidens of Brindaban (*gopis*) to him, enchanting them with the sound of his flute, their union is expressed in the form of a dance—the cosmic dance of erotic power. When the dance of divine love brings sexuality and spirituality together, elements of ecstatic joy, laughter, and overt sexual passion combine. Other symbolic representations convey the chaotic, out-of-control nature of this passionate display—the frenzied state of the participants, clothes and hair in disarray, rolling about in the dirt or plunging into the water, unaware and unconcerned with the rules of propriety that would, under normal conditions, be strictly obeyed.

An excerpt from the *Harivamsa*, an appendix to the influential classical epic, the *Mahābhārata*, illustrates this ecstatic union of sexuality and spirituality:

> As she elephants, covered with dust, enjoy the frenzy of a great male . . . so those herding women—their limbs covered with dust and cow-dung—crushed about Krishna and danced with him on all sides. Their faces, laughing, and their eyes, large and warm as those of dark ante-lopes, grew bright as they drank ravenously the wonder of their dear friend. . . . And their hair, coming down, cascaded over their bounding breasts as the young god, thus among the Gopis, played, those nights, beneath the autumn moon.[155]

This passage celebrates Krishna's power to generate ecstatic adoration.

Female erotic potency is also evident in Hindu literature, where the female element is not only celebrated but deified.[156] Radha, Kali, Sita, and Savriti all embody *shakti* energy, a power having considerable status in Hindu culture.[157] Female erotic power is evident, for example, in writings such as Jayadeva's "The Song of the Cowherd" (c. 1175 C.E.), depicting the union between Krishna and Radha. In this poem, Radha rather than Krishna is the central object of devotion.[158] The twelve odes tell of Radha's attraction to Krishna and of Krishna's promiscuous dancing among the gopis. However, Krishna becomes troubled and leaves the gopis, longing for Radha. When he comes to her, she supposes him false and rejects him. Her servant intervenes on his behalf, and Krishna begs Radha for her love:

> The luster of your teeth, bright as the moon, scatters the darkness of my fear. The fire of desire burns in my soul: let me quench it in the honey of your lips. If you are angry, stab with your eyes, chain me in your arms, and rip me to tatters with your teeth. You are the pearl in the ocean of my being. You are the woman of my heart. Put away your fear of me, who inspired it. There is no power in my heart but love.[159]

Eventually, love conquers the divine one completely. After the lovers have finally met in an astonishing battle of love, the Lord Krishna, manifestation of God Himself, humbly obeys Radha's request to assist her in repairing her dress and ornamentation.[160] Radha manifests *shakti*—primordial female sexual/spiritual potency.

Why is sex such an important element in Hindu literature and art? As Benoy Kumar Sarkar explains, "Herein lies the Hindu conception of the dignity of sex,—the sacredness of sex as an organ of the human system."[161] The joys and griefs of love are as sacred as those of other spheres of life.[162] "Sensuous love, when most glowing, utters itself in terms of spiritual or religious or mystical ecstasy. To men and women under the influence of this passion there is nothing higher than love, love is their 'highest good,' the only reality."[163]

Whether or not sexual union represents the ecstatic route to the highest of all spiritual planes, the fact remains that even the most otherworldly experiences are expressed in sensory terms. That the love between Krishna and Radha is human love does not diminish its sacred value.

Krishna's sport with Radha and the milkmaids unites the divine and the human. Their lovemaking also becomes the symbol for *lila*, the dance, or play, which the divine enjoys with humanity. An enormous body of Hindu literature and art has developed "around the joyous dalliances of Krishna with Radha and the gopinis sanctifying the most human of urges and desires among the populace."[164]

Walter Spink comments that the religious views of India also affirm the role of the erotic in creating and transforming *identity*. For example, the relationship between sexuality and spirituality is transformed when creation is understood as an act of the One in copulation with Itself, surrounded by cosmic ocean.[165] In this cosmogonic vision, creation comes about from the self-expression (which is also the divine union) of primordial male and female forces—from this conjunction (*purusa* and *prakriti*) all things arise.[166] "This concept of a primal intercourse undertaken in urgency and delight, this concept of the creation of the manifest phenomenal world from the very substance of the source ... is diametrically opposed to the Western view of a creator who in every essential remains apart from the thing which he has made."[167]

Another manifestation of sexual/spiritual interrelatedness in Hindu literature is the *Kama Sutra*, traditionally ascribed to the sage Vātsyāyana and compiled some time between the third and fifth centuries C.E. This text contains detailed classifications of sexual techniques and types of love along with instruction in the sexual arts. It represents the sage's attempt to fit *kama* (love and sexual pleasure) into the fourfold Hindu scheme of life: *kama*, along with *artha* (prosperity), *dharma* (moral righteousness), and *moksha* (liberation) are viewed as both complementary and mutually exclusive goals.[168] According to Mulk Raj Anand, the hypothesis of this work contends that, since sexual curiosity may either awaken one's sensibility toward Reality or cause perversion of the mind, "it must be satisfactorily explained and analysed, so that such education can lead not only to healthy enjoyment of the variegated pleasures of the body but also clarify the mind of all filth attached to the secret act."[169] The *Kama Sutra* is also devoted to the elimination of hidden longings that might hinder those who seek *moksha* from making spiritual progress.[170]

The erotic merging of sexual and spiritual themes is also evident in Hindu erotic sculpture, especially in the depiction of Maithuna (loving) couples. These images appear in settings that range from the earliest cave temples to works of the eighteenth century. They are most stunningly revealed in such massive displays as the temple sculptures of Khajuraho and the Sun Temple at Konarak. These sculptures depict an incredible array of sexual activities and combinations in intricate and graphic detail. The participants seem completely unrestrained in their sexual expression, yet the figures also convey enormous spiritual power. Their entangled limbs hold, connect, embrace, caress, and reach to pleasure one another. Their faces are serene, full of tenderness, devotion, and unharnessed love. The effect is quite the opposite of the pornographic image.

What can we conclude from the multiplicity of sexual/spiritual images in Hinduism (beyond the fact that such a vast array can never be adequately contained or described)? The images themselves shatter fixed assumptions. For example, although the union of male and female is emphasized as representative of the union of the individual soul with the divine, this depiction does not necessarily impose a strictly heterosexual dyadic model. Tantrism, a religious movement that emerged around the sixth century c.e. in both Hinduism and Buddhism, emphasized that each human body contains both male and female elements, and that these, through sexo-yogic practice, might "unite into the non-dual state of Absolute Reality."[171] Since male and female spiritual elements are both contained in every being, many combinations are possible, and Indian erotic sculpture overtly reflects this variety.

Sexuality, from one perspective the epitome of activity bound to the physical, actually has the capacity to transcend all dualisms. The sex act provides insight into "the metaphysical mystery of the non-dual entity which has been made manifest as two."[172] The delight of sexual union confirms the intrinsic unity and metaphysical identity of human and divine:

> For through the sexual act, the creatures of the outside world come into touch with the metaphysical sphere of the non-dual source. Of course, the latter is not apart. In fact, it is their own essence which they experience in every impulse of compassion. Only in the sex act, the supreme realisation of compassion takes place at its supremest height, the great delight.[173]

Although Hinduism celebrates female power, the ecstasy of erotic union, and metaphysical transcendence through the sex act as depicted in literature and art, misogyny is evident in some of the same material. Hindu myth sometimes depicts female figures as temptations and distractions who diminish the power of gods and men and stand as barriers to enlightenment.[174] In addition, the joyous celebration of sexuality as a sacred expression of divine eros is tempered by concern that one's spiritual journey not become mired in the realm of the sensuous. Hindus value pursuit of *kama* (pleasure and love) as a sanctified activity, but *dharma* (moral righteousness) and *moksha* (release from delusion/liberation from rebirth) are typically to be given priority.

The role of sexuality in Buddhism, and its cultural understanding of women's place, adds another perspective on Eastern tradition. Lorna Rhodes AmaraSingham points out in her study of Sinhalese Buddhism that sex, although not associated with sin, remains problematic in Buddhism because it represents such a strong tie to the "world of impermanence."[175] One of the first steps in detachment from desire is detachment from the sensual pleasure embodied in women, who are viewed as great barriers to salvation.[176] Women are also connected to the world of attachments that must be transcended through their close association with the household and with childbirth. In the great tradition of Buddhism, women represent "sensuality, desire, and attachment," characteristics that, as AmaraSingham asserts, imply "suffering, death, and rebirth."[177]

On the other hand, according to Junko Minamato, the Buddhist concept of emptiness (*sunya*) negates all separations, including the divisions and dualisms created by language.[178] Consequently, when men and women become empty, there is no longer any separation between them.[179] "This concept does not negate the difference in gender, but removes all discrimination against both genders."[180]

Rita Gross suggests that the view of Buddhism as otherworldly or world-denying is partly due to Western misperceptions.[181] From within the tradition itself, one "can just as cogently see Buddhism as a path to freedom *within* the world process as a path to freedom *from* the world process."[182] Gross suggests a feminist reconceptualization of Buddhist theology based in the feminist emphasis on relationality

Dancing after the Whirlwind

and the centrality of community. Toward this end, she calls for a deeper appreciation of the *Sangha* (the Buddhist community, one of the Three Refuges in Buddhist life) as "the indispensable matrix of spiritual existence."[183] Without the Sangha, there can be no Buddha, no dharma (teaching). Gross's reconceptualization associates Sangha with such feminist values as "community, nurturance, communication, relationship, and friendship," values that have had no significant place in the more traditional understanding of the Sangha's role.[184]

Another aspect of Gross's reconceptualization is a revisioning of the traditional Buddhist hierarchical dichotomy between spirituality and "ordinary" existence. Her view affirms domestic and work-related activities "as sacred—as spiritually significant."[185] This does not mean a mere nonreflective immersion in daily activities but pursuit of a path along the "razor's edge," valuing all parts of one's life as important to one's overall spiritual well-being. Gross would agree that these views may not represent mainstream Buddhist practices, but they *are* deeply rooted in Buddhist tradition.

Rita Gross and other scholars pursuing feminist postpatriarchal interpretations of Eastern religious traditions, like feminist theologians of Western religion, do not deny the deeply rooted misogyny and patriarchal oppression within these traditions. Hindu texts, for example, frequently express the view that women cannot attain enlightenment while in female form; their best hope is to be reincarnated as a male. Some forms of Buddhism allow for the possibility of female enlightenment but not for the possibility of a female Buddha.[186] A woman who attains enlightenment must therefore become male.[187]

Control is also an issue in Eastern religious traditions, and even in India, a state of passion is not the ultimate ideal. Erotic pleasure can be "used" by humans and gods, but it is an aspect of existence that should eventually be transcended.[188] Thus, although certain Eastern religious traditions affirm erotic power, the effects of denial and projection are visible as well. The cultures in which these traditions predominate are hardly exempt from patriarchal suppression of women and nature. Many Eastern religious traditions also degrade the natural world, regarding it as inferior to the spiritual or as a realm of deceit and illusion.

Are there Indian religious traditions which did not historically debase or degrade women? Although the social structures of India are usually viewed as thoroughly patriarchal, if not misogynistic, certain religious views do suggest a different understanding of women. *Saktism* (goddess worship), for example, emphasizes female deities, but it also regards women as embodiments of divine female power.[189]

In her study of Tantric Buddhism, Miranda Shaw notes the profound influence of the Sakta element. Both Saktism and Tantrism tend to view the cosmos "as generated by female creativity, a recognition of femaleness as ontologically primary and maleness as derivative and dependent and a deference to women in social and ritual contexts."[190] Texts in both traditions urge respect for women and threaten transgressors with severe punishment.[191] The Sakta theme that women possess a special spiritual potency and therefore both contain and disburse the energy (sakti) that gives rise to life and well-being became deeply embedded in Tantric Buddhism.[192]

Among religious beliefs affirming the connection between sexuality and spirituality, Tantric Buddhism has a unique place. In contrast to those who champion asceticism, emotional restraint, and removal from the world, Tantrics "insisted that desire, passion, and ecstasy should be embraced on the religious path."[193] Self-mastery was to be tested amid the activities and dangers of everyday life: practitioners sought to conquer desires by immersion rather than avoidance. Their task was to "bravely dive deep into the ocean of the passions in order to harvest the pearls of enlightenment."[194] Since enlightenment could be found in the midst of activity, sexual intimacy served as a major Tantric paradigm and the basis for ritual practice.[195] Tantric monks abandoned vows of chastity and pursued their religious practices in the context of life with a spiritual compan-

Dancing after the Whirlwind

ion.[196] This sexual/spiritual union also reflected the divine union of enlightened beings.

Sexual communion in this sense was not understood as a self-serving or isolated activity. Rather, divine spiritual/sexual union, "although exquisitely blissful, is ultimately undertaken out of compassion for the world. The sacred communion of male and female Buddha generates waves of bliss and harmony that turn the world into a *mandala* and showers forth a rain of nectar that satisfies the spiritual hunger in the hearts of living beings everywhere."[197]

Tantric influence led to the inclusion of female Buddhas in the Buddhist pantheon, an explicit affirmation of the possibility that Buddhahood could be attained in a female body.[198] Female Tantric practitioners might incorporate into their practice meditations in which they envisioned themselves as female deities.[199] The concept of a female Buddha was also critical to the Tantric doctrine that Buddahood could be attained in a single lifetime, avoiding the exclusion of women from attaining this goal.[200]

Here again, sexual/spiritual integration and a specific affirmation of female divine power combine. But does this tradition, like many others, incorporate worship of the female divine while at the same time practicing misogyny and overt oppression of women? Does incorporation of divine eros help to mitigate the need for absolute control over the female, who represents chaotic disorder? Many scholars of Tantric Buddhist practice have suggested that women served as mere prostitutes or servants in this tradition, used sexually by men in order to fulfill their sexual/spiritual needs.[201]

In her well-documented study, Shaw takes exception to this point of view by claiming that Tantric Buddhist texts acknowledge the sexual/spiritual bond and display a "profound and appreciative metaphysical understanding of female embodiment."[202] Refuting the position taken by some scholars that Tantric traditions were exploitative and degrading to women, Shaw notes that Tantric writings lack the traditional condemnation of women common to much religious literature:

There are no pronouncements of women's inferiority or religious inca-
pacity. Conspicuously absent are portraits of submissive, oppressed
women and depictions of abusive, exploitative relationships. The texts
do not seek to legitimize or justify male authority or superiority, nor do
they suggest that women should not practice, teach, or assume leadership in Tantric circles.[203]

In Tantrism, respect for women, although enjoined upon all,
had different implications for men than for women. Men were urged
to respond to a woman's divinity with attitudes ranging from respect to ritual worship.[204] Women, on the other hand, "must discover
the divine female essence within themselves."[205] For women, the relationship is one of identity with the divine. A woman possesses a divine energy and power that cannot be extracted or stolen, although
she may choose whether or not to share it in order to enhance her
own spiritual development and that of her partner.[206] A woman does
not choose a partnership to attain self-approval or social respectabil-
ity, or to maintain the moral order, but "solely for her own enlightenment."[207]

Shaw argues that this understanding of gender represents a renewal of the Buddhist commitment to egalitarianism "by offering a
new strategy."[208] In place of misogyny or gender neutrality, Tantra
stresses "gender polarities" that give greater emphasis to the female
pole. Thus, through identification with the female divine, women receive "an unassailable basis for self-confidence" that "seems to have
empowered [them] to speak the truth fearlessly, to be physically and
mentally adventurous, and to be argumentative and aggressive
when it suited them."[209] This "gynocentric arrangement" does not
result in female dominance, however, but in "psychological parity
between men and women."[210] This privileging of the female in theory leads to achievement of a balance in practice, because it serves
"to counteract an erosion or total loss of the balance by even the
slightest male strategy of appropriation."[211]

If Shaw's interpretation is correct, women within the tradition

Dancing after the Whirlwind

of Tantric Buddhism historically maintained a position of equal partnership with men. Giving priority to the spiritual power of the female overcame patriarchal assumptions. And by identifying with the erotic energy of the female divine, women possessed their own divine energy and pursued their own enlightenment rather than merely reflecting the divine power of another.

What Has All This to Do with Denied Identities?

Clearly, we cannot divide the world into traditions that alienate sexuality from spirituality and traditions that bind them together. But where sexuality *is* cut off from spiritual life, whether in theology, religious ritual, or cultural practice, the result is often increasing oppression and violence against women, children, and nature, and increasing cultural and personal denial.

Can this knowledge help an individual woman struggling to know and affirm herself? Has Inanna's Boat of Heaven anything to offer a married mother of three who is falling in love with the woman next door? Do Augustine's anguished failure to control his sexual appetites and his equation of lust with sin have any relevance for the woman whose nightmares and flashbacks convey the terror of childhood sexual violation? Can a woman struggling to understand her own sexuality in light of a positive HIV test get any help at all from the glowing serenity of Konarak lovers?

These specific images may or may not connect with the lives of individual women, but I would contend that we must understand sexual/spiritual alienation in order to understand the dynamics of cultural denial. Likewise, we must recognize the erotic power born of the dynamic interplay of sexuality and spirituality as we struggle against the shattering effects of that denial—as we struggle to know ourselves, to heal ourselves, our cultures, and the wild wonder of our planet.

When we are taught through our religious institutions to fear or to hate our own wild, erotic power, this denial chews at the foundations of our sexual identity. As we suppress our deep, embodied power, we suppress knowledge of ourselves. We create a gap these same religious institutions then fill with guilt, shame, and self-doubt. But when we are taught that our deepest erotic connections with one another reflect the erotic bond between human and divine—the creative burst of power released when the cosmos makes love to itself—we have a way to affirm our loving, lusty unions as integral to identity.

There may well be no contemporary religious institutions that unambiguously and wholeheartedly support the incorporation of the sexual into spiritual growth and identity, just as there are probably none completely devoid of violence and oppression. Are we then to assume that theology is antithetical to eros, that we must choose either religious institutions or a healthy relatedness between sexuality and spirituality? Both Eastern and Western traditions have clearly contributed to the alienation between body and soul and to patterns of denial and projection. However, alternative voices within these institutions challenge any facile conclusions or condemnations.

I include the "sex-positive" view in each tradition to illustrate the point that one need not abandon religious institutions, even those that are profoundly patriarchal (which is to say most, if not all) in order to recover the sexuality/spirituality bond. Yet this restoration is critical to recovery from the damage of denial and to the development of personal and spiritual identity. Before we can further consider treatment, however, we must further understand the symptoms. Before we can plan the rebuilding, we must view the damage.

Obviously, denial, projection, and suppression of erotic power and the sexuality/spirituality connection are damaging at many levels. My focus here, however, is on a particular consequence of these processes: the denial of certain aspects of identity, especially sexual identity, and the impact of that denial on spiritual identity. Because of deeply established cultural fears, certain aspects of women's lives

Dancing after the Whirlwind

disappear. This denial leaves holes in our lives. Cultures reward us for what we seem to be while denying what we are. We survive by participating in this denial, but at the deepest level of self-awareness, alienation and invisibility may deepen. Who are we? Who are we really?

Chapter Three

The Consequences of Denial

I am not free of the condition I describe here.

I cannot be certain how far back in human history

the habit of denial can be traced. But it is at least as old as I am....

All that I was taught at home or in school was colored by denial,

and thus it became so familiar to me that I did not see it.

— SUSAN GRIFFIN, *A Chorus of Stones*

_____ *Denial. How does it affect* the process of learning (and forgetting) who we are, of finding out (and failing to see) who we can be together? Is it really only a cultural joke—a flake of psychobabble originating in Freud's obsession with repressed sexual urges and now transformed into a social weapon against all who refuse to interpret their own experience the way we see it? Is it a much-maligned but valuable coping mechanism employed by the suffering in order to survive and transcend past atrocities? Is it a dangerous tool of oppressive cultural forces that negates what cannot or will not be destroyed? Is it the undoer of identity, the great unraveler of humanity's fabric of connectedness?

It is, of course, all of these and more. However we come to understand denial, we must take its profound effects on the formation and maintenance of identity into account. Denial is about more than rejecting or blocking past or current experience. It is about unknowing who we are. It is also about enabling us to continue to be.

It is one of denial's stranger habits that it denies itself, thus reinforcing its own invisibility and rendering us invisible to ourselves. Some general preliminary observations will help to illustrate the deep implications of denial for the formation and development of spiritual identity. These views will also point toward spiritual transformation and renewal by illustrating the connection between affirmation of our sexual/embodied lives and maintaining spiritual (and relational) health and growth.

Martin Buber, the early twentieth-century Jewish existentialist anthropologist, philosopher, theologian, and ethicist, provides a useful perspective. For Buber, true awareness of another person is not possible through detached observation. Only as a partner can we perceive another as "an existing wholeness." The individual must become fully present to us through the complexities of relationship.[1] To illustrate this connection between relationality and awareness, Buber distinguishes between two types of human existence: being and seeming. "The one proceeds from what one really is, the other from what one wishes to seem."[2] When we are being, we give of ourselves spontaneously, without reserve, without thinking about how we are perceived. When we are seeming, on the other hand, we are concerned with the image our appearance produces in the other. We "make" a look that is designed to appear spontaneous and reflect a personal life of a particular kind.[3]

In terms of the current discussion, "seeming" is denial in action. By appearing to be other than we are, we conceal critical truths about ourselves from others. In the process, we can also conceal these truths from ourselves. Rather than acknowledge and confront our duplicity, we convince ourselves that we are as we seem to be.

According to Buber, the tendency toward seeming rather than being destroys the authenticity of life between one person and another: "Whatever the meaning of the word 'truth' may be in other realms, in the interhuman realm it means that [people] communicate themselves to one another as what they are."[4] Where the authenticity of the interhuman is absent, the human element itself cannot be authentic. A great deal is at stake here, because in Buber's ontology the self is fundamentally relational: "in the beginning is the relation."[5]

Ironically, our concern with appearances stems from our need to be confirmed by others, and "seeming" deceptively appears to offer help. Buber therefore refers to seeming as humanity's "essential cowardice" and to its resistance as "essential courage." Attaining true being is always possible by struggling "to come to oneself—that is, to come to confidence in being."[6] In our significant relationships, we long to be confirmed in our being as what we are and nothing else.

The process of coming to oneself is, of course, the process of recognizing and claiming one's identity, which is, at its deepest level, a *spiritual* task. In childhood, lies and secrets might actually be part of the process of developing an identity, since they are among the first things that are truly "ours."[7] But when we become aware of discrepancies between appearance and reality in our adult lives we enter into a period of crisis, continuing to maintain outward appearances ("seeming") while attempting to remain true to ourselves within. Anyone who practices conscious deceit on a daily basis (lawyers and spies come to mind), even in conformity to social expectations or survival needs, knows how difficult it is to live a double life and still maintain one's integrity.

We can more clearly understand why claiming our full identity requires integrity by bringing in a third term: fidelity. Fidelity is a value-laden term referring to the faithfulness or truthfulness demonstrated in a relationship. Just as being true may include both loyalty and accuracy, fidelity is related to constancy as well as authenticity (as in that now archaic phrase of the early recording industry, "high fidelity"). To demonstrate fidelity is to bring integrity and identity into right relationship with one another.

As the multiple meanings of fidelity suggest, being true to others and being authentically ourselves are interdependent. It's a chicken/egg thing. As we move from a preoccupation with appearances to being more open with others, we also may become more true to ourselves. Carter Heyward rightly cautions against identifying integrity with "a self-possession." We are only fully ourselves "insofar as we are trying to live in right, mutual relation to others. Integrity is a relational blessing, given as we become centered, at home, in the particularity of who we are."[8]

The interaction between being true to others and true to ourselves highlights the strong connection between authentic being, including sexual being, and spiritual identity. If spiritual identity includes, at the most foundational level, our deepest and most meaningful relationships, then denial undermines integrity in a twofold sense: we are prevented from *being* who we are with others, and we are prevented from *knowing* who we are, from claiming our spiritual identities.

As Buber's insights demonstrate, both individual integrity and relational fidelity depend upon overcoming denial, being as we are rather than as we wish to seem. Culturally speaking, we must also overcome denial in order to affirm the authentic being of others, and this may include resistance to social and religious structures that deny erotic power and ban the dance between body and soul.

All my adult life I have witnessed the impact of denied sexual identity on women and pondered its spiritual consequences. If authentic being is indeed at the core of our spiritual and relational lives, such denial will affect us at the deepest level. This point returns us to the core question of this book: *What happens to a woman's spiritual identity when key aspects of her sexual identity are routinely denied?* In order to address this question, we must consider the consequences of denial as it operates in individual human lives. We must enter the realm of memory and story, of events and interpretations.

Feminists have known and forgotten and remembered that the

personal is political, and we continue our efforts to fathom what that means. What it will mean here, among other things, is that the experiences of women—especially the ways in which individual women interpret these experiences for themselves—is a relevant source of knowledge. I will therefore draw on personal narratives as well as research to consider the processes of denial and identity formation. If we want to know who a woman is, what happened to her and why, how she manages and understands her experience, she may well be unable to provide us with all the answers. But it would be wise to ask.

The dynamics of denial cannot be separated from identity formation, maintenance, and renewal. We never establish who we are once and for all, nor do we entirely overcome the impulse to seem rather than to be, to deny rather than to confront, to erase what we cannot acknowledge, or to slip away into psychic places where we feel invisible because our eyes are closed. If the processes of denying and forming identity are dynamically interrelated, then *spiritual healing is an ongoing process that continues throughout our lives*. The goal is not to overcome denial completely but to develop an integrated sense of ourselves that acknowledges the dynamics of growth and allows us access to our deepest internal resources.

Lesbian Identity: The Crisis of Incongruity

The existing research on lesbian identity formation provides an immediate example of the problems that arise in generalizing about human development: the contradictory findings do not always clarify how discovering and affirming a lesbian self takes place. They do, however, help to illustrate the identity issues at stake.

One model, much debated since Vivienne Cass's landmark 1979 study, envisions lesbian identity development as a series of stages or levels of self-realization. Stage-based models have served as the basis for research on gay and lesbian identity and have been frequently critiqued and revised.[9] Certain aspects of these theories are relevant to the impact of oppression and denial on lesbian identity development.

Cass bases her developmental stages on a person's perceptions of her own behavior and the actions she takes as a result. She proposes six stages of development toward a gay identity that is "fully integrated within the individual's overall concept of self."[10] In developing the approach, Cass makes a crucial distinction between public and private aspects of identity, which brings to mind Buber's concern with being and seeming.

Lesbians and gay men often walk a wire between a public identity as a heterosexual and a private homosexual identity. To reach the final stage of "overall and integrated homosexual identity," the public and private spheres must become congruent with one another. Without this congruence, as Buber suggests, genuine human interaction may be impossible. When incongruence becomes too intense, and stress reaches an unbearable level, the result will be either "identity foreclosure" (the choice not to develop further) or movement to another stage of identity development.[11] Identity foreclosure typically involves some form of denial, since the actions or feelings that have caused the crisis must be suppressed or denied.

Cass begins with the observation that initially, virtually every woman holds a view of herself as heterosexual.[12] The culture denies that a lesbian identity option exists. Although people may encourage their children to be anything they choose, certain options are suppressed or rendered invisible. Children are rarely exposed to positive lesbian and gay role models and certainly, they are not encouraged to imagine that their future partners might be of the same sex. Congruence is maintained by denying those thoughts, feelings, or images that might reflect anything but heterosexual relations.

Adrienne Rich has explored the impact of this "compulsory heterosexuality." Challenging the assumption of "innate heterosexual-

Dancing after the Whirlwind

ity," Rich notes that in a culture that erases lesbian possibilities, heterosexuality is not a "preference" but "something that has had to be imposed, managed, organized, propagandized, and maintained by force."[13] Enforced heterosexuality assures the male right of access to women physically, economically, and emotionally.[14] Lesbians have therefore been written out of history or dismissed as mentally ill.

Given the virtual absence of alternatives to an assumed heterosexual identity, it is no surprise that the first of Cass's developmental stages is identity confusion.[15] A woman becomes aware of her own lesbian thoughts, feelings, or behavior, which are incongruent with both her experience of the world and her previously stable assumed identity as a heterosexual. Her sense of incongruence is associated with feelings of confusion, alienation, and isolation. She may pursue several options to try to resolve this incongruence, such as matching society's denial with her own, attempting to suppress her thoughts or feelings, or rejecting the portrait of herself as a potential lesbian. At this stage she rarely discusses her feelings of turmoil with others.[16]

From identity comparison, Cass's stages move to identity tolerance and, finally, for those who have not foreclosed a lesbian identity along the way, to acceptance, pride, and synthesis. Every stage presents numerous options for handling the incongruence between the way we see ourselves, the way we interpret our behavior, and the way we believe we are perceived by others. Although total cognitive and affective congruence is probably not possible, given Western heterosexist assumptions, incongruence can be reduced to tolerable levels.[17]

Cass's model highlights those life situations in which the pieces refuse to fit together: our feelings do not match the expectations or perceptions of others or even our perceptions of ourselves. Incongruence brings us to the brink of a realization. What we have always assumed about ourselves may no longer be—or may never have been—true. In such a crisis, we may choose to deny the incongruent data and attempt to live as if the pieces fit. What we may gain by this option is the ability to go on. What we may lose is a sense of integrity. Eventually, however, our increasing awareness of the discrepancies in our lives may prove too great a stress upon the fragile identity structures we have created.

For many women, this is the time when things fall apart. Old assumptions disintegrate in the face of new feelings and experiences, and the whirlwind of chaotic change sweeps away assumed structures and models. Attempting to hold the pieces together may involve denial and projection. We may attempt to suppress all erotic feelings, inadvertently cutting ourselves off from the very power source we need to navigate these turbulent waters.

Joan Sophie makes the important observation that women typically avoid identifying themselves as lesbian, regardless of their own experience, until they have been able to construct a positive understanding of lesbian identity.[18] This identity foreclosure poses a serious threat to the development of a positive sense of self, since the attempt to "keep it together" also prevents the achievement of personal integrity, of congruence between thought, values, and behavior. For many, the beginning is a feeling of being different. Socialization provides human beings with certain categories for self-definition, but the roles and models that surround us often feel awkward and ill-fitting. With no way to connect feelings of same-sex attraction to an acceptable place in the world, many women experience a vague sense of not belonging anywhere.

Obviously, feeling lost, alienated, or out of place is not the exclusive domain of lesbians (and gay men). However, without cultural models or social support, lesbians may find it especially difficult to develop an integrated sense of self. When feelings of same-sex attraction might result in rejection and ridicule, we protect ourselves from our own emotions and perceptions through various defense mechanisms, repressing or sublimating our desires and rationalizing our feelings.[19] Self-awareness itself becomes seeming rather than being.

Even if a woman acknowledges a lesbian identity, concern with appearance may be necessary not only for acceptance by others but for survival. Forces of oppression and denial may *require* public seeming, but the result is a struggle between public and private spheres that entails both psychological and spiritual consequences.

Lou Ann Lewis points out that this sense of alienation may promote self-blame and self-hatred. When women begin to have concepts and language with which to interpret same-sex attraction, the shame, anxiety, and ambivalence resulting from the conflict between socialized expectations and emotional reality further exacerbate negative feelings.[20] The agony of this experience cannot be overstated, and the appearance of a few ambiguously positive gay and lesbian media images has done little to ease it. These emotions come in waves that overwhelm the ability to consider future hopes and expectations rationally. To be a lesbian is to live outside the acceptable social structures, which acknowledge and reward only heterosexual options.

If these realizations come early, the fairy tales fall fast. There will be no Prince Charming, no societally supported marriage and family. Although she may be able to form a successful, even joyous life without the standard models, happily ever after never happens. When this realization comes later in life, the fairy tales have probably already fallen by the wayside, but a woman who has long thought of herself as a wife and mother may find it very difficult to understand herself as the lover of a woman.

If she has been raised to expect a life that includes the financial support of a man, a woman may be shocked to realize that she will very likely be her sole source of financial support for the rest of her life. Even in contemporary culture, where collapsed marriages, intrafamily violence, and lack of support are reality, many women still assume, perhaps unconsciously, that someone will be (or ought to be) there to take care of them.

Again, these realizations are hardly the exclusive domain of lesbians, but the virtual absence of socially acceptable structures or models for coping with them can cause multiple crises in identity formation. Accepting a lesbian identity may involve the annihilation of long-held and valued assumptions at the core of personal identity.

Since Cass's original study, several other scholars have proposed stage theories, all of which refer to an awareness of difference as an early step.[21] Without discussing other stage theories in detail, certain generalizations can be made. Joan Sophie summarizes six stage-theory proposals as follows:

> In keeping with other developmental research, the tendency has been to propose stage theories of development of homosexual identity which are inherently linear: one begins with no identity, or with the presumption of heterosexuality, proceeds through a series of stages of development and ends with a gay or lesbian identity, proudly held and fully integrated with other aspects of one's identity. Although it is clear that not everyone who begins at stage one ever arrives at the final stage of positive gay or lesbian identity, the paths chosen by those who do not proceed through the stages, or who go through further change in identity after adoption of gay identity, tend to be ignored.[22]

Sophie's research centered on fourteen women who were currently experiencing a shift in their sexual orientation. Although her research results indicate considerable conformity to stage theory in general, especially in early stages, she also notes important discrepancies, including significant variations in the order and timing of events and the important fact that, for some women, a lesbian identity did not represent the final stage of development.

Sophie's observations amply demonstrate the dangers of oversimplification. They also reinforce the view that the process of identity formation is ongoing. The way we see ourselves can change and change again, with or without a loss of integrity. In her personal account, Caryl Bentley refers to her own coming out as a lifelong process of connecting feelings, ideas, and experiences to her identity as a lesbian.[23] Confronting discrepancies, overcoming denial, and affirming an emerging awareness are complex steps in a dynamic process.[24] Individuals achieve integrity and fidelity not by becoming complete but by allowing and *acknowledging* the cycles of disintegration and renewal as they unfold.

With each realization, we face choices regarding whether to own or to be what we see. And this touches on an issue lesbians share with other disenfranchised groups, the practice of *passing*. For lesbians, the passing option, seeming rather than being, is almost always available. The cultural tendency to assume heterosexuality provides extensive camouflage. Lesbians (and gay men) can actively reinforce these cultural assumptions. Dissembling techniques, such as controlling personal information, avoiding association with gay and lesbian lifestyles, and conveying a falsely heterosexual image, have at least two functions: they protect us from personal confrontations with those who may react negatively to our sexual preference and they give us time to absorb and manage the incongruence we feel as we come to terms with our sexual identity.[25]

Passing techniques can also cause harm to those who practice them. They might cut us off from areas of our lives that usually represent sources of love, friendship, and support. Family and workplace are often viewed as providing security and a safe framework for developing personal identity and self-esteem. These areas, however, are usually the last bastions against an integrated lesbian identity, since here, rejection and discrimination are most intensely felt.[26] In the environment of denial necessitated by homophobic culture, they become dangerous ground where a degree of distance and evasion must often be maintained.

Aspects of lesbian identity that involve choices about professing or passing, declaring or distancing, are often encapsulated under the term *coming out*. For both lesbians and gay men, coming out is something like a rite of passage in reverse. The passing is over. To come out is to demonstrate fidelity to one's own identity—to be (and feel) authentic. It is often also an act of commitment to relationality and love. As Heyward puts it: "We can come into our power as lovers by coming out. There is a great power in naming ourselves. For you to come out will contribute to the well-being of us all insofar as you are participating in shaping the Sacred among us."[27]

This spiritually creative emergence begins by "coming out" of an apparently mundane space that is actually filled with secrets. Like gay fashion and gay dance, gay slang has entered the culture in disguise. "Coming out of the closet" has become idiomatic for any slightly risky (or risqué) self-revelation. One can "come out" as a watcher of daytime television or as a "closet" Republican. But it is important to remember exactly who it was that first "came out" and exactly what it was they came out of: the closet. The original occupant was perhaps the ubiquitous skeleton (Aunt Bertie lived with her "friend," Anne, for thirty years, although the family did not discuss it). But there are all sorts of other items in the closet—uniforms, hats and coats, bags and shoes—from which one can design any number of disguises: the suitable suit, the appropriate "drag," the right attire for looking "just like everybody else." As lesbians struggle to leave the closet behind, they emerge still wearing the disguises they first "tried on" within the dark and narrow confines of that hiding place.

There is the expectation, especially from inside the gay community, that a person who has come out is now more free to pursue self-expression. This is probably true. But that person first learned self-expression behind the closet doors, and those roles and costumes are difficult to set aside. There are, of course, outfits from which to choose in lesbian life, "images" ranging from the power butch to the lipstick lesbian (with all the inherited problematics of heterosexual gender expectations), but these may prove an awkward fit.

Models of identity formation may help clarify these issues, but they cannot convey emotions. In order to understand more about this crisis of authenticity, I turn to specifics. Every story is, of course, unique, but over the course of several personal narratives, the shared threads of experience provide a pattern for greater understanding. In a sense, although these are actual stories of individual women, they are also "typical" scenarios.

Sharon has been attracted to other girls since she was twelve. Her emotional involvements were always intense. She "fell in love" with her camp counselor, and her PE teacher, and Patty Duke, and her best friend. She has always known that she is "different," but she does not know how to understand the difference. She feels that she doesn't fit.

Ann has been pleasantly (if not happily) married for fifteen years. It occurs to her one day that her emotional relationship with her best female friend is much more intense and satisfying than the one she shares with her husband. She asks herself which one she loves more deeply, and the answer frightens her.

Susan dates several men and has an active sex life. She thinks she is missing something that must be connected to finding the right man, so she keeps looking. A relationship with a particular female friend becomes increasingly intimate, and eventually sexual, but she does not define herself as a lesbian. This one particular relationship with her friend is special.

Mary has been actively involved in feminism for several years. She has been living with the same man for some time, and although they frequently argue, she feels that she has about as good a relationship with him as a woman can have with a man. She makes frequent references to how hard he tries to understand and support her. One day she stops in at a meeting of lesbian feminists ("just out of curiosity") and continues thereafter to attend their meetings. She tells them that she enjoys their company, because they know how to laugh. No one asks her if she is a lesbian. If they did, she is not sure how she would respond.

These cases have certain features in common. None of them bears the stamp of sudden, overwhelming revelation—no lightbulb coming on over the head, no sudden, thigh-slapping "That's it!" Rather, they express a kind of collapsing and confusing of identity, a state of mind and heart in which the answer to "Who am I in relation to others?" is up for grabs.

Although the term *coming out* describes an extremely complex range of discoveries and disclosures, it can be broken down initially into two broad categories.[28] The first is personal realization, usually not one overwhelming insight but a growing awareness of one's sexual identity with varying degrees of self-acceptance. The second is disclosure to others, which also takes place and expands over time. The process of establishing one's own lesbian identity typically precedes disclosure to others, although some women integrate the two, developing their sexual identity in conversation with other supportive individuals.

These two senses of the term *coming out* are related to various forms of denial. Denial may refer to a refusal to acknowledge a particular situation, characteristic, or identity. This refusal may be a self-defense mechanism that protects us against anxiety by shutting out the existence of some threatening realization. Women overcome denial in this sense when they confront and acknowledge their own lesbian feelings.

Second, denial may refer to denying charges or accusations leveled by others, including facts that might bring harm if revealed. Denial of lesbian identity can be active in response to a specific accusation ("You're a queer! No, I'm not!"). Much more often, however, when circumstances, events, or identities are concealed (passing), denial takes a passive form. Denial in this form recalls the second sense of coming out, disclosing one's lesbian identity to others.

Finally, denial may involve a refusal to grant entry, recognition,

Dancing after the Whirlwind

or value to another. This is the form of denial practiced in a hetero-sexist society. Alternatives to denial may range from tolerance to acceptance to affirmation, and even celebration.

Interestingly and ironically, lesbian identity is often both accepted and denied. That is why we can make sense of two different meanings of "coming out": What is admitted within is often denied in interacting with others, as Cass's distinction between public and private makes clear. In fact, the problem of presumed heterosexuality extends far beyond our own early self-identification. To an extent, most adult women *continue* to be public heterosexuals, since without disclaimers to the contrary heterosexuality is assumed. A lesbian colleague once noted that she has to decide when "not to pass." Because she is presumed to be heterosexual, she "passes" unintentionally.

Our relationships with others may also be narrowed, in Buber's terms, by a need to *seem* other than we are. Such a situation guarantees a continuing sense of incongruity, and therefore, I would claim, a sense of lost integrity. Unfortunately, *some* level of denial is usually essential to ensure survival and continued sanity, but it may derive less from a sense of shame or self-hate than from an awareness of the potentially brutal consequences of disclosure.

Public opinion surveys repeatedly refute the suspiciously tenacious fallacy that public tolerance for gay and lesbian lifestyles has increased to a point where such denials are no longer necessary. A 1982 Gallup Poll indicated that 39 percent of those surveyed felt homosexual relations between consenting adults should not be legal, and 51 percent felt that homosexuality should not be considered an acceptable lifestyle. More recent polls show no significant change in attitude. A 1993 CNN-Gallup poll reported in *USA Today* indicated that 48 percent of those interviewed felt that civil rights laws should not include homosexuals. Interestingly, more recent polls indicate a significant gender gap: 56 percent of the women polled agreed that civil rights protection should be extended to gays, but only 35 percent of the men.

Gay men and lesbians may be the last acceptable scapegoats for the projected fear and hatred in U.S. American culture. This situation is neither accidental nor coincidental, but closely associated with the cycles of alienation, projection, and denial I have been describing. Sexuality is the focus of such fear and fascination that overt expressions of embodied sexual life in everyday life, let alone in spiritual life, are viewed with horror. As Nancy Wilson observes, "Society's hatred and loathing of homosexuals is really about the collective shame, guilt, fear, and self-hatred in our culture at large, especially as these are related to issues of sexuality."[29] When lesbians and gay men honestly express their sexuality, they challenge the fundamental power structures of patriarchal culture.

Fear and hatred take various forms, including the intentional dissemination of lies and distortions.[30] The research carried out by Hetrick and Martin demonstrates that society expresses negative attitudes in negative verbal statements and beliefs, discrimination, and violence.[31] Gay men and lesbians have been called predatory, a threat to the survival of the race, criminal seducers, and a danger to children, and considered incapable of forming and maintaining mature relationships. They have been accused of causing anorexia nervosa, crime in the streets, cultural genocide, the Second World War, the Holocaust, AIDS, and lowered SAT scores (this last by Jerry Falwell).[32] Most of these accusations have been leveled during the past twenty years.

Gay men and lesbians share experiences of disenfranchisement and oppression, but as in most other areas of life, these experiences are greatly affected by gender. In fact, many lesbians feel that they have more in common with women as a group than with gay men.[33] Mary Hunt cautions against generalizing gay and lesbian experience: "trying to talk about lesbian/gay anything is like trying to speak of a Judeo-Christian culture. It simply obscures the differences and results in muddled and ultimately disrespectful discussions."[34]

Certain aspects of the struggle to develop and maintain an authentic sexual identity are shared, but it is important to note those

Dancing after the Whirlwind

aspects of coming out that are specific to lesbians. For example, social expectations may thwart attempts to experience life as an adult with a mature sexual identity. Relatedness, nurturing, and emotionality, often central to identity development in women, are labeled by patriarchal culture as less mature or less differentiated, and devalued. Lesbians thus find themselves in a particularly stressful double bind. If the "'ticket' to psychological maturity and entry into adulthood" is available to women only in the form of heterosexual marriage and motherhood, "obviously," notes Christine Browning, "for the lesbian there is no acceptable way to achieve adulthood as defined by traditional theories and cultural expectations."[35] These maturity issues are complicated by the fact that the developmental tasks of coming out—integration of adult sexuality into one's personality and coming to terms with society's sexual norms and values—are similar to those usually experienced in adolescence. As a result, in one sense "coming out is an adolescent phenomenon at whatever age it occurs."[36]

There are other differences between men's and women's experiences of the coming out process. Many studies stress the importance of the presence of an emotional bond in sexual relationships among lesbians.[37] A relational context may indeed be supportive in coming out, but this emphasis on the emotional bond can also be an effective mechanism for denying a lesbian identity. First sexual relationships with women, for example, may be viewed as special or unique friendships without calling sexual identity into question.[38] Caryl Bentley elaborates on her own coming out process by describing overwhelming feelings toward another woman: "I attributed my love for Biz to her rare and wonderful qualities, as though she were a goddess fallen into my Midwestern life whom I was compelled to adore. I had no experience or conceptual tools to help me see that my feelings for her came from my identity rather than hers."[39]

If women are conditioned to lead with their feelings, they have also learned from experience to be certain before taking any action. Lesbians, experiencing the confidence-undermining influences that affect all women, hesitate to enter into lesbian relationships, or even to adopt a lesbian identity, until they are able to develop sufficient intellectual certainty about their feelings.[40]

Gender differences in the coming out process often highlight the issue of control. Women have traditionally been socialized to give control to others and to put the feelings and concerns of others above their own. The coming out process adds a dimension of fear, which may exacerbate loss of control. But if a woman is to develop a sufficient sense of self to overcome the forces of denial in herself and in society, she must be able to realize some level of control over her own life. Thus, decisions regarding coming out, whether they involve establishing her own sexual identity or disclosing that identity to others, must belong to her.

For women entering into lesbian relationships, the issues of identity and control become even more complex. Women who have experienced difficulty in coming to terms with their own sexual identity may fear that their newly established identity will be swallowed up in the relationship. Women socialized to be relational may find that their intimate relationships with women are deeply entangled with issues such as codependency, fusing, and loss of identity.[41]

The methods of denial and oppression employed by the culture also differ along gender lines. Although certainly not immune from overt harrassment or assault, lesbians are less likely than gay men to be attacked directly. There is a stereotype that discrimination against lesbians is less severe and that even openly homophobic individuals are more likely to be tolerant of lesbians than of gay men. Many heterosexual men express less hostility to lesbian sex than to sexual relations among men. Some of the reasons for this belief are obvious. Since women in patriarchal culture are taken less seriously than men and are generally less valued, their sexual lives are also devalued. I once heard a man say that although he would kill any man who had sexual relations with his wife, he was not threatened by the idea of her sexual involvement with a woman. "She doesn't garden or

Dancing after the Whirlwind

belong to a bridge club," he declared. "I think it would be good for her to have some activities outside the marriage." Clearly, the idea of a sexual relationship between his wife and another woman was not something that he took at all seriously.

But are woman/woman *sexual* relationships really less threatening to men? I would suggest that when lesbian relationships are both sexually expressed and exclusive of men, they represent one of the most serious challenges to patriarchy, and they are profoundly threatening to patriarchal power structures. The more overtly sexual the lesbian relationship, the greater the threat.[42]

According to one common view, lesbians are more tolerated because women are freer to express physical affection toward one another than are men. However, patriarchal culture is established on the principle that women are available for male use. Sexual relationships among women, *when they exclude men*, are neither acceptable nor nonthreatening. This raises the issue of the "lesbian fantasy" theme in pornographic literature. Men who find gay male sexuality repulsive may claim to be strongly attracted to lesbian sex. The key here is that pornography involving lesbian sex makes women available to men and thus sabotages the power of lesbian sexuality to remove women from sexual use by men. Pornographic images of lesbians restore women's availability by inviting the man into the picture as a voyeur or as a participant in a "threesome."

Lesbian Sex

The pseudo-tolerance extended to lesbians in fact reflects cultural denial. Lesbians are tolerated only if the specifically sexual aspect of their identities and relationships is negated or coopted for male use. But lesbian identity incorporates far more than sex acts between or among women, and it is important, especially in a society that minimizes female sexuality, not to ignore or diminish the power of lesbian lovemaking in lesbian life.

Lesbian sex is wild sex. It takes place outside the borders of accepted societal norms. It is absolutely natural and absolutely abnormal, the physical expression of woman/woman wilderness attraction. Lesbians are boundary crossers. When women touch one another sexually, they leave behind the civilized structures of cultural order and enter the unbounded. The experience is enhanced by the nature of women's sexuality, which tends to be more diffused throughout the body than genitally specific, more focused on contact and context than on event, more capable of multiple orgasmic variety and connection, all of which clearly threatens the separation and alienation upon which patriarchal culture depends. The erotic connections of lesbian sex bring together pleasure and love, sexuality and spirituality, sensuality and tenderness. When lesbian sex separates itself from structures of dominance and submission (often though by no means always a characteristic of woman/woman lovemaking), it challenges the foundations of patriarchal social structures, the very basis of the social order. To preserve the established boundaries and borders, it must be vigorously denied.

Lesbian sex must therefore be made to disappear. So lesbians are depicted as "trying to be like men," thus mitigating the threat of the excluded male. Or their sexual lives are minimized. They are viewed as roommates or good friends or even lifetime partners, not as passionately aroused, sexually active, fully embodied women who love and touch women. This was brought home to me many years ago when my lover and I both received matching nightgowns from each of our respective mothers for Christmas. This was hardly an affirmation of our sexual relationship. Rather, the sexual dimension of our lives together had been so thoroughly erased in our mothers' minds that even bedtime posed no threat. We were to be roommates or best friends at an extended pajama party, decorously clad in matching flannel, forever asexually munching popcorn or putting each other's hair up in pincurls.

This form of denial fixes lesbians in an eternal preadolescence,

Dancing after the Whirlwind

but there is another view of lesbians as R-rated, for adults only. Insofar as lesbians are understood as sexual beings, this sex is taboo, and decent people must be kept from exposure to it. Until very recently, lesbian subject matter in the media—such as women kissing or demonstrating even the mildest sexual attraction—was sufficient to restrict access or exposure.[43] Lesbian sex, by its very nature, raises the specter of something that is at its most benign a "mature topic" and at worst fundamentally depraved.

_____ *Children*

Restricting lesbian sexuality as particularly prurient has been coupled with the false stereotype linking gay men (and sometimes lesbians) to child abuse. The result is yet another example of the power of denial to alienate us from resources essential to healing and spiritual growth. Adult gay men and lesbians are often cut off from children.

Once, more than twenty-five years ago, I took a walk with my friend Bill, just as I was going through the process of coming out myself. On a Southern California pier, at about sunset, we observed two women walking along holding hands. My memory-picture of these lovers is still perfectly intact, their hair caught and tangled together by the gusting wind. They had that air of people in love, too preoccupied to pay much attention to those around them. We followed them at a distance along the pier. As they passed two older women standing with a young boy, one of the older women deliberately turned the boy away from them and covered his eyes. I will never forget it.

Constantly confronted by both overt and covert cultural messages that children are "off limits," lesbians and gay men have, until very recently, generally accepted the estrangement. Nancy Wilson suggests several underlying reasons for this acceptance: internalized homophobia that unconsciously buys into the child-molestor lie and reinforces the assumption that we really should not be around children; the associated tendency to assume that we are more likely to be accepted by mainstream culture if we keep children from our midst; the tendency to dissociate gay and lesbian lifestyles from procreation (in the early days of the gay liberation movement, for example, heterosexuals were referred to as "breeders"); and, a very interesting point, the continuing existence, for many of us, of a wounded child within.[44]

I think Wilson is right that "our resistance to children is our resistance to our own healing."[45] In order to be safe with ourselves and with each other, we must welcome children among us and continue to create a safe place for them.[46] But healing is also something we must extend to the children themselves. Children who grow up with feelings of same-sex attraction carry scars of isolation and alienation that will never be healed until we make a place for them to understand that they are not alone. Children of gay and lesbian parents must themselves confront issues of denial as they struggle to find safe ways to be themselves with neighbors, friends, and schoolmates.

My own experience bears this out in ways that raise strong feelings in me. When I came out in the midst of the gay liberation movement of the early seventies, children were rarely in evidence. There was also great concern (not to mention paranoia) that associating with children would encourage homophobic assumptions and should therefore be avoided. I have no children. I had no friends or lovers with children until I was over thirty-five. Although my sister and brother both have children, I have not had much contact with my nieces and nephews, largely because we live in different parts of the country. I never thought I needed or wanted children in my life.

Since moving to the Midwest, children have entered my life. I have become very close to several lesbian friends with children.

(One just became a grandmother!) Most significantly, I have spent the past eight years helping to raise David, my lover's now thirteen-year-old son. While he is not a child of my blood, he is and will always be a child of my heart. I have witnessed his own struggle to affirm the relationship between his mother and me, to let me know that he loves me, and to survive the conflicts he encounters in his homophobic surroundings. I know now that we need children, that we will not survive without children, that we cannot grow or heal without children. And we absolutely must resist the cultural divisions that keep us away from them and them from us.

The Power of Resistance

When our identities are denied, when our most meaningful relationships are degraded and demeaned, when the beauty of our bodies and our many ways of loving are distorted, believing in ourselves and in one another is an act of defiance. As Hetrick and Martin point out, "the most devastating acts of social discrimination are those that corrode one's self-worth and self-esteem."[47] In claiming the authentic passion of our embodied sexual connections, in affirming the significance and the appropriateness of our close relationships with children, we combat the continuous assault of denial on our sense of self.

Affirming lesbian identity involves resisting cultural oppression, and resistance, as Alice Walker knows, is the secret of joy.[48] Yet many other factors affect the degree to which we truly resist the patriarchal system of privileges and punishments—a system that uses categories of race, ethnicity, class, gender, and sexual orientation to threaten and divide disenfranchised communities.[49]

According to Wilson, passing may reflect a desire to maintain mainstream cultural privilege: "Being able to be closeted means that gays and lesbians have been able to pass and use race, gender, or class privilege, where possible, to get the goodies here on earth."[50] But one is obviously only able to evoke this privilege to the extent that one *can* pass. Even affirming our lesbian and gay identities will only foster patriarchal divisions if we do so while denying the existence of poor, working-class, and nonwhite lesbians and gay men.[51] Wilson relates this tendency to the growing stereotype of gays and lesbians as a "white wealthy minority" with a particular political agenda and significant economic and political clout. That the white, middle- and upper-income, gay and lesbian political establishment encourages this stereotype may represent an effort to maintain privilege at the expense of those who are further disenfranchised on the basis of race or class.[52]

Sexual Identity Affirmation and Spiritual Health

Coming out is a story of rocks and hard places, but successfully navigating this terrain may be one of the most critical journeys of lesbian life. Richard Troiden has noted a number of factors that combine to infuse homosexual identity with increased significance. Many gay men and lesbians, at some point in their lives, come to "view their sexual identity as defining characteristics of self that are relevant to all situations." Being gay overshadows other attributes and becomes a key component of one's identity.[53]

The tendency to view one's sexuality as a highly significant aspect of one's identity is neither obsessive nor misguided. As Carter Heyward states, "the celebration of the erotic and of our desire to express it sexually *ought* to be a major issue in our life together because it is the primary wellspring of our capacity to be creative together" [emphasis in original].[54] The critical relationship between affirming one's sexual identity and maintaining spiritual health and growth again raises the question I posited earlier in another form: *What happens when that which one considers to be a central aspect of one's own iden-*

tity is simultaneously that which is persistently denied? The negative
forces of oppression and discrimination tend to highlight the importance of that aspect of personal identity toward which they are directed, especially if that identity is concealed or suppressed. This explains why remarks like "Why do you have to flaunt it?," "Why are
labels so important?" and "What you do in the privacy of your own
home is none of my business" are so infuriating.

Overcoming both internalized and culturally-imposed homophobia simultaneously is a daunting task. But when one succeeds in
breaking through the barriers, the consequences of developing a positive lesbian identity reach far beyond simple recognition and acceptance. Changes in sexual self-understanding also "involve changes
in the meanings of the self-concept, of the concept 'woman,' of religious beliefs and values, and of future expectations."[55]

With so many conflicts and ambiguities, so much confusion and
danger, and so many changes in our fundamental assumptions
about who we are, what we mean, how we live, and what we value, is
it really worth it? As the whirlwind rises, taking apart what culture
teaches, what we assume, what we have always "known," we come
to weigh the burdens and benefits. What does affirming one's sexual
identity offer? Congruency among various aspects of our lives: who
we perceive ourselves to be, how we live, and how others perceive us.
Authenticity and fidelity in our relationships. A stronger self-
concept and higher self-esteem. An odd but insistent feeling of
greater safety as we choose being over seeming, and thus trade living
a lie for living the challenges of our lives within cultures that still
deny us. And *healing.* Wilson makes a powerful observation: "truth
is our spiritual equivalent of an immune system."[56] Lying may help
us slip past some of the more overt forms of cultural oppression, but
it compromises our spiritual health.[57] The lies of omission, the lies of
silence, finally offer us no great solace. As Audre Lorde put it so succinctly, "We can sit in our safe corners mute as bottles, and we will
still be no less afraid."[58]

Denial and Sexual Identity

Of the significant differences among the three communities of women in this book, one of the most important has to do with the nature of what is denied. Lesbians suffer oppression because of their sexual orientation, but at least for most, being a lesbian is not in itself bad news. In spite of media and literary portrayals of gay and lesbian life as full of suffering, guilt, and misery, being lesbian is not a tragedy. As Nancy Wilson puts it, "The sad and lonely stuff is about oppression, not about sexuality."[59] Being a woman with a history of childhood sexual abuse or a woman with AIDS is quite another matter.

Many women seek—and find—positive aspects in even the most horrendous circumstances or experiences. Corinne Squire, for example, notes the observation made by many women that "HIV and AIDS have had good effects on many individuals and communities, provoking transformations in ways of thinking, ways of life and ethics."[60] But this does not mean that being sexually abused as a child or being HIV-positive is a good thing.

I do not celebrate sexual abuse, nor do I wish to make facile proclamations that women should shout their HIV-positive status from the rooftops. Women who have been hurt, women who are facing illness and death, need to be seen and heard as they are. And some of them are women who were sexually abused as children. Some of them are women with HIV/AIDS. Those circumstances are not good news, but they are significant, they are real, and they may be critical to all of us as we seek to know ourselves—a key to spiritual healing.

When a woman with a history of childhood sexual abuse struggles with denial, more is at stake than whether the traumas she remembers actually occurred. These experiences, together with the experience of remembering them, affect her at the core of her being, especially in terms of her sexual identity. She may identify herself as a woman who associates sex with pain and fear or as a woman who is struggling toward sexual health while wrestling with the demons of the past. Meanwhile, the surrounding culture may view her as a neurotic, weak, or vindictive hysteric rather than as the woman she understands herself to be.[61] Struggling against her own internalized denial, who is she really?

Similarly, HIV-positive women must deal with more than the denial that AIDS exists or that their lives are affected by it. They must deal with the negation of their sexual being. To the surrounding culture, the sexuality of an HIV-positive woman is something dangerous or even evil, something she ought to suppress or conceal. She may be taught to have sex "safely" or not to have sex at all, but her sexual desires, emotions, and activities are either ignored or treated as something to be feared.

Abuse, Reversals, and Soul Shattering

There is a silence that belongs not to intentional secrecy or to protective withdrawal but to the empty spaces of memory where body and mind conspire to make experience go away. This silence is often the legacy of severe trauma and abuse. Our past no longer speaks to us because we cannot know what happened and survive. This erasure of memory is a loss, not because it is good to remember pain and horror but because these experiences represent continuity, moments that were and are ours. We lose them because keeping them would bring about a crisis in congruency too great to resolve. We forget, or we remember and know that some of our life experiences make no sense at all. So we forget.

For many years, as I researched and wrote about the spiritual consequences of childhood sexual abuse, I assumed the stance of a concerned friend and scholar. It was something of a shock to realize that certain events in my own life fit the description, and that these patterns of denial were even more familiar to me than I had been willing to acknowledge.

Childhood sexual abuse, whether by a parent or a trusted caretaker, is a terrifying reversal: a vital source of love and protection becomes a force of violence and violation. This is the first of many reversals that survivors confront in the process of recovery.[62] Faced with the impossibility of perceiving those on whom she absolutely depends as dangerous, an abused child may unconsciously erase what she cannot absorb. Survival often takes the form of denial mechanisms, including various forms of splitting, also known as dissociation. The term *splitting* is used in two ways in survivor language: first, following a more clinical understanding, the splitting of the abusing parent into "all good/all bad" categories (the child's perspective may switch back and forth between trusting love and fear, or the child may actually perceive the parent as two different people, one a loving caretaker, the other a mysterious monster); and second, the survivor's own splitting. Sometimes her abused body remains behind while she goes "out" into the wallpaper, through the ceiling, into the light fixture, through the wall socket. At other times, she may dissolve into fantasies, read long books, perform intense scholarly or household tasks, work to the point of exhaustion in one helping profession or another, trying to be good enough to be safe.[63]

We begin to divide our experience into categories of "good" and "bad" as infants. These divisions help children learn to put events together, rather than "split" them apart.[64] As adults, we need to be able to absorb ambiguity, but severe trauma and abuse may diminish that ability. We return instead to the absolute categories of childhood: This is all good; that is all bad. I am here; I am not here. If I close my eyes, you can't see me.

A thirty-five-year-old woman wrote the following poem recalling her own childhood experience of coping by "going away":

> As I lie on my back, looking up at the mashed potato
> swirls of my ceiling, I wish. . . .

I wish that the trembling would stop just enough. . . .

just enough so I could jump up and down,
up and down on my cold, narrow bed.

And, reaching up, I would grab handful after handful
of the white, fluffy comfort. . . .

and eat and eat until the shaking quit
and the fear went away.

But stuck to my bed the way my wet fingers stick
to the bottom of my mommy's metal ice cube trays,

I cough out, "Daddy, sweet Daddy, I'm afraid.
"Come lie down with me. . . . Pleeeeeee . . . ase."

But the monster crawls into my bed, and I obediently turn
to my side. I see the daisies, the daisies, the daisies.

It pushes and presses and shoves me closer,
closer to the yellow and white daisies . . .
daisies on my wall.

I can't stop it . . .
I fall. I fall into the daisies and float
up . . . higher and higher. . . .
swirling and swirling. . . .
smelling like daisies,
feeling like daisies.

I am a daisy. . . .
light, airy, carefree, fragrant.

But suddenly, I am falling again.
Down, down, down to my bed.
My petals wither and fall off and die.
My daddy is gone.
Where did he go?

Legs and bottom, all wet and sticky....
like the time my orange Popsicle melted in
my lap as I sat on the swing in my backyard.

I must have wet the bed.[65]

After suffering for years in abusive adult relationships without any recollection of past abuse, the author of this poem began to have dreams depicting incidents of abuse. Later, her memories took the form of intense flashbacks during which she would vividly experience these abusive incidents as if they were reoccurring. She had also been suffering from serious physical difficulties, including symptoms of multiple sclerosis. She suffered loss of bowel and bladder control, facial paralysis, and eventually total paralysis and seizures. Her own interpretation of her illness is that her body could no longer contain her secret. These symptoms may be another manifestation of denial: the only means of keeping back her fear and pain was paralytic stillness.

Clearly, the consequences of child sexual abuse can be horrendous. Physical symptoms may include difficulty with swallowing, gastrointestinal problems, headaches, fatigue, seizures, joint problems, and gynecological disorders. Possible psychological consequences include severe depression and anxiety, inability to trust, problems with setting boundaries or expressing feelings, intense fear and phobias, sexual dysfunction, relationship conflicts, fear of intimacy, hypervigilance, feelings of alienation and abandonment, feelings of confusion, insecurity, and helplessness, low self-esteem, nightmares and night terrors, eating disorders, drug and alcohol abuse, self-destructiveness, including suicide attempts and self-mutilation, and various forms of dissociation and revictimization.[66] The sociologist Pat Gilmartin also notes spiritual consequences, including loss of faith in anything and a feeling of being dead or hollow inside.[67] Many of these symptoms can be directly or indirectly linked to a woman's denial of her own abuse.

Dancing after the Whirlwind

Dissociation may provide the survivor with distance from overwhelming memories, but it may also disturb or alter her integration of identity, memory, or consciousness. If integration of identity is disrupted, the survivor may forget her own identity and assume or impose new ones, as in multiple personality disorder (lately renamed Dissociative Identity Disorder), which is strongly linked to severe sexual abuse. If memory is disturbed, the survivor may completely block out important personal events including, but not limited to, events of abuse.[68]

Children often begin to forget abusive incidents even as they are occurring. This amnesia might extend for years, lifting only when the survivor finds a way to recover and cope with her past experience. Even when she knows what happened to her, a survivor may not reveal what she knows. This form of denial is directly related to the silence imposed on the child at the time of the abuse. Why doesn't the child tell someone what is happening to her? Here is a brief but representative list of responses offered by children themselves:

I didn't know anything was wrong.
I didn't know it was illegal.
I didn't know who to tell.
I did tell and no one believed me.
I was ashamed.
I was scared.[69]

Scared of what? Here is a representative list of threats:

If you tell, I will kill you.
If you tell, you'll be sent away.
If you tell, I'll kill your little sister.
If you tell, I'll molest your little brother.
If you tell, I'll kill your dog.
If you tell, it will kill your mother.
If you tell, no one will believe you.

If you tell, then you will go to the insane asylum.

If you tell, I'll go to jail and you'll starve.

If you tell, they'll give you to someone who will really hurt you.

If you tell, you'll go to hell.

If you tell, I won't love you anymore.[70]

Perpetrators may not actually intend to carry out these threats; usually, no overt action is necessary. As Roland Summit of Harbor-UCLA Medical Center has observed, small children, like other small creatures, deal with overwhelming threat by freezing, pretending to be asleep, and playing possum.[71] If you scare her sufficiently, she *will* be quiet.

Denial of overwhelming evil or severe trauma is not, of course, perpetuated by survivors alone. Therapists responding to severely abused clients are constantly challenged by their own denial mechanisms. Summit notes a persistent tendency among therapists "to overlook the role of child sexual assault and other specific victimization as a precursor of emotional and behavioral dysfunction."[72] Histories of assault are often difficult to discover, and these difficulties may be compounded by the therapist's own hidden avoidance.

Professional denial has a long history, involving such figures as Tardieu in the 1860s, Ferenczi in the 1930s, and Freud. Many are now familiar with Freud's turnabout from his earlier position that early childhood seduction was the central basis for neurosis to the development of his Oedipal theory suggesting that dangers to our emotional health are universal and intrapsychic rather than environmental.[73] Referring to denial among therapists, Summit comments:

> Looking squarely at sexual abuse requires a sacrifice of comfort and an exercise in humility. The vagaries of dissociation insult the last foundations of logic, blurring the boundaries of already tenuous assumptions.... The scholar and the healer are no more immune from misguidance than the student and the patient. The parent may be more blinded than the child.[74]

Dancing after the Whirlwind

Summit also notes the appearance, since the early 1980s, of reports of multiple victim, multiple perpetrator cases, involving female perpetrators, pornography, sadism, bondage, coprophagia, drugs, and blood rituals. Such reports may strain the credulity of therapists more accustomed to stories of "ordinary" abuse.[75] To these horrific accounts Kathy Steele adds recollections by survivors of being "buried alive, physically tortured in unimaginable ways, sexually mutilated and abused, bound and gagged, starved, force-fed (sometimes even involving cannibalism), sleep-deprived, systematically degraded and humiliated, drugged, brainwashed, left alone in utter darkness."[76]

I include these accounts not to shock, but to illustrate our aversion to direct confrontation with evil. Although I have been researching the consequences of child sexual abuse for several years, my eyes still tend to blur or skim the words when I read such a list. In studying ritualized child sexual abuse, I find that I am only capable of reading a few sentences before my mind refuses to absorb the words. For therapists hearing these accounts directly from survivors, this aversion may be much more intense.

Steele also comments on the response of therapists to patients with histories of particularly bizarre or sadistic forms of abuse. Most therapists are "blindsided" at some time in their practice by the horror and savagery they must confront in responding to these clients.[77] Facing "these new dimensions of evil and suffering" raises old existential questions: "There is a vicious jolt that comes as we hear the unspeakable, as we know the unknowable, as we sit with someone who has experienced the intolerable. What can we do when all our carefully constructed answers to the questions of life and death, of good and evil, crumble around us like a house of cards?"[78]

Therapists may also be forced to confront their own Shadow selves. Faced with what appears to be the active embodiment of evil in the lives of others, one must ask how a human being can do such things and what it is that prevents us from behaving in this way.[79] If these factors contribute to denial on the part of therapists, the behavior of sexually abused clients further complicates matters, since individuals with such histories initially tend to tell their stories through their bodies rather than their words. As the list noted earlier confirms, many of them have been threatened with brutal consequences should they ever tell. "Besides, they think, saying the words will only underscore the despair, the horror, the shame. Silent screams only."[80]

Therapists may respond to this encounter with evil with their own "protective maneuvers":[81] "We deny. We close our eyes and ears, we deftly change the subject without knowing it ourselves. We do not look too closely at their eyes so that we cannot see the searing pain. We call them psychotic. We disbelieve. We tell ourselves the facts may never exactly be determined."[82]

The tendency to deny may be reinforced by cultural and professional pressures. Mental health professionals who do raise these issues are scapegoated. Increasingly, clinicians who report such cases may be sued by accused perpetrators.[83] As Summit notes, even if they remain anonymous, therapists involved in such cases "suffer an assault to their sense of decency, safety, and trust. If they choose to believe in even a limited version of the atrocities described, they are plunged into uncertainty, fear, powerlessness, and silence, much like victims themselves."[84] Challenging the denial in order to treat survivors of childhood sexual abuse responsibly is likely to be personally painful and professionally dangerous. Given these circumstances, it is not surprising that therapists approach clients who report histories of severe abuse with increasing trepidation.

We also encounter denial on a massive, societal scale, and discussions of the topic stress its nature as secret, hidden, covered in silence. Silence reinforces the child's sense that these experiences could not have happened to her.[85] It also reinforces the adult woman's inclination to respond to memories of abuse as symptoms of psychosis rather than as recollections of actual experiences, and the willingness of some therapists to accept this response. In addition to the language of secrecy, verbal responses that negate the survivor's pain under the guise of providing comfort seem insensitive, even

Dancing after the Whirlwind

stupid: "Look on the bright side." "Focus on the positive." "Things could be worse." "You must be very special for God to havė given you such a challenge." "Surely you can find some good in this." "There's a reason for everything."

As a culture, even as concerned individuals struggling to find meaning in horror, whom are we trying to fool when we address survivors in this way? Whom are we trying to help? If we honestly examine our motives, we may find other hidden agendas beneath our empty optimism: "Don't hurt in front of me, because it scares me." "I need to believe this happened to you for a reason, because then maybe it won't happen to me." "I can't sit with your wounds. Please cover them for me so that I can stay with you." "If this tragedy is your fault, I can make sense of the world."

Increasingly, however, social denial of childhood sexual abuse is taking overt and vocal forms. There is a growing tendency to view recovered memories of childhood sexual abuse not simply as psychotic symptoms of severe emotional disturbance but as "false memories" that have been planted or coerced by incompetent or intentionally duplicitous clinicians. According to this view, survivors are victims of hallucinatory delusions or dupes of conniving therapists, but also people incapable of accurately or responsibly describing their own lives.

The Question of Recovered Memory

Cultures have a phenomenal ability to skew evidence in order to maintain the established order, even if the resulting structures conceal deep disturbances or social evils beneath the surface. One false recollection or accusation of childhood sexual abuse makes a greater impact than many true ones, since society does not want these recollections and accusations to be true.

Since early 1992, the mainstream press has repeatedly taken up the theme of false abuse complaints and so-called "false memory."[86]

These stories typically rely on anecdotes, speculation, and "expert opinions" from a small group of professionals to challenge the reliability of survivors and the competence of mental health professionals. The result has been "to favor the position of those accused of sexual abuse, allowing them to claim the support of educated opinion, while relegating their accusers to the realm of 'mass hysteria.'"[87] Thus, the public shock and horror at growing evidence of epidemic levels of child sexual abuse is giving way. Some complacently embrace the notion that most accounts of abuse are the disturbed and misguided ramblings of "False Memory Syndrome." I believe that this response represents yet another form of denial—one with dangerous consequences for survivors.

False Memory Syndrome (FMS) is not a recognized medical or psychological syndrome but a term created by members of the False Memory Syndrome Foundation (FMSF), a support and advocacy organization comprised of several thousand members who claim to have been falsely accused of committing sexual abuse by their children. The prime target of FMSF members is what they consider the "sex abuse industry," the political activists, therapists, and social service providers who (they claim) are utilizing mind control techniques to dupe their clients into believing they were sexually abused.[88]

Opponents and supporters of recovered-memory therapy generally agree on some basic facts. Most acknowledge that child sexual abuse exists, that it is more common than previously thought, that such abuse is a criminal act, that perpetrators should be punished, and that survivors typically need and should seek treatment. Both sides also agree that some people hold false beliefs about past experiences, that incompetent or manipulative therapists may be guilty of incorrect diagnosis, that normal memory is often vague, distorted, or confused, and that scientific data on traumatic memory is incomplete.[89] At this point, the views diverge considerably.

FMSF members and their supporters take the position that victims of serious traumas do not forget their pain or its causes, that such memories need not be "recovered" because they have never been buried.[90] But research does not support this view; there *is* substantial evidence of memory disturbance in situations of severe trauma.

One very interesting study by Linda Meyer Williams follows a group of two hundred women who had reported sexual abuse in the early 1970s.[91] At the time of the abuse, these women (then aged from infancy to twelve years) were brought to the hospital emergency room in a major northeastern city for treatment and collection of forensic evidence following sexual abuse. Interviews and detailed medical records were obtained at that time. Seventeen years later, one hundred of these women, now aged eighteen to thirty-one, were interviewed in a clinically controlled study designed to investigate the extent of amnesia for the abuse. Williams's team found that 38 percent of the women interviewed did not remember the abuse or chose not to report it seventeen years later, although many were willing to reveal other personal experiences. In fact, over half of the women amnestic for the abuse reported other childhood sexual victimizations. Although this research does not address the issue of recovered memory, it strongly supports the position that sexually abused children are likely to block out memories of abusive incidents. Williams concludes that "retrospective studies which rely on self-reports of childhood experiences of sexual victimization are likely to result in an underestimation of the true prevalence of such abuse."[92]

Opponents of recovered memory therapy believe that statistics on the incidence of child sexual abuse are greatly inflated. However, experts in the treatment of child sexual abuse note that survivors typically deny rather than exaggerate both their memories of abuse and the resulting damage. Even those who remember the abuse often discount their experiences or blame themselves. Here, the "planting" of responses may be of another sort, since this response is often the result of specific threats or suggestions on the part of perpetrators.

[S]urvivors have been well taught by their abusers to distrust their own feelings and perceptions. Even when the evidence of the abuse is unmistakable and externally well corroborated, even while coming to believe and accept the reality of their memories, survivors of abuse have moments of doubting what they know. And the expression of doubt in others evokes the same sick, desolating sensation they had as abused children—that nobody believes, nobody understands, nobody accepts them.[93]

This tendency toward self-doubt or self-blame may also be related to the human inclination to seek some kind of meaning or explanation behind tragic or traumatic events. As I noted in chapter 2, Elaine Pagels associates this inclination with Western culture's acceptance of the doctrine of original sin. Survivors may avoid feelings of helplessness or meaninglessness by assuming that they did something that would logically cause the abuse to occur.[94]

Although opponents of recovered memory contend that memories of abuse are induced by therapists, most memories of abuse occur outside the therapist's office. Judith Herman suggests that of the various triggers for delayed recall, "suggestion by a therapist is probably at the bottom of the list."[95] More common triggers are becoming involved in a new relationship, having sex, getting married, becoming pregnant, or having one's child reach the age when the abuse commenced. Other possible triggers are the disclosure of abuse by another victim of the same perpetrator or the perpetrator's illness or death.

Instead of first experiencing memories of abuse while in therapy, survivors typically seek therapy because they are *already experiencing* troubling nightmares and flashbacks. Steele speculates that although one *could* conceivably make up such stories, "it takes an awful lot to shatter a soul, this shattering one cannot feign."[96] As she notes, anyone who has been in the presence of such a shattered soul knows that "The moment you connect with the reality of that shattering it pierces you with a hot stab, sucks your breath away in a vor-

Dancing after the Whirlwind

tex of permeating sadness and horror, then fills you with a heavy coldness—maybe just for a moment, but you'll know it, and you'll never forget it."[97]

In my view, such experiences are not likely to be created by even the most incompetent or manipulative therapists. Perhaps the tendency to blame therapists is related to victim-blaming. Christine Courtois also suggests that the tendency to scapegoat therapists "parallels the same displacement of guilt we see in the incestuous family, in which the victim is blamed for disclosing the abuse."[98] Therapists find themselves in a double-bind: they can be sued both for "implanting" false memories and for failing to correctly diagnose abuse-related trauma.[99]

The consequences of social denial are most devastating, however, for survivors. Keith Russell Ablow, medical director of the Tri-City Community Mental Health Center in Lynn, Massachusetts, writes: "The danger in a label like false memory syndrome is that it can be politicized and used to silence real victims, reproducing the trauma they suffered when they were harmed as children and warned never to tell a soul. It can neatly close the circle of abuse by defining accusers as unreliable."[100] These levels of denial conspire to hinder survivors of child sexual abuse in forming and maintaining the positive sexual identity that is a significant component of spiritual well-being.

Once survivors have overcome their own denial and completed the process of recovering the memory of their experiences, their memories are often both internally consistent and externally verifiable. In Herman's study of 53 survivors, 74 percent were able to validate their memories by obtaining confirmation of the abuse or corroborating evidence from another source. Only 6 percent could obtain no corroboration.[101] Most of the subjects in this study (64 percent) also experienced at least some degree of amnesia about the circumstances of the abuse, with just over one quarter indicating severe memory deficits.[102]

That these recovered memories are accurate, however, is rarely mentioned in media coverage of the issue. Survivors typically do not seek publicity, nor do they wish to discuss their experience publicly. Friends, therapists, and social service workers are personally or professionally obligated to maintain confidentiality and thus cannot respond to public declarations of innocence on the part of those accused of abuse. Since the accused have a major interest in publicly promoting their innocence, media coverage is skewed in favor of perpetrators.[103]

According to Herman, this phenomenon illustrates one of the major insights of feminism: the rules of the public, patriarchal world are not made for "the private world, the world of sexual and domestic relations, the world of women and children." They consistently give the advantage to the empowered over those without power and status in the public realm.[104]

The Power Dynamics of Denial

Survivors of abuse and the helping professionals who work with them often collude with perpetrators and the general culture, however unintentionally, in perpetuating cycles of reversal and denial. In order to understand this dynamic, we must reach behind the treatment of symptoms to the sources of the "dis-ease."[105] This territory is not for the squeamish. Often, it is all we can do to keep from covering our eyes or turning our faces away. Overcoming denial requires our deepest commitment and resistance.

Much has been written in the struggle to understand the motives, urges, and actions of perpetrators, and I will not review that material here. I do believe, however, that certain issues must be addressed if we are ever to understand the pervasiveness of this form of violence and the cultural denial associated with it.

First, we must deal directly with power. Here, Carter Heyward's association of perversion with reversal is again helpful: "When our eroticism is perverse—turned away from its empowering purpose in our lives—sex is dangerous, possessive, and violent."[106] When we focus on sexual violence, we discover a series of reversals: power, responsibility, and blame are turned upside down and inside out; our sense of who we are, what we know, and how we relate to one another is distorted and reversed. To affirm identity and effect transformation, we must reveal and then reverse the reversals.

In traditional patriarchal scenarios of conquest, heroes gain power by conquering powerful foes. Legends of knightly valor highlight the fierce strength of opponents, whether dragon or enemy warrior, in order to emphasize the greater power of the conqueror. This notion of power, dependent as it is on hierarchy, violence, and the need to diminish the power of another in order to establish one's own, has long been a staple of patriarchal culture, and it is obviously problematic. However, it is also based on notions of "fair play," however distorted, and an apparent (though odd) sense of justice.

When power structures are perverted, literally turned upside down, the picture becomes even grimmer. As perpetrators themselves often reveal, it is the very innocence and helplessness of the child victims that becomes overwhelmingly attractive. When asked why they engaged in sexual abuse, many offenders offer no complex explanations. One man's response is typical of many: "Because I could. And I could do it again and again, and nobody could stop me. It felt very powerful." Perpetrators frequently indicate that their sense of power is directly related to the *powerlessness* of their victim. Here, even the most primitive notions of fairness in power relations are completely reversed. Power is acquired not by conquering powerful foes but by overwhelming helpless victims. This is perversion at its most terrifying.

Sexual abuse may also involve a reversal of identity, our most fundamental sense of who we are. While perpetrators project their fear and hatred onto their victims, they also attempt to exchange identities, projecting their own blame on the victim and assuming the victim's innocence and purity for themselves. The helplessness and innocence of infants may represent the characteristics most desired by those who sexually abuse them.

The roots of these reversals of identity and power are neither simple nor superficial. They do not exist only in the deluded minds of a few perverted individuals. Rather, it is my contention that these reversals are themselves an extremely effective means of maintaining the patterns of violence that undergird patriarchal oppression. Strange as it may seem, it may be easier to convince someone else that black is white than that black is gray. When facts are slightly distorted or altered, we may engage our perceptions and our reason to determine the actual situation. But when reality is reversed, we can lose our ability to trust our senses, our intuition, our feelings, and our reason.

Mind games like these are the tools of race, class, and cultural oppression as well as sexism. Although sexual victimization is carried out—and often culturally institutionalized—against girls and women of all ages and cultures, this form of violence becomes particularly virulent when forces of racism, classism, and sexism combine. Women of color and third world women suffer disproportionately in view of the "multiple jeopardy" they face. According to Cheryl Gilkes, sexism both reinforces racial privilege and sharpens the consequences of racial oppression.[107]

The Spiritual Consequences

The world of a sexually abused child is both private and powerless to prevent the distortions and reversals that affect her sexual identity from the beginning. Acts of sexual abuse and violence are negations of erotic connection. *They are a sacrilege, the greatest possible defilement of the sacred bond between spirituality and sexuality.* Through sexual abuse, eros is perverted: it should be the very ground of connectedness, creativity, and love, but it becomes the source of alienation, brutality, betrayal, and power dominance. Survivors of child sexual abuse are left with a disastrous legacy: sexuality, potentially the most natural source of pleasure and expression of love, becomes a source of pain and betrayal.

The acts of the abuser, like the acts of the pornographer (and the embodiment-negating religious institution), project hatred and fear of the body and sexuality and then oppress, or assault, the object of that projection. The abused—those who bear these projections—need to reclaim their sexual identities as their own. But this is not an easy task to accomplish from the place of pain. In reenacting the sexuality/spirituality divisions described in chapter 2, survivors often associate sex with evil and pleasure with guilt. Relationality and embodiment, the potential keys to erotic power, become the realms where danger and betrayal are magnified. What is sexual identity to a woman with such a history? What is the process of healing, of developing a spiritual identity that incorporates and affirms her sexuality?

Again the whirlwind rises. As memories surface, souls are shattered and lives come apart. This is hell the hard way. Survivors of sexual abuse are drawn to images of the Holocaust. How could this have happened? How could people do that? How shall I understand this? How shall I go on?

Women and AIDS: Epidemic Ironies

I have been well educated by the friends I have loved and lost to AIDS. What they have taught me has often been surprising and unexpected. I anticipated that I would learn about my own mortality, my own suppressed fears and projections, my capacity—or lack of capacity—to face the unknown and to be there for others in need. I learned much about these things. But I also value other unanticipated gifts of awareness.

I learned to pay attention to the fact that even those who are suffering often have a deeply felt need to be needed. I remember my friend Mark commenting about how much he needed someone, anyone, to ask him a favor. He was surrounded by so much loving support, so many who were willing to help, but we forgot that he also needed to be himself, a man to whom others could turn for care or help or just a little attention.

I learned that we assume a continuity in daily life that is far more tenuous than we realize. I went with a friend to a bookstore in Greenwich Village some years ago. While wandering through the stacks, my friend encountered an acquaintance whom he had not seen for some time. They greeted each other warmly. "I'm so glad to see you," said my friend. "I thought you had gone." As we left the store, I asked him if he had thought his acquaintance had left town. "No," he said, "I thought he was dead. We're always so happy to see someone we haven't seen for a while. When we don't see them, we figure something has happened." I was struck by the immediacy of it—every chance encounter intensified by the realization that those who are out of sight may never be seen again.

I learned a powerful new context for wisdom I had earlier derived from the lesbian and gay liberation movement: perhaps the single greatest weapon in the battle against devastating fear and loss is a good sense of humor.

And I learned that denial is at its most powerful when fear joins forces with racial, sexual, and class oppression. This last awareness was not a surprise, but I have discovered deeper, more dangerous levels of denial in the cultural response to AIDS. While I grieve deeply for *all* who have lost loved ones and feel solidarity with those men simultaneously living with AIDS and combating societal ignorance and denial, I focus here on women who are seropositive for HIV or living with AIDS. As a culture, we have done our best to annihilate their image or to view them as "vessels" or "vectors" of infection and disease. We need to see and hear and touch them. We need to learn from them. We need to know that they are here with us.

I met Krista Blake, a student in my introductory course on world religions, in 1990. A couple of weeks into the course, Krista approached me after class and advised me that she was HIV-positive and was becoming symptomatic. Neurological problems were affecting her memory, and she was having a difficult time retaining what she was reading for the course. For the next several weeks, Krista and I got to know one another as we worked through the course material together. She would read from the course text and then immediately come into my office to discuss what she had read. Krista was fascinated by the religions of the world and often related the material to her own feelings and circumstances. Not surprisingly, we often veered from discussion of doctrines and rituals to more philosophical and theological concerns. Questions about the reasons for suffering, divine intentionality, faith and practice, take on a different tone when one of the discussants is facing a limited future uncertain in every aspect save one.

Although Krista did well in my course, increasing physical and neurological difficulties soon made it impossible for her to continue her college education. She reached out for another level of learning, however, and in the remaining years of her life became a teacher for many of us. She became a well-known educator and activist on behalf of people living with AIDS. She lectured, participated in panels, made public appearances, and "made the cover of *Newsweek*." She was "out." Unlike many in the earlier days of AIDS awareness, Krista received general support from family, friends, and community, but she was very aware of public opinion. She said, "They all call me 'that girl from Columbiana with AIDS.'"

This brings to mind another subtle form of denial—the denial of all other aspects of one's identity *except* the offending characteristic. Krista encountered that form of denial every time she appeared in public, and she worked hard to help others see her as more than a woman with a terrifying disease. I learned much from Krista, and I loved her. She was particularly concerned about the lack of information and awareness about women with HIV and the failure to provide adequate assistance. This concern was and is well founded.

Krista's face on the cover of *Newsweek* underscores one of the many ironies associated with women and AIDS. The cover story featuring Krista ran in August 1992, and its focus was not women but teenagers and AIDS. The blurb on the cover reads: "Krista Blake had a 'basic, white-bread' American life until an older boy gave her the virus. She was 16." I never asked Krista what she thought of it, but I know she was often angered by those who made distinctions based on the cause of infection. Her face on the cover is haunting—pale, thin, and agonizingly young, she stares out from the black background. To me, her eyes say, "Can you handle it that I, too, am the face of AIDS?"

Krista's face and story evoke sympathy. She is depicted as a model citizen of a small Midwestern town, the victim of an older boy who took advantage of her youth and ignorance. The text of the story on teenagers and AIDS emphasizes the fact that now even "good kids" are at risk. The message to readers of *Newsweek* seems to be "This could be your kid."

By now we have become familiar with some of the other faces of AIDS: Rock Hudson, Ryan White, Magic Johnson, Arthur Ashe, Greg Louganis. Somehow we manage to lift cultural icons above the taint enough to grieve. We forgive them their sins, or we highlight their blamelessness. Louganis, as a gay man, is perhaps more suspect than the others. The generic face of AIDS in popular culture is male, white, gay, probably middle class, with a history of sexual promiscuity.

But where are the faces of the women? Although comparisons are of little value in considering the impact of denial, it is crucial to acknowledge that women with AIDS are among the most culturally invisible people on the planet. Statistically, women with AIDS are more likely than men to be people of color and poor. Many positive women are employed as prostitutes, have a history of drug use, or have had drug users as partners. Mary Hunt notes that "the racism, sexism, and classism that underlie an unjust society are mirrored in the greatest public health problem of the twentieth century."[108]

These are the women that we, as a culture, cannot see, the ones whose very being we most profoundly deny. When we do acknowledge their existence, they become the object of our projected hatred, fear, and shame. We cannot even see their illness and their suffering, let alone their anger and their pride, *and certainly not their sexual desires and emotional and spiritual needs.* So we bypass their lives, their feelings, and their experiences completely, reducing them to carriers of infection to men and to children. As Alexandra Juhasz observes: "Somehow AIDS has become just one more systematic oppression for the already oppressed in our society, exaggerating and multiplying the compromised positions under which many women already live their lives."[109]

Most of the forms of denial I will discuss are related to recognizing the existence of HIV-infection among women and acknowledging the needs and feelings of women who are HIV-positive. But there is still another level of denial that threatens not only their physical and emotional well-being but their fundamental sense of themselves. We fail completely to acknowledge HIV-positive women as sexual beings, greatly inhibiting their ability to define their sexuality in positive ways. This is most evident not in overt rejection but in the absences and empty places where affirmation of HIV-positive women as sexual (and spiritual) beings ought to be.

It is not surprising that AIDS, certainly one of the most intense cultural experiences of our time, presents in distilled form many of our most perverse cultural and personal patterns. AIDS is a virtual case study in denial. By now many are aware of the appalling societal failure to respond to AIDS and the ongoing devastation that has resulted: the initial refusal to acknowledge its existence; the prolonged belief (against all scientific evidence, all data, all reason) that the disease infected only gay men and IV-drug users, that it would not spread to other elements of the population, and that it was therefore not a public concern; the failure to dedicate sufficient funds to research; the projection of blame onto those who become infected (and are thus potential carriers of infection to others) instead of the cultural patterns that encourage and support the transmission of the disease.

But in terms of women and AIDS, denial has been so extreme that even the denial is denied, even the cover-up is invisible. Many members of the general public are still under the impression that women are unlikely to become infected with HIV, and few are aware of the reasons for this false impression. I count myself among those who have practiced selective denial and chosen to remain ignorant. My research into cultural and medical responses to women and AIDS has often made it difficult for me to refrain from bouncing books and papers off walls in my anger over this hidden history.

The Invisible Others

According to Gena Corea, the AIDS virus thrives because of "the notion of 'otherness,'" which permeates the U.S. medical system. "This is also called 'sexism,' 'racism,' and 'homophobia'—words too puny and mild-mannered to convey the savagery they represent."[110] Otherness allows us to fail in our response to the disease and its spread, to withhold care from those who are afflicted, because they have brought this disease on themselves through their "tainted" lifestyles. "Certainly we don't have to worry about catching AIDS ourselves if it is something 'others' get."[111]

And woman, as Simone de Beauvoir has made clear, is fundamentally "other." When we factor in race and economic class, HIV-positive women are so ultimately other, they have already been annihilated by definition. Even after AIDS finally became a public concern, "women remained invisible in the epidemic."[112] In her well-researched—and emotionally devastating—chronicle of the cultural failures in recognizing the relationship between women and AIDS, Corea notes that a number of women professionally employed in prisons, hospitals, and social service and government agencies raised concerns as early as 1981, but the medical community continued to insist that there was no significant risk of HIV infection in women and that funding of medical research on women and HIV was unnecessary.

As late as 1985, the surveillance definition of AIDS (the definition used in the United States for reporting the extent of the disease) included no gynecological symptoms. When gynecological symptoms of AIDS were found (chronic pelvic inflammatory disease, refractory chronic candidiasis, vaginal candidiasis, cervical dysplasia leading to cervical cancer, chronic urinary tract infections, recurrent genital warts, abnormal pap smears), they were not added to the AIDS surveillance definition. These omissions inhibited recognition of the disease in women and prevented many infected women from qualifying for the governmental assistance available to infected men.[113] Without a Centers for Disease Control-defined diagnosis of AIDS, extremely sick women were denied benefits for food, shelter, and medical care, since disability benefits were often women's only access to Medicare and Medicaid.[114]

In 1987, when the CDC added conditions found only in HIV-infected children to the surveillance definition, the proportion of women diagnosed with AIDS increased by 39 percent. Conditions appearing only in women, however, were still excluded.[115] In fact, the first and only female genital complication of AIDS established as an AIDS-defining diagnosis, invasive cervical cancer, was not added until January 1, 1993, a full twelve years into the epidemic.[116] Corea quotes an activist participating in a demonstration at the Department of Health and Human Services: "The only way women were meeting the government AIDS definition was on autopsy."[117] Another activist slogan illustrates the ironies of denial: "Women don't get AIDS. They just die from it."

The strong climate of denial did not protect some women from being put in an impossible position: they were required to prove that they were *not* HIV-positive, even before the HIV test was generally

available. Corea tells several painful stories: A woman with an unmarried son living in Greenwich Village is fired, because her boss assumes that her son must be gay and she must therefore be a carrier of
AIDS; a woman is suspended from her employment until she can
prove she doesn't have the disease, because she confided in some coworkers when her boyfriend died of AIDS.[118]

The Data of Denial

Statistics can be used to conceal individual suffering behind a blur of
numbers, but they also reveal the data of denial. Diagnosed AIDS
cases among women are a rapidly growing proportion of the total in
many parts of the world, including Europe and North America.[119] In
both the United States and Europe, AIDS is increasing more rapidly
among women than among men.[120] In 1991, the World Health Organization estimated over a million cases of AIDS worldwide and
about ten million cases of HIV infection, a third of which are likely
to be women.[121] Half of those diagnosed with AIDS in Africa are
women.[122] In a 1992 study, the Centers for Disease Control reported
the number of women registered with an AIDS diagnosis as 22,607,
and an estimated five times that many women who were HIV-
positive.[123] AIDS is the leading cause of death for all women between
ages fifteen and forty-four and the sixth leading cause of death for
women of reproductive age in the United States.[124] The comparative
rate of infection for women has increased steadily since data collection commenced.

In addition, despite the stereotype that AIDS is a disease of gay
people and IV-drug users,[125] the rate of HIV-positive women who
were infected through heterosexual contact has jumped from 12 percent in 1982 to 34 percent, making this the fastest growing transmission category for women.[126] Women may be as much as three times
more likely than men to become infected through heterosexual in-

Dancing after the Whirlwind

tercourse.[127] As we enter the new millenium, global projections suggest that the typical person with AIDS will be "a heterosexual woman with dependent children in a country now known as the 'two-thirds' world."[128]

Women with HIV/AIDS have less access to medical treatment, receive less treatment, and die sooner than infected men.[129] Data collected in 1985 indicated that far more women than men were likely to die during the same month they were diagnosed, and that women diagnosed with AIDS died twice as fast as men with the same diagnosis. Among other things, these data imply that women are likely to be diagnosed much later than men.[130] Correct diagnosis may not be made until women develop serious illnesses—or it may not be made at all. This problem is exacerbated by doctors who fail to indicate an AIDS-related diagnosis on death certificates, listing only the specific opportunistic infection that caused death.[131] Obviously, early diagnosis will result in more immediate and more appropriate medical care.

Ironies and Abuses

From the earliest days of HIV/AIDS awareness, the circular ironies of denial with regard to women and HIV/AIDS have multiplied. Failure to believe that women were at risk led to a failure to support research funding, which in turn contributed to lack of awareness. The poverty, medical problems, and limited resources of many clients and research participants further inhibited both concern and funding. Medical theories assumed a male model, which further marginalized women, and the general cultural failure to represent the lives and circumstances of women adequately, coupled with racism and classism, negated the existence of HIV-positive women.[132]

Western feminists have also been slow to see AIDS as a women's issue. Corinne Squire suggests that this situation may be linked to their predominant concern with the interests of middle-class women. In addition, some feminists do not consider AIDS their issue. They even criticize lesbians for their concern and involvement, claiming that those organizing around HIV/AIDS are becoming "wives to the gay men's AIDS movement."[133]

AIDS, Women, and Power

But AIDS *is* a woman's issue, and the situation must be understood in the wider context of patriarchal power structures and women's place in society.[134] Hortensia Amaro cites "institutional sexism" as "the factor that has most powerfully framed the United States' response to HIV infection and AIDS in women."[135]

One illustration of gendered power structures and their impact is the relationship of women to the health care system. As nurses, home health aides, and family caretakers, women are, almost universally, the primary providers of health care, although their positions are usually lower paid and lower status, and they are underrepresented in decision-making bodies in the health care services.[136] Women's daily contributions to health care are generally unrecognized and unrewarded, yet they bear almost exclusive responsibility for maintaining the ongoing health of family members.[137] A further complication is the fact that the male-run medical establishment still assumes, for the most part, that the male body is the norm, and regards women's bodies as "anything from a complicated, troublesome variation on the norm to an innately pathological entity."[138] Women are also more likely than men to receive a psychological rather than a physiological diagnosis for physical symptoms such as fatigue, dizziness, or headaches. "Men seem to be regarded within medicine as intrinsically more honest, more reliable, more stable and more likely to have 'real' health problems than women."[139] At the same time, the medicalization of all facets of women's sexuality and reproductive life further relegates women to the realm of patient in a male-dominated medical profession.[140] The realities of medical research and treatment underscore the gendering of AIDS. Gena Corea notes that "for many medical professionals women are dark shapes in dark shadows who don't come into focus unless they are seen as endangering either men or fetuses."[141]

Given their significant role in providing health care to others, it is also ironic that in the early and mid-1980s as the epidemic gained momentum, women hospitalized with AIDS were frequently subjected to miserable treatment. Their beds and clothing went unchanged, they were not bathed, and their food trays were not delivered to them directly but left in the hallway.[142] The health needs of infected women were—and still are—considered by both the medical profession and the general public to be secondary "to their supposed role as 'transmitters' of infection."[143] Corea writes, for example, of Elizabeth Prophet, an imprisoned prostitute who became a media symbol of the threat of AIDS to the male heterosexual community: "It wasn't Prophet's health that was a concern. It was the health of the men who used her."[144]

Other gender issues also illustrate the massive cultural failure to respond adequately to the needs of HIV-positive women. Public discourse on AIDS "tends to ignore, sideline, or pathologize women."[145] The "common cultural erasure of women" continues as gender issues for women dealing with HIV/AIDS are minimized or denied. At the same time, however, this discourse also "reproduces cultural definitions of women as incarnations of sexual danger, biological power and victimhood."[146]

The association of women and female genitalia with contamination and disease parallels the linkage between women and death-wielding seduction. "The ages-old image of sexual woman ... is of a deathtrap, as the honey-pot luring men to die from syphilis, gonorrhoea and now AIDS."[147] Corea notes the intense irony of blaming women for spreading a disease while simultaneously reassuring them that they are unlikely to get it.[148]

We have seen these patterns of projection and denial before. Here, denial and a hatred of erotic power are projected onto the bodies of seropositive women, erasing the reality of their suffering while crafting phenomenal structures of reversal to blame them for it. This amounts to the denial of women's sexual identity through obliteration of everything but disease. No longer a resource for healing, female erotic power acquires the death's head. A woman's love, says the patriarchal powers that be, is death.

Prostitution and AIDS

As the case of Elizabeth Prophet illustrates, the image of women as vehicles of sexual contamination has assumed a peculiar intensity in the lives of prostitutes. Although some cultures are making headway in providing prostitutes with education and medical services for HIV, the safety of many of these women is outside their own control. Governmental collusion in the sex industry underscores prostitution's economic and political function by reinforcing women's economic subservience.[149] Meanwhile, in a "truly startling feat of irrationality," guilt is shifted from the man who uses both wife and prostitute to one of his victims.[150]

Denial thrives at every level of the prostitution industry. Women's sexual identity and their sexual needs are denied; they exist only to service the needs of others. Their risk and their suffering as a result of dangerous sexual practices (and the economic and social conditions that necessitate them) are denied; their experience is invisible. The male role in spreading HIV through prostitution is also denied. A woman is a vessel, the bearer of pleasure or illness, gratification or threat, children or disease.

Although the individual needs, feelings, and identities of HIV-positive prostitutes are denied, another irony of the cultural response to HIV is the tendency to assume that *all* HIV-positive women are prostitutes. Corea notes, for example, that a 1985 study of HIV in women launched in San Francisco by a team of woman medical doctors was referred to by their male colleagues as "The Prostitute Study," even though less than a third of the women included in the study were prostitutes.[151]

_____ *Sex and Danger*

In fact, in cultures where sexual assault, rape, and coercion are commonplace, it is usually women who are in danger. In a sexually violent culture, women's sexual practices and desires often have little impact on the sexual transmission of disease. Tamsin Wilton notes the irony of promoting safe sex within the context of a culture in which sex "has never been safe for women."[152] Women are always at risk, not only from sexually transmitted diseases but from the contraception, pregnancy, abortion, and child support issues they must face. Men can and do "expect free, spontaneous sex" yet remain unwilling to take responsibility for unplanned results.[153] And celibacy and abstinence have little relevance to women's HIV-positive status "when violence is the transmission mode."[154] According to Corea, "male supremacy provides the wings on which the human immunodeficiency virus flies around the world."[155]

Wilton cites research on a global level suggesting that for most of the world's women, sex is "more often than not uncomfortable, painful, embarrassing or humiliating, far from pleasurable, and that they are seldom willing and equal partners."[156] Factors such as illiteracy and poverty increase women's dependency on men, and sexual refusal puts women at risk of being ostracized, turned out, raped, or killed. "Sex is widely understood to be something which men do to women, and a service which men feel they have a right to demand of women."[157] Although this picture may be changing, it is changing only for a tiny minority: "'Negotiation' and 'consent' are concepts which have very little relation to the heterosexual lives of most women," although they are crucial to the practice of safe sex.[158]

Furthermore, studies show that men lie to women in order to have sex and that they disclose intimate information much later than women do. Corea cites research evidence that 20 percent of men would lie to a woman about whether they had been tested for AIDS and that two-thirds of men with a higher risk for HIV did not think they needed to use condoms. Deception is another contributor to the spread of HIV.[159]

Men's inclination toward sexually motivated deception is perhaps the ultimate illustration of the destructive role of denial. These lies and secrets literally kill, while love, fidelity, accountability, and the other precious elements of relationality fall victim to the ultimate in sexual/spiritual alienation. The death's head actually glares from another direction. Denial can be terminal when sexual activity is completely isolated from the communal bonds of eros.

Lesbian Issues and AIDS

Lesbians have a unique relationship with the HIV/AIDS virus, one replete with contradictions. In terms of the potential for sexual transmission of HIV, lesbians may be the cultural group at lowest risk of infection, but homophobia and ignorance combine to lump them erroneously with gay men as among those most likely to be infected. The tendency to invoke lesbians as women at high risk in media discourse about AIDS may be associated with "the power social fears of homosexuality and female sexuality have in this epidemic over epidemiological knowledge."[160] Wilton comments: "Those who proclaim that AIDS is the just deserts of perversion, or divine retribution on unnatural sex, do not distinguish between male and female 'deviancy.'"[161]

The low risk for sexual transmission of HIV between lesbians has an unfortunate by-product rooted in sexual stereotypes about lesbian lifestyles: the failure to diagnose HIV in lesbians who may have been infected by blood transfusion, needlestick injuries, or heterosexual contact. Because of their assumed low risk, minimal educational information about safe sex is specifically directed to lesbians.[162] And, perhaps most odd, there is virtually no existing research into why lesbian sex is comparatively safe. As Wilton observes, "It is worth recognizing that, were it not for social and political considerations, medical common sense should suggest that any group whose behaviour puts it at risk of contracting a potentially lethal condition could do no better than to seek advice from a group whose behaviour clearly protects it from that condition."[163]

The costs of the disease are enormous for gay men and for lesbians. Mary Hunt points out the erosive effect of the AIDS specter on gains made by the lesbian and gay communities: "It has provided a homophobic society with the medical excuse necessary to do its dirty deeds to lesbian/gay people, and that same society has taken every opportunity."[164]

Reproductive Issues

Reproductive issues are enormously complex for HIV/AIDS, and it is impossible to consider all of them here. Since pregnant women receiving prenatal medical care are most likely to receive HIV antibody screening, and since there is intense social concern about the economic and social costs of HIV-positive babies, "it is in discourse and practice around pregnant women that the characterization of women as the vessels of HIV infection obtains its greatest force."[165] Cultural gender divisions reinforce the assumption that pediatric AIDS is a woman's problem.[166]

As research provides more information about transmission risks during pregnancy, delivery, and breast-feeding, the assumption that mother-child transmission of the virus is almost inevitable is being seriously questioned. Although all babies born to HIV-positive women have antibodies to HIV in their blood, current estimates suggest that as few as 10 to 15 percent of these babies are themselves infected with the virus. Additional research challenges other previously held assumptions. For example, pregnancy and childbirth may not significantly increase the progression rate of AIDS-related illness. Although theoretically, breast milk may transmit the virus, existing studies indicate that the risk is very small.[167]

These new data further complicate the issue of whether or not women with HIV/AIDS ought to be discouraged (some would even suggest prevented) from becoming pregnant and bearing children. Amaro mentions potential abuses: the use of prenatal HIV antibody testing to pressure seropositive women to abort and support for forced sterilization and involuntary antibody testing.[168] The psychological, cultural, and social characteristics of the women at highest risk for HIV infection must be considered: "For many HIV positive women, a 70 per cent chance of having a child who is not infected may be the best odds they have ever had."[169]

It will not do to declare that no woman who is HIV positive has a moral right to become pregnant and bear a child. The histories of many cultures reflect enormous intervention into the reproductive lives of women. In the United States, many women, a disproportionate number of them women of color and women labeled mentally deficient or mentally ill, have been coercively sterilized. While white middle-class women have had to fight for the right to terminate a pregnancy, poor women and women of color are pressured not to bear children and suffer cultural ostracism if they do. Often, they are encouraged to abort their children or are required to consent to sterilization as a condition for termination of a pregnancy.[170] In such a climate, restricting the reproductive rights of any woman raises complex issues of race, class, and physical and mental ability.

Another HIV/AIDS-related concern that deeply affects the lives of women is society's response to drug addiction, in particular, the view that drug addiction is a moral issue rather than an illness.[171] Corea summarizes the implicit U.S. policy on drug addiction: it is designed to "keep addicted women drugged."[172] Because drug-addicted mothers who seek treatment for their addiction risk losing custody of their children, they may avoid the treatment they need. Punitive actions against drug-addicted women for prenatal child abuse are also on the rise. While pregnant drug-addicted women may be criminally charged or lose their children, they are also routinely rejected from drug treatment programs.[173] In addition, few treatment programs provide child care or residential facilities for children.[174] "While we are horrified at the sight of drug-addicted newborns," Corea concludes, "we make it nearly impossible for a pregnant woman to break her addiction."[175]

Drug use has a significant effect on the spread of HIV infection, especially through needle sharing among IV-drug users.[176] The horrendous increase in crack addiction since 1986 has also affected HIV transmission, especially among women, since they may be forced into dangerous sex-for-drugs exchanges. Corea notes the impact of the cultural setting: Inner-city women may have switched from heroin to crack because of their desire to keep their anger (which heroin suppresses) and to feel good. Heroin users, on the other hand, may "adopt intravenous drug use as an escape from sexual trauma into an asexual world," since heroin also suppresses the sex drive, and women with sexual abuse histories might want to cut off sexual thoughts and desires.[177]

The difference between recreational drug use and addiction may ultimately lie not in the drug but in how women feel about themselves and how much hope they have. In addition to the combined ravages of sexism, racism, and classism in their lives, hopelessness may be associated, as we have seen, with a history of abuse. In fact, there is a high correlation between histories of child sexual abuse and being drug addicted and/or positive for HIV/AIDS.[178] Corea describes the cycle:

> A female is sexually assaulted. She uses a drug to numb the pain of that experience. To procure the drug, she submits to further sexual degradation and humiliation. Now an even greater pain requiring anesthesia throbs within her. The attacks through abuse, on a woman's spirit, on her self-esteem, on her very capacity for developing an ego, an identity, a self, a sense of "I am," plow the ground for drug addiction. This, in turn, creates an environment ripe for HIV infection.[179]

Sexual exploitation in relation to crack addiction is not limited to past incidents of sexual abuse. Corea cites the experiences of Marilyn (T. J.) Rivera, a former addict from New York City, who describes crack's sexually stimulating quality. She believes women started using crack because men gave it to them to make them more sexually available. The men wanted the sexual stimulation; the women often wanted the drug-induced sensation of power: "Sex was a tool they sometimes used to get the drug; the drug was a tool they used to make the sex endurable."[180] Drug dealers would often offer a woman along with the drug, and drug-addicted women might be kept at crack houses as virtual slaves of the drug and the dealers.

Bartering sex for drugs ("tossing") differs from other forms of prostitution in that it involves a much smaller payment (for example, vaginal intercourse for a three-dollar vial of crack), even less negotiating power on the part of women (who may be forced to perform degrading or dangerous acts in order to obtain even a small amount of crack), and a particularly degraded social position (women who exchange sex for drugs are referred to as "crack hos," "skeezers," or "toss-ups").[181] The intense euphoria crack users experience can induce them to do anything to obtain a hit. One addict reveals the depth of her degradation and humiliation: "I sucked his dick, right, and he came in my mouth and I was spitting out—and he gave me $4. I was crying and shit because I knew how bad I [had] gotten. I was like, oh my god, $4 and I was out there begging for a fucking dollar."[182]

Control issues are again relevant here. In the lives of women addicted to crack, the drug is in control. The need for the drug will take precedence over basic survival drives (food, water, and self-preservation), over concern for others, even one's own children, over concern for appearance, even the desire to be clean. Lown et al. note that women addicted to crack blamed themselves not only for the sex for drugs exchange but for the loss of "womanliness" resulting from their addiction. In spite of their struggle to fulfill gender-role expectations, "they described losing battles in which crack overwhelmed their capacity to be the 'women' and 'mothers' that they were expected to be."[183]

All these issues illuminate the interaction between projection and denial. With gay men, lesbians share the scapegoat role, bearing the projected sins of the culture in relation to HIV and yet simultaneously denied adequate education and medical care. Pregnant HIV-positive women are blamed for transmitting the disease to their children but their own needs and desires are overlooked. Drug-addicted women are viewed as dangerous and evil, yet the most basic elements of human identity and dignity (including treatment for their addiction) are denied them.

Spiritual Starvation

What is at stake in confronting cultural denial regarding women and HIV/AIDS: gender, sexuality, power, and identity. The lens through which most, if not all, cultures of the world view the AIDS epidemic is tinted—and tainted—with the politics of patriarchy. Alexandra Juhasz observes that "even when men scrutinize nature, other men, the HIV virus or knowledge in general, this activity is already codified by tropes of gender, sexuality and power: the seer is a man, that which is seen is a woman, and the act of seeing is sexual."[184]

In fact, the cultural response to women who are positive for HIV/AIDS negates their sexual identity and redefines them in terms of their disease. As I have already noted, even the most supportive literature on women living with HIV/AIDS includes almost nothing about sexual feelings or identity aside from safe-sex guidelines. The *Woman's HIV Sourcebook*, for example, an otherwise thoughtful work designed to assist seropositive women in self-help has nothing, even in the section for husbands and partners, about *feelings* related to sex.[185] The text refers only to specific sexual practices. Not surprisingly, there is also very little in the literature about spirituality. The same book has only one paragraph on "prayer or contact with a higher power." Women living with HIV/AIDS are not encouraged to explore or to develop their erotic power, to love and be loved, to passionately connect with the wild power of life in the world. Rather, they are carefully instructed to view themselves and their sexuality as death-dealing weapons that must be contained and controlled.

One critical issue in prolonging wellness among those who are HIV-positive is maintaining body weight. Weight loss is a severe threat to seropositive individuals, and the bodies of individuals with advanced AIDS often appear to be in the last stages of starvation. This image brings me to reflect upon the starvation that is not so easily observed in women with AIDS, unless we are strong enough to gaze directly into their eyes: the starvation of the soul.

Spiritual nourishment is fundamentally relational, and erotic power is an essential wellspring. That we cannot tend to the body without tending to the soul is a cliché. That we cannot affirm the spirit of a woman without seeing her as fully embodied and sexually valuable ought to be as obvious.

Erotic power is sacred, and denial of that power is sacrilege. In order to recover from the damage of denial and renew our sexual and spiritual identities, we must reverse the reversals. Lesbian sexuality

Dancing after the Whirlwind

is not perverted. Rather, patriarchal culture perverts sexual loving between women, turning it completely around. If lesbian sexuality cannot be erased, it can be distorted into something sinful, sick, or depraved. Child sexual abuse perverts the natural, spontaneous development of sexual identity with overlays of threat, fear, and pain. And the cultural response to women with HIV/AIDS turns love and pleasure against themselves. Just as the HIV virus penetrates and destroys immune systems, images of danger, disease, and death invade and seek to destroy the passion and pleasure we take in loving one another. The balance of life and death is upended. But whether we fear it or rejoice in it (or both), Eros will not be overcome.

Spiritual Recovery and Transformation

I am beginning to believe that we know everything,

that all history, including the history of each family,

is part of us, such that when we hear any secret revealed . . .

our lives are made suddenly clearer to us,

as the unnatural heaviness of unspoken truth is dispersed.

For perhaps we are like stones; our own history and the

history of the world embedded in us,

we hold a sorrow deep within and cannot weep

until that history is sung.

— SUSAN GRIFFIN, *A Chorus of Stones*

The songs of our lives. We need them. Even broken or bitter histories belong to us, and claiming them, no matter how painful, is part of the process of recovery and renewal. But reflecting on the losses and damage of the past, even claiming our identities in the teeth of the whirlwind, is only part of the story. I want to turn now to the spiritual side of the dynamic, to what Andre Guindon would have us understand as tenderness. Even as our histories are sung, even as we weep for all that has been shattered and lost, there is always the dance.

Contemplating the process of healing and recovery, however, initially leads not away from suffering but deeper into spiritual crisis, the shattering of souls. Recovery and renewal are never a linear process. In each of the communities that concern us here, individual spiritual growth and renewal involve passage through these crises and emergence into new levels of spiritual awareness. This journey cannot be described without including the painful moments of departure.

There is currently a lively debate in feminist theory over the practice of focusing on women as victims. On the one hand, we struggle to move beyond the image of women as perpetual victims, unable to stand against the onslaught of patriarchal violence, and to celebrate the strength and joy of women's lives. On the other, we strive to identify and to resist forces of oppression and abuse rather than deny their damage.

I do not consider the women in this book to be resourceless victims, wandering helplessly about in a patriarchically structured world with no sense of identity or direction. They *are* encumbered by the processes of denial. They *do* struggle when key elements of their identities are both personally and culturally denied. They may also experience soul shattering: the forces of the whirlwind literally take them apart. But in the midst of the storm, there are sources of spiritual replenishment. Each of the communities I have described has well-established support structures and spiritual resources, although they are more accessible to some women than to others. These structures often provide not only support but focal points and frames of reference for resistance against continuing oppression.

Now I come to the dance of recovery, healing, and renewal. As I considered questions about identity and denial, I found myself reflecting on a Christian Bible story that has long intrigued me.[1] I have always been able to picture Peter vividly, crouching by the fire in the courtyard, confronted by the bystanders who accused him by association, Peter insisting, "I do not know what you mean. I do not know the man."[2] Even when all the bystanders confronted him at once, saying that his accent betrayed him,[3] he continued his denial. And then the cock crowed. "And he went out and wept bitterly." The consequences of denial. But that is not the end of Peter's story. The cock's crow woke him up. He found catharsis and renewal in affirming that which he had once denied, and this affirmation empowered him to spiritual renewal and great work.

This story illustrates two key elements that are critical to recovery from denial and spiritual rebirth. Both are relevant to each of the communities of women whose struggles I have described. Neither is a new idea, but their intertwining activity in our lives takes on new power when we explore their intricate relationship. The first is *authentic being*. We must know who we are and be who we are. As simple as it may sound, this is probably the fundamental description of every meaningful spiritual quest, and it has never been easy. The second is *transformation*. We must feed our old structures and patterns to the whirlwind, dancing the wild dance of erotic change until we are reborn.

The ironies in the relationship between these two processes are complex. Authentic being implies a stability of identity that transformation is already undermining. How can I be myself when my self is coming apart? Is this new emerging self an authentic one? What will I do when the fit of this new skin is tested by future changes? If there is no permanent and stable "me" here, how can I possibly be true to my self. How can there *be* a true self?

Still, even in the face of this paradox, both processes are critical. To claim our own being is to undo the tangle of duplicity that has knotted our lives. When we live authentically, the complicity of our silence, our subtle and overt deceptions, is revealed. This connects us to the power of our own internal resources, certainly, but as Martin Buber makes clear, it also enables us to develop and maintain authentic relationships—perhaps the most potent resource of spiritual strength available to us here, in this mortal place.

And even as we come to know ourselves and to own what we know, our spiritual journeys are already taking us across the borderline into wildness. It is here in this uncharted terrain that we dance to the drumbeats of our hearts' changes—in the space between being and becoming.

But these metaphors, bounding as metaphors do beyond our ability to focus on specifics, need grounding in the particularities of women's experiences. Perhaps I can best work toward resolving the tension between identity and change by focusing on each community in turn.

Lesbian Spirituality: Tribal Songs

To begin, then, what does being an authentic lesbian have to do with spiritual identity? Affirming the value of personal experience, what do lesbians have to do with Peter or Peter with lesbians? We can begin to explore this question by considering lesbian identity in the context of religious and spiritual life. For lesbians, spiritual recovery and healing require an affirmation of lesbian identity as a core component of who we are.

Why is it necessary to affirm lesbian identity as fundamental to a basic sense of congruence? In order to recover from the illness of denial through celebration of the rich spiritual traditions of the gay and lesbian community. In order actively to resist physical, mental, and emotional oppression. In order to conquer fear. Coming out may be an act of rebellion against dominant power structures and practices of denial. *It is also an act of love.* We need congruence in order to function and to grow, but we need authentic being to be true, to demonstrate fidelity, for ourselves, but also for one another. As a community, lesbians passionately desire to affirm, and to celebrate, the power of erotic love among women.

Perhaps most important, coming out works to enhance and promote integrity. By this I mean more than truth telling. I mean the creation and preservation of a sense of integration and connectedness with others that is most possible within a context of fully realized identity. Lesbian spiritual identity is the expression of those who will no longer deny or be denied.

Such a celebration of lesbian identity may seem naive. Let me hasten to add, then, that coming out, like many other acts of love, is also difficult and dangerous. Given these ambiguities and the pressures of heterosexist society, it is likely to be a conflicted process: "Coming out involves being stretched between these urges—to come into a wild, erotic ecstasy, a full celebration of our bodyselves and those of others; and, at the same time, to hold on to ourselves, keep the lid on, lest we simply disintegrate in the midst of a culture hostile already to who we are."[4]

Alienation from Mainstream Religious Traditions

Although I have discussed the consequences of denial in gay and lesbian life in some detail, the spiritual aspects of recovery require a bit more reflection. One obvious source of the alienation and projection that reinforces internalized homophobia is the profoundly (and, in many circles, increasingly) negative and destructive attitudes of mainstream religious institutions.[5] These attitudes are not exclusive to Christianity but deeply entrenched in the principles and practices of many religious structures. However, as I have indicated, Christianity has often been particularly inclined to cut erotic power and embodied pleasure off from spirituality, and these attitudes reflect that alienation.[6]

In his 1960 antigay manifesto, for example, Michael Buckley specifically condemns religious bodies and individual moralists who, "by confusing the purposes of matrimony, put sexual fulfillment and mutual help and companionship on an equality with the primary purpose of procreation."[7] This moral error is particularly loathsome to Buckley because it "plays into the hands of homosexuals."[8] He is especially concerned that holding sexual pleasure and companionship equal with procreation will weaken the Catholic position against homosexual unions "where there is genuine affection."[9] Even though Vatican II departed somewhat from these distinctions, the attitude has not changed much.

Whether or not lesbians and gays ought to be gay, call themselves gay, or have gay sex has been much discussed within various religious traditions. Many exclude lesbians and gay men from membership, leadership, and religious life, and the damage to the spiritual lives and identities of lesbians and gay men is of concern. However, the endless debates within these religious communities over whether one should hate the sin and love the sinner, banish the evil from one's midst, or open one's heart to all people without judgment do not provide much insight into the processes of forming and maintaining lesbian and gay identity.

In my opinion, the entire discussion of *cause*, which sometimes emerges within the broader debates, is fruitless if not dangerous. Whether a lesbian was born a lesbian or became one, she still has to make choices that concern her self-understanding, her life, and her relationships. She must choose whether or not to self-identify as a lesbian, whether or not to publicly name herself a lesbian, whether or not to make love with a woman. In all of these decisions, the processes of identity and denial unfold their many layers. And throughout the process, choices have spiritual consequences.

Authenticity and Transformation

In the process of coming out, lesbians often engage in a self-exploration deeper than any they have undertaken in the past. Obviously, this journey is immensely personal—an attempt to establish contact with one's innermost feelings. The struggle for congruency is, however, also a relational effort, an attempt to integrate self-knowledge into one's public life. As sexual beings, lesbians can take nothing for granted. The search for identity is also the effort to meet one another face-to-face rather than from behind the facade of heterosexual assumptions.

Striving to seem rather than to be results in alienated relationships, and fear of exposure forces continual strategies of disguise. Peter huddled in the courtyard, Peter denying his most fundamental identity and relationships—these are poignant images of soul-loss and suffering. Similarly, self-hatred in lesbian life resides primarily in the closet. It is much less evident among "out" gays and lesbians than among those who live "passing" lives.[10]

Where does transformation come in? As old images and assumptions crumble, our first impulse is to shore them up. Finally, as the coming out process illustrates, the center will not hold. We must discard what does not fit, let go of what we can no longer sustain, sweep up and dispose of facades broken beyond repair. Lesbians and gay men must release long-held and often treasured expectations about their place in the culture, their relationships with coworkers and family members, their "fit" in places of employment, religious structures, and community. The process of recognizing and accepting loss is painful. It is also transformative.[11] The surrender and release of old expectations engages us more deeply with others and with ourselves. Gay men and lesbians meet that moment when they must finally acknowledge that "This is no longer my story; the old self-description is no longer mine." There is certainly grief in this, but there is also an accompanying psychic shift. Reformulated loss leads to consolidation among disparate elements of our lives and a sense of coming to terms with our deepest feelings.[12]

At the same time, this very process also *unbinds us from any sense that we can establish a fixed identity completely and forever*, without any further experiences of loss, grief, and renewed transformation. Rather, our own self-understanding becomes more open and fluid in the face of ongoing change.[13]

Although confronting and transforming our losses is only part of the spiritual recovery process, these developments amply illustrate the dynamic interaction between authentic being and transformation. A new understanding of what it means to be ourselves emerges, one that acknowledges the flow of change and releases fixed concepts, but simultaneously acknowledges the need to affirm our authentic being: I am this changer, this dancer. These are my moves. This is my history. This is my way of loving. This is who I am as I change.

Betty Berzon's personal "coming out" story, told in the first chapter of *Positively Gay*, poignantly illustrates these experiences.[14] She writes of living with loneliness "that begins at one's core and permeates the entire field of one's being." The core of this emotion is a loss of connection to the self brought about by fear and accompanying denial: "It is the loneliness of alienation from the true self, as if deep in one's center there is a truth pleading for acknowledgment but lost in denial and dread of exposure to the unknown. Risking the acknowledgment of my gay feelings, the expression, the being known for what is true and so long denied, had been terrifying for me."[15]

Upon moving to a new city and affirming her own lesbian identity, Berzon experienced a transformation:

> With the living out of that truth came a sense of new strength and optimism, came new prerogatives I had only dared dream of before. I could open my life to lesbian women. . . . I could (and did) make myself available to deeply involving emotional and sexual experience in which I could give up control for the first time and allow another human being access to the inner reaches of my sensuality. When that happened, and it was really different than it had ever been before, I knew I had made the right decision, that my re-invented self was one I would want to spend the rest of my life with, hold up to others as evidence of the rewards of struggling for truth in self-definition.[16]

As Berzon's story illustrates, this transformation is more than personal. It expands her ability to relate to others, to open herself up to deeper levels of authentic relationship, and it enables her to share the benefits of affirming her lesbian identity. Working through our own denial processes inevitably draws us into a deeper level of personal engagement with others.

Even as we are already transforming, however, we must confront the forces of denial that reject not only our self-descriptions but the erotic power of our emotional and spiritual lives. Throughout this process, the spiritual journeys of identity affirmation and transformation gay men and lesbians undertake may serve as effective examples for others who are engaging in this spiritual work from different particularities.

Spiritual Contributions

Until very recently, most of the Christian literature about lesbian and gay spirituality has been apologetic. Writers have taken up scripture and church doctrine, religious ethics and cultural beliefs, in order to wrestle with questions such as whether or not lesbians and gay men should have a place in church life, whether or not lesbian and gay lifestyles and sexual practices are sinful, and how the institutional life of the church and its congregational members should respond to the presence of lesbians and gay men in their midst.

More recently, a few writers have considered the spiritual *contributions* of lesbians and gay men to religious life and the possibility that lesbians and gay men have something to offer or to teach spiritual communities out of the particularities of their sexual orientation and experience.[17] This seems to me a more fruitful course. While no amount of scholarly commentary on scripture or doctrine, however well researched or argued, is likely to change the attitudes of homophobic elements in religious institutions, we *can* develop our own spiritual lives from a deeper understanding of our own spiritual identities. And we can teach what we have to teach to those with the body and soul openness to receive and respond. This process, in turn, will undoubtedly be transformative for those who undertake it.

Positive theological reflection on the contributions of lesbian and gay life from outside the lesbian and gay community is rare. Yet, given that such considerations actively relate the spiritual gifts of lesbian and gay life to the greater culture, not only demonstrating but *participating in* their contribution to the spiritual lives of nongay people, it is worth pursuing one of these perspectives in greater details.

Andre Guindon makes some important observations in his reflections on "gay fecundity or liberating sexuality."[18] His initial comments reflect a fairly typical liberal religious pattern of acceptance: the life and ministry of Jesus are entirely "alien to a religious worldview in which the word of God is used to clobber people," the Gospel is not served by conducting "murderous pogroms against gays," lesbian and gay lifestyles and identities are for many people "their only sane choice."[19]

However, Guindon also explores what spiritual resources the gay and lesbian perspective might offer to other Christians. Again, his observations stem from his understanding of sexual language as the means for each individual to grow "into a whole self."[20] First, he acknowledges that gay and lesbian sexuality represents "a gratuitous celebration of love."[21] This conforms to my own observation that gay men and lesbians form sexual partnerships not because of social expectations or advantages but solely because of a desire to express erotic attraction and affection. Recognizing that nongays may partner for the same reason, Guindon observes that, as a group, lesbians and gay men tend to display "a sensual approach to sex."[22] This sensuous celebration is, for Guindon, a valuable reflection of "Christ's sensuous humanity and love's sexual body." Gay men and lesbians can help the whole body of the church to "rediscover sensuousness."[23]

Guindon is particularly troubled by Christianity's alienation from the body and from sensuous life. Too many people "act as if they were not their bodies, as if their bodies were not their own intimate selves whom they are supposed to love as God does."[24] Christians acting on the very un-Christlike premise that "self-hatred is the path leading to the love of others" abuse their own bodies and deny their own needs. "They must be taught to look at their body, to know it, to touch it, to reclaim what is theirs" as a basic condition of intimate and truthful communication.[25] For Guindon, lesbian and gay relationships can be valuable models of sensuous love in committed partnerships that can both deepen the sensuous experience and liberate it from the weight of shame.[26]

What spiritual value might *lesbian* experiences in particular offer? Several possibilities appear once we affirm our lesbian sexual / spiritual identities and fully claim our own particular spiritual journey. Much has been written arguing for the acceptance of lesbians into spiritual community based on the understanding that we are human beings "just like everyone else." This direction might be helpful in overcoming the most blatant and stereotypical forms of oppression, but it misses out on the possibilities that unfold when we consider what might be different, even unique, about lesbian experience.

Considering lesbian life in particular leads me to radical relationality. Since Carol Gilligan's *In a Different Voice*,[27] there has been much debate about her findings—whether or not in making ethical decisions women generally demonstrate more concern for relationships or caring than men do—and whether this focus on relationality represents a valuable approach to ethics or merely reinforces stereotypical gender distinctions.

This debate has been lively but inconclusive. I believe that women as a rule are more effective than men in developing, preserving, and maintaining relationships, that women *are* often more relational. That there are some less relational women and more relational men is obvious, but I think the generalization still holds.

This is not to say that men do not *want* and *need* loving and nurturing relationships. More than twenty years ago, at an Experimental College class on gay life and liberation at Cal State Fullerton, a number of us were discussing the quality and duration of gay and lesbian sexual relationships. "Everyone raise your hands," said one young man laughingly, "and put them down when I get past the number of sexual relationships you've had." We all raised our hands, and he began to count: "One, more than five, more than ten, more than fifteen...." At about that point, there were no more female hands in the air (this was Southern California in the early 1970s), but most of the men were still in the game. A number of women were blinking with astonishment as the numbers got higher and higher, into the hundreds. After it was over, I remember thinking that perhaps gay men and lesbians did not have much in common when it came to our sex lives. We were all gazing at one another in confusion.

Then another young man spoke softly: "OK, but how many of us really *want* one person we deeply love to love us back?" Virtually every hand in the room shot into the air, and we all breathed a sigh of relief. We had common feelings after all. Still, yet another gay man had the last word: "So how come women are so much better at that?" Nobody had an answer for him.

I do not believe that this gender discrepancy in relational inclinations comes about because of immutable forces of nature, or child-rearing practices and women's less rigid boundaries alone.[28] The socialization of women to relational roles is undoubtedly a complex process, as is the socialization of men to autonomy, more clearly defined boundaries, and a stronger sense of self. I really do not know why this is the case, and I support no existing hypotheses. However, I strongly suspect that for the most part and in most cultures, it *is* the case.

Lesbians therefore often find relational congruence in their sexual relationships. That is, since both (or all, in the case of alternative partnering arrangements) participants are likely to be strongly motivated toward preserving and maintaining relationships, concern for the stability and growth of the relationship is likely to be a very high priority for all involved. This in turn is likely to support the endurance of a relationship over time, but it can also be a problem. The literature about lesbian relationships typically includes discussion of "fusing," the tendency of the partners to disappear into their relationship and to dissolve their individual identities into one an-

Dancing after the Whirlwind

other.[29] However, where care is taken to affirm our own individual sexual and spiritual identities while tending to the well-being of the relationship, extraordinarily enduring, passionate, and spiritually connected love bonds can and do develop and grow. This model of mutual relationality may be one of the spiritual gifts lesbians have to offer to the greater culture.

Consideration of lesbian relationships also raises the question of sameness and difference. What are the spiritual consequences of being of the same gender? Might one find one's own inner light through love for another who is similar enough to effectively reflect one's own beauty? Do I see the goddess in my beloved and recognize her as myself? Well, yes, in a way. But I think it is perhaps a mistake to overemphasize the function of similarity in lesbian love or to assume that lesbian relationships are certain to be partnerships of likes rather than differences. As women we may be able to more deeply understand certain emotional responses from our women lovers, but every person is full of mysteries, and being of the same gender will not automatically solve them.

Lesbian partnering is spiritually significant. Cultures typically offer lesbians no support in partnering, making commitments to one another, or staying together. In view of the punitive cultural responses to lesbian ways of loving and the virtual absence of cultural support, lesbians wouldn't do it if lesbians didn't *want* to do it. Stated positively, this observation becomes a resource of spiritual power: We love, we connect with one another, because we know we want to connect, to be together, to live with one another and celebrate our sexual and spiritual lives with one another. Lesbians do not realize cultural advantages from being lovers or partners, they do not receive financial or social benefits, and they do not usually please their family members. They please themselves ... and one another. Ironically, this reinforces what seems to me to be the only sound, stable, and authentic basis for a relationship: mutual desire, *the primacy of the erotic bond.*

This brings up another relational issue in lesbian experience that has received insufficient attention: forming and maintaining close friendship bonds with former lovers. I know of no other social community in which this phenomenon is so pronounced. There is, of course, a sort of common sense about it. If women seek to preserve relationships, they will have a stronger tendency to develop some form of continuing connection even after a sexual relationship is no longer successful or desirable.[30] But in lesbian relationships this phenomenon, while perhaps not so pronounced as it once was, is still quite remarkable. Ex-lovers are of best friends. Communities of mutual support and friendship, especially in urban areas, often include complex friendship networks among former lovers. When cross-connections become this complex, traditional relational categories begin to fade. This phenomenon—closely knit groups incorporating individuals formerly involved in sexual relationships with one another—may well be unique to lesbian experience.

The usual disclaimers are necessary here. There are, of course, bitter breakups, nasty jealousies, and undying animosities in lesbian life. There is also woman on woman violence. We hurt one another, we even batter one another, and we sometimes experience such deep conflicts with one another that no amount of relational concern can heal the damage. Still, there are so many women calling their former lovers on the telephone, shopping and camping and talking late into the night with women who are no longer sexual partners; they have not in the course of relational transformation lost their connection to one another.[31]

Another possible cultural contribution of the gay and lesbian communities emerges from the need to create new partnership patterns rather than draw on stereotypical cultural expectations. Where no preassigned roles structure the relationship, issues of power, control, and authority must be constantly negotiated and negotiable. Everything from the distribution of household tasks to the expression and satisfaction of sexual desires must be actively sorted out in the context of unfolding relationships. In the process, lesbian and gay partners may challenge social assumptions about hierarchy, dependency, family, and the relationship between the partnership and the surrounding culture.

This departure from role-based partnership may represent a spiritually helpful alternative to traditional ways of relating. Of course, as I have already noted, it is a mistake to assume that anyone in any cultural matrix is role-free. In fact, lesbians assume many established cultural roles, including but not limited to those associated with gender. Given that I constantly negotiate social expectations about what it means to be a parent, a college professor, a neighbor, and a community member, as well as a woman, the degree to which I do or do not conform to feminine stereotypes is hardly my greatest concern. I do find myself redefining all these social roles in the context of lesbian life, but I am not free of the pressures applied by those expectations.

In fact, we may never be completely free of the gender roles and expectations society has carved for us, because socialization begins so early. Obviously, the culture provides a detailed set of moral principles, laws, guides, and traditions that can be adapted to lesbian experience. But sometimes this can feel like navigating the Amazon while referring to a map of Youngstown, Ohio.

Because almost without exception society's role models for women assume heterosexuality, lesbians are in a unique situation. They do not face the dilemma of accepting or rejecting various social roles, models, images, guidelines, instructions, and cultural expectations. Rather, as most come to realize, these options just do not apply. Adrienne Rich describes "a country that has no language, no laws," charting through wildness "unexplored since dawn." Whatever we create in the process of going this hard way together is "pure invention."[32] Although there are gay and lesbian subcultures (with a variety of roles and social rules), they may not be available to women living apart from active urban centers. And for many women, the visible surface of these subcultures may appear even more ill-fitting than heterosexual roles. Hence, one collection of lesbian life stories is appropriately entitled *Inventing Ourselves*.[33]

Since most cultures do not view lesbianism as a viable (or visible) option, there are no alternative models—no sterling templates of lesbian womanhood, no dyke of the month. Although recently, a few public lesbian models have become visible—the good soldier, the two-mommy household, the lesbian sitcom character, the lesbian feminist activist—these models are often tainted by homophobic assumptions. The absence of images to which one can respond, whether with acceptance, rejection, ambivalence, or apathy, is closely associated with feelings of isolation and alienation, of being alone with emotions no one else experiences or understands.

In her own coming out story, Julia Penelope Stanley describes her realization of her gay identity as an overwhelming relief. Her words express recovery from the sense of isolation so commonly described by lesbians: "It's hard to explain now the tremendous freedom that word bestowed in those years. More than anything, I now knew for sure that I was *not* alone, that I wasn't the only 'one' in the world."[34]

The sense of alienation caused by cultural denial—and the relief and joy of recognizing what had formerly been concealed—underscores the importance of the denied characteristic. As I noted in Chapter 3, lesbian *sexual identity* is highlighted in a manner quite unlike that of heterosexual women when they assume or reject very visible sexual roles. Although a heterosexual woman might view her sexuality as important to her identity, she is unlikely to focus upon its specifically heterosexual dimension as a key component of her sense of self. Similarly, unless infected with blatant racism, white people typically do not emphasize their skin color as a key component of their identity. By contrast, sexual identity is the *focus* of society's hatred and oppression of lesbians. For many, it has taken on a unique intensity and centrality in the development of personal identity.

Dancing after the Whirlwind

The lack of social models, together with the associated experience of uniqueness, has important spiritual consequences. In order to clarify this point, I will misappropriate a term from Soren Kierkegaard because it aptly expresses this aspect of lesbian experience. A principal characteristic of lesbian spiritual development is "entangled freedom."[35] Identity struggles often lead lesbians to the development of two affective states, usually in this order: the first is fear, the ancient feeling of being lost in the woods, not knowing how to act, arriving in strange territory with no passport or knowledge of the local customs; the second, one I believe to be a direct result of struggling toward authentic being outside the framework of cultural support, is freedom. This is not so much a freedom *from* as a freedom *for*—the freedom of a pathfinder, a pioneer, an eccentric, a risk-taker. It is the freedom of the invisible woman to move through the social sphere without fitting into established categories and thus to create new structures for relationship, a new language, new rules. This freedom, however, is "entangled"—in social structures and moral codes that assume heterosexuality and reward it, in covert and overt oppression and denial of lesbian identity, and, of course, in the fear and silence that often accompany it.

Within the parameters established by this entanglement, alternative life-affirming models can and do emerge. As I have noted, the process of developing a successful relationship without reliance upon typical cultural expectations requires communication and negotiation. This "processing," although it may be carried to such extremes that it has become a subcultural joke, also has the potential to foster nurturing mutually empowering relationships without dominance, tyranny, or brutality.

Gay and lesbian conflict resolution strategies also foster spiritual renewal and growth. Although lesbian and gay friendships and partnerships are not immune from violence, significant effort to negotiate nonviolent resolutions to power struggles is a common thread in gay and lesbian relationality. In addition, gay activism has historically been pursued through nonviolent means. While critics rave against the "outrageous vulgarity" of bare-breasted women, men in dresses, and leather drag at gay and lesbian parades and demonstrations, they fail to note that these demonstrations are typically friendly, nonviolent, and (in marked contrast to many political demonstrations) full of people having fun and doing no harm to anyone. A nonviolent style is certainly not unique to gay activism and undoubtedly has its roots in earlier liberation movements. But the pursuit of change through nonviolent means is a choice, and the example set by lesbian and gay activism provides a valuable social model—especially when set in contrast to increasing antigay violence.

This observation calls attention to a final, and perhaps most significant, locus of spiritual identity, recovery, and transformation for gay and lesbian people—the community, the common bond among us, which Nancy Wilson, following the lead of Judy Grahn, associates with tribal consciousness and tribal memory: "Sometimes, in my deepest self, I feel like we are some ancient tribal remnant that has survived and that now appears to be dispersed among every other earthly tribe—a transtribal tribe."[36] Lesbians and gay men take this tribal awareness in two directions: "*healing our tribal wounds* and *boldly exercising our tribal gifts.*"[37]

Wilson writes from her experience within the context of Metropolitan Community Church in Los Angeles, but this tribal identity extends far beyond any particular church, social group, political movement, or community organization. Her suggestion illustrates the dual aspects of the spiritual renewal process in lesbian spirituality—identity affirmation and transformation. On the one hand, we confront the task of healing the wounds caused by denial and oppression. Coming out to ourselves and others, celebrating woman-loving lives, means acknowledging what we have lost along the way and who we have become in the process. On the other hand, we affirm the erotic power of our own sexual / spiritual relationality through the particularities of our lives. As Judith McDaniel expresses it in her own account of the coming out process, "I feel more comfortable with my own body and sexuality now than ever before in my life . . . finding a natural and spontaneous expression of my deepest, most intimate feelings."[38]

Sharing our spiritual gifts of creativity and relational power with our wider communities transforms pain and loss into renewed energy and mature and loving interactions. The activity of healing requires authenticity and fidelity. The activity of affirming and exercising our gifts requires transformation.

The rhythm of the tribe is the percussion of my heart. Same song, same dance. The rhythm that tongues know, the beat that vibrates along skin touch, that settles and sings in curves of elbow and knee, in arches and wrinkles and folds and fur. Do planets really turn to the same syncopation that stirs us to dance or to kiss or to swim ecstatically through layers of loving to the center of ourselves? I think so. The sexual union of women is not barren. Songs are born.

Spirituality and Recovery in the Belly of the Beast

The processes of affirmation and transformation are also relevant to spiritual healing and renewal for women whose personal histories involve sexual abuse. Overcoming denial requires that we see what there is to see. Recovering—or developing—a sense of integrated sexual / spiritual identity after such trauma requires restoring erotic power to the sexuality / spirituality relationship.

In *Dancing with Daddy,* her account of her own struggle toward recovery from child sexual abuse, Betsy Petersen considers the importance of recollecting the past.

> Is it necessary to remember? My therapist asked me, and I said: Maybe not, not to heal. But it's a spiritual challenge. I've spent my life denying evil. . . . I wanted to be an island. I didn't want to hear the bell tolling for me.

Now I want to choose. I want to go willingly into that place, terrified but not powerless. . . .

To confront evil is to see it whole: sight, smell, sound, taste, touch. Not only the facts and feelings but the sensations. And what it means.[39]

Another survivor connects her healing process directly with the process of overcoming denial: "We have to speak out and break the silence, especially in our own families. I know *I have been able to heal because I'm not being silent*" (emphasis mine).[40]

Ultimately, however, the damage is so deep, the betrayal so profound, that the healing process must involve not only the individual struggles of survivors but a commitment of support and affirmation from everyone who seeks to resist and break the cycles of sexual abuse and betrayal. Whether or not we have personally experienced such abuse, every caring person is called not only to recognize the damage but to participate in the transformative process.

In order to heal and recover, survivors and supporters must avoid denial and despair. As a culture, we must no longer pretend that sexual violence to children is not happening or that it will go away. But we must also resist the sometimes even more attractive option of giving up. "'Leave every hope behind, ye who enter,'" says Shaw's Don Gonzalo, contemplating the gates of hell, "Only think what a relief that is!"[41] Resisting the forces of oppression, domination, and reversal that contribute to and deny the reality of abuse often seems so overwhelming that we are tempted to lapse into withdrawal, depression, or apathy. We become like children, covering our eyes in order to make whatever disturbs us disappear.

Survivors, helping professionals, and all who desire to resist patterns of sexual abuse and violence need to understand how reversals function in order to combat them. We need to recognize our own internal fears, projections, and denial before we can overcome them. And we need to discover our own visions of healing in order to implement them.

Dancing after the Whirlwind

An important aspect of this healing is spiritual. All sexual experiences have spiritual implications, but, as Joan Timmerman observes, the first carries particular weight:

> In my view the meaning of first intercourse as spiritual peak, moment
> of integration, final ending of inactive sexual existence, clear begin-
> ning of adult relational genital experience carries in itself, whether or
> not it is acknowledged, connotations of sacredness. Because it is a ritual
> moment, it participates in more than literal time. It is sacred passage,
> initiation into sacred sexuality of adult spiritual life, ... [F]irst inter-
> course, in the appropriate aesthetic and psychological context, can be
> the liturgy that heals and restores the person to spiritual centeredness,
> and so performs the deepest meaning of spiritual virginity: being a per-
> son who possesses herself, who is neither owned or taken away from
> her own vocation by someone else.[42]

Even if we do not fully realize it at the time, our initial sexual encounters can bring us into sacred space. The consequences of violence and betrayal at this critical life-turning are obvious and profound. My work in this regard is strongly influenced by that of Kathy
Steele, and I incorporate some of her ideas here because of their value
in revealing the deep-seated existential issues involved and because
her work has not received the scholarly attention it deserves.[43]

Steele has shown that the survivor's spiritual journey is one
from "existential crisis" to "existential comfort." Confronting memories of child sexual abuse precipitates a crisis at the most fundamental level of her identity. Developing a positive sense of self must
therefore involve coming to terms with this experience. In the process, survivors encounter certain issues that are particularly relevant to this discussion.

Meaning. Humans tend to attempt control over events by finding
some meaning or explanation for them. Survivors often seek this
meaning through what Steele calls "traumatic reenactment," the

tendency to seek mastery over the abuse by repeatedly creating situations that reenact the trauma or perceiving life events as reenactments. The unconscious hope is that by reenacting the trauma one can eventually understand it—why it happened, what it means, and (ironically) how to prevent it. Survivors of child sexual abuse are at increased risk for revictimization, in part because they may unconsciously place themselves in dangerous situations or pursue relationships with abusive partners as adults. On the other hand, survivors may experience nonabusive adult relationships as repeating or threatening to repeat the abuse patterns of their childhood. Even gestures intended to be affectionate may be perceived as an assault. Alicia Mendoza (a pseudonym) describes the effect of recovered memories of abuse on her relationship with her partner: "There were times in the process that I would forget he was Joe and react to him as 'generic Man.' He had never hurt me in any of those ways, but I would confuse his identity completely. We'd be lying in bed at night. I'd be trying to go to sleep, and I'd have to get up because I felt 'I can't lie here with this male body. It's too terrifying.'"[44] Unfortunately, because present events and relationships are always distorted by responses and interpretations carried over from traumas of the past, the attempt to gain mastery or understanding through reenactment is rarely successful.

Death. The dissociation, or splitting of mind and body, some survivors use to tolerate memories of childhood sexual abuse is often viewed as a good, or at least helpful, mechanism that keeps them from becoming overwhelmed and nonfunctional. Steele points out, however, that the circumstances of dissociation are often experienced by survivors as terrifying—as a form of "mini-death." Survivors of severe abuse sometimes undergo an intense flashback or reliving of the abuse, often precipitated by some unexpected "trigger" event in the present. During such an experience, survivors may pass out or go into trance, entering into a state of "semi-death." Survivors often indicate that they do not expect to live long or predict their death before a particular age. These encounters with themes of death and dying underscore the existential struggle to attain a meaningful and fulfilling life.

Identity. Many survivors tend to identify themselves primarily with their trauma or dwell on it to the exclusion of their present experience. Other aspects of the self that might otherwise function well in the present are thereby ignored, disowned, or disenfranchised. As Steele observes, the survivor must face the question "Who am I after I know?"

Intolerable Pain. Survivors must establish for themselves some way to integrate meaning into both their memory and their present experience of profound pain and suffering.[45]

_____ *Shattered Souls in Spiritual Crisis*

These crises of meaning and identity require spiritual resolutions. However, in order to renew ourselves, whether this renewal is viewed psychologically or spiritually or both, we must be able to perceive ourselves in relation to others. But what if we have no self? What if we feel unreal, nonexistent? What if we have multiple selves, and the connections among them are missing? These are feelings often expressed by women who have survived severe sexual abuse.[46]

How will denial affect the spiritual life of the survivor? First, we must ask, "Where is her spirit?" For example:

> They tell you to discipline a child, but not so much that you break her spirit. Abuse shatters the spirit, so there's nothing left. I often think of myself as a house that has been hit by a tornado. The structure is demolished, all the pieces are scattered around. So you try to rebuild, but some of the pieces are destroyed—too broken to use again. And some of them are missing. So you can't ever get it back the way it was.[47]

This survivor reports being altered in a fundamental way. Writing about survivors of exceptionally severe abuse, Kathy Steele states that "These kinds of trauma often fragment the psychological collage we call the 'self.' I believe it also shatters, or at least deeply wounds, the soul—that essential being of a person that is more than the psychological self."[48] This "essential being" to which Steele refers is not a fixed core but a dynamic sense of who we are at the deepest level—it is what I mean by spiritual identity.

Dissociative Identity Disorder is one possible aftereffect of severe abuse. The dissociation is so intense that identity literally splits into parts. These selves function more or less autonomously, and one or more of them may be unaware of the existence of the others. Not only do their personalities vary; their moral values, physical characteristics, including body temperature and blood pressure, and memories may as well. What can soul or spirit or spiritual life mean for these women? What can we mean by relationship, by love, by wholeness for such women?[49] By identity and transformation?

Where all integrated sense of self is lost, there is a death—a murder. Child sexual abuse threatens the image of the loving and rescuing parent children desperately need. Overwhelmed by helplessness and rage, the child must suppress these feelings in order to survive. In the process, the child's identity submits to that of the abuser, a process the psychologist Leonard Shengold calls "soul murder." The identity and power of the victim are totally subsumed.[50]

"Soul murder" involves more than the loss of one's personal sense of self. It is also the loss of one's ability to relate—to love and trust others. What, for example, about God? Many people take refuge in a personal relationship with God as an all-powerful, all-knowing, loving, and protecting parent. Monotheistic traditions also conventionally teach that this most-powerful deity is entirely blameless for the evils of the world, which arise as a consequence not of divine malevolence but of human sin. But how are we to interpret these teachings if our all-powerful human caretakers are sexually abusing us? What if they tell us, even as they are abusing us, that the blame lies not with them but with us—in something we have done, some way we look, some way we are? Are we not likely to conclude that the blame rests not with the powerful perpetrator but with some fault of our own? Identity reversal is again at play as the (godlike) abuser assumes the guise of innocence and projects guilt upon the (sinful) abused. *Is this where we get our social habit of blaming the victim?*[51]

Religious messages about human sin and divine blamelessness can reinforce a survivor's awareness that she must accept the blame in order to survive, that she cannot perceive those responsible for her as unable or unwilling to care for her and keep her safe. Children are often programmed by abusive families to accept the blame. Even those with no memory of abuse may feel as if they have done something wrong. Other kinds of role reversals are frequent, as abused children often take on the tasks of caretakers, mothers, and housekeepers for the family.[52]

While perpetrators may acquire a feeling of power from the abuse, survivors suffer a continued sense of powerlessness.[53] The needs of abused children for security, guidance, and appropriate limits are not being met, and they are also unable to predict or control the actions of parents or to secure their own safety. In adulthood, this childhood powerlessness translates as "learned helplessness."[54]

Survivors may also suffer from a profound sense of guilt: they may assume the blame for the abuse or they may feel guilt because some aspect of it was accompanied by feelings of pleasure and they therefore, in some way, must have "asked for it." If perpetrators frequently project blame onto the victim, church, family, and society may contribute to this process. For these reasons, a woman's choice to decline the blame is a critical component of recovery. But even those who have come to terms with and rejected guilt may still face a sense of shame.

Sam Kirschner and his colleagues connect the pervasive sense of shame among survivors with two different forms of betrayal. Knowing that she has been betrayed by a trusted family member, the survivor blames herself for the change in the perpetrator and for somehow "polluting" those around her.[55] She may also feel shame because of a sense that she has betrayed her real self. In denying the abuse and remaining loyal to the family, she has sold herself out: "She knows that she is no longer being authentic—and she cannot run far from that knowledge."[56] These authors connect the experience of the shame-bound survivor with the psychological theorist Abraham Maslow's "Jonah complex." Just as Jonah flees from God's call and hides, "the survivor, having learned to mistrust herself, flees and hides from her authentic self in the shame-filled belly of the whale." In this way, she avoids pursuing her true path in life.[57]

To claim that childhood sexual abuse has spiritual consequences is to say that it affects us at the very deepest center of our reality. When we are told to forget, to put the past behind us, we experience society's refusal to acknowledge that a shattered soul cannot be healed by ignoring the damage.[58]

Where death has occurred, survival requires rebirth.[59] The key to renewal through the cycle of death and rebirth is transformation. Survivors must, of course, define this process for themselves, and each woman's experiences and spiritual life are unique. However, certain themes of transformation emerge: from a feeling of being split, shattered, or dismembered to a sense of integrity; from the bind of guilt and shame to reclaimed power and authenticity; from soul-death to new life.

Let me be clear about this. Being reborn is not a walk in the park. Hell may be transformative, but it is also . . . hell. But as we struggle to overcome personal and social denial of these violations, wilderness pathways open.

The Forgiveness Debate

Some of these pathways are found in traditional religions. Marie Fortune, founder and director of the Center for Prevention of Sexual and Domestic Violence, has written extensively, from a Christian perspective, about spiritual recovery from sexual violence. As she points out, survivors often assume that the abuse is God's punishment for their sinful nature. (And, as I have noted, this assumption may well be reinforced by the perpetrator.) These assumptions also shift the blame from where it rightfully belongs—on the offender.[60]

Rejecting the notion that the abuse happened for "no good reason," survivors often seek a reason for their suffering.[61] Fortune suggests that the theology of the cross and the resurrection may be helpful; like Christ, survivors face suffering but also the possibility of new life.[62] Rather than justify the suffering, the realization that God is present even in the midst of profound suffering redeems it. Through this image, survivors may eventually be able to view their experiences as "an occasion for new life, i.e., the occasion to become a survivor."[63]

Another path toward healing that some Christians recommend is forgiveness. Since survivors often feel abandoned by God, many experience overwhelming anger toward God as well as the perpetrator. Fortune contends that forgiveness can help survivors to let go of destructive anger and pain.[64] However, she is quick to stress that forgiving does not mean condoning or excusing the actions of the offender. Furthermore, Scripture is clear that forgiveness must be dependent upon the offender's repentance.[65] Even when genuine repentance is present, forgiveness cannot be rushed or forced; it must come from within, when the victim is ready to let go.[66]

The issue of forgiveness has stirred a lively debate among those concerned with the spiritual aspects of recovery from sexual violence. Sheila Redmond claims that many Christian values and virtues, including the emphasis on forgiveness and repentance, actually hinder the process of recovery in children and in adults. "Forgiveness for the perpetrator is not a requirement for resolution of the abuse, and lack of forgiveness does not entail the need for revenge."[67]

Kyos Featherdancing, another survivor, confirms this position with her own personal statement: "A lot of people believe forgiveness is the ultimate healing. And to me, that's bullshit. The man doesn't deserve my forgiveness. *I* deserve my forgiveness. . . . If you're looking to forgiveness as this goal, then you're still believing the lie that keeps you under control."[68]

Confronting the issues of blame and forgiveness, the Jewish theologian David Blumenthal traces a "theology of protest" through Jewish tradition. Here, the relevant metaphor is not Jonah but Job, who acknowledges God's existence and power but "questions God's justification, God's morality, God's justice."[69] Exploring this position in relation to survivors of childhood sexual abuse and to Holocaust survivors, Blumenthal acknowledges the survivor's right to refuse both self-blame and forgiveness, and to adopt distrust and suspicion as appropriate religious responses. Blumenthal calls for a "post-holocaust, abuse-sensitive faith"[70] in which survivors overcome the conspiracy of silence and "tell the truth—to ourselves, and to God."[71] His "religious psychotherapeutic healing"[72] progresses through stating the truth, rejecting the blame, and expressing justified rage and grief to the self-empowerment that comes with accepting the painful memories of the past and developing a new understanding of God. Authenticity and transformation. "This form of religious healing is not a reinsertion into the hierarchy of divine authority. . . . Rather, it is a confrontation with a real but terrifying past, set in the context of acquiring the spiritual and religious skills necessary to deal with God as well as with that past."[73]

The religious messages many of us grow up with—forgiveness is divine, honoring one's parents is God's law, self-sacrifice is the perfect manifestation of the divine will—can reinforce early experiences of powerlessness and forced submission. If we have also internalized guilt and sinfulness through these messages, perceiving ourselves as blameless for the abuse may be a desperate struggle. Recovery may require not only refusing to accept the blame for the abuse but clearly attributing it to those who are responsible. For example, many survivors find that directly confronting perpetrators is a healing experience. However, I cannot accept the contention that forgiving the offender is essential to healing, even though it may be a healing choice for some survivors.

Spiritual Resources

For many survivors, the images, metaphors, and values of traditional religions are insurmountably problematic. But alternative spiritual resources are available, and some survivors have found support and healing by connecting with these emerging movements.

I have already discussed the value of goddess imagery in restoring the deep bond between spirituality and sexuality and in providing a positive female image of the divine to women struggling with issues of identity and esteem. The mirror of the goddess has the power to reflect a woman's sacred embodied beauty back to her, and this reflection can be deeply healing for survivors of childhood sexual abuse. Noting that sexual traumas are profoundly registered upon the body, Patricia Reis utilizes goddess imagery to heal the Abused Body.[74] The body's memory remains, even when cells die and are replaced. "This is the truth of the body, which does not lie. Thus, the female body is inscribed with its own truth and has many stories to tell—both ancient and new."[75]

Reis recommends reclaiming Aphrodite as a "sexually affirming Goddess for women."[76] Recovering Aphrodite involves reestablishing inner balance and embodied strength. By claiming the image of this sexually affirming Goddess as activating "the creative imaginations of women,"[77] women can recover their lost erotic potential, once devastated by abuse. "Female erotic energy is aphroditic, and it is a resource that lives deeply within all life. . . . It is the name for the empowered creative energy that can inform and infuse all aspects of our life."[78] According to Reis, the image of Aphrodite is helpful to survivors in several ways: it renews a sense of intactness and integrity; heals sexual dysfunction; assists in learning to love and cherish other women in order to find and claim our female selves; and restores a sense of the sacred value of the body and of erotic love.

Although the connection has not previously been much explored, insights from ecofeminist theory may also be helpful to survivors of abuse in restoring the body / mind / soul connection. The damage brought about through severing the connection between spirit and nature, mind and body, has already been much discussed here. Ecofeminists emphasize that healing the earth depends upon restoring sacred value to nature.[79] Likewise, healing the abused body / soul depends upon reclaiming the sacred value of the body.

Survivors are already making these connections. The life-affirming activities in which survivors engage as part of the healing process often reveal a new awareness of life's value as reflected in other living things. One woman relates her healing to a new experience with caring for plants:

> It's a small thing, but I never had plants before. It's just my way of trying to keep something other than me alive. It gives me a lot of pleasure. . . . I got my first plant about six months ago. Now I have all sorts of flowers on my porch. . . . It's real Latina, all these colors. . . . I was scared about it at first. But now I know I can nurture them and keep them healthy. . . . After I've been so rough in my life, I can still take care of something so delicate. Even though I've been knocked around, I can still keep them alive.[80]

Ynestra King makes this association between earth and body explicit. Noting that ecofeminist theory takes as a starting point an analysis of "interrelated dominations of nature—psyche and sexuality, human oppression, and nonhuman nature,"[81] King recommends an ecological approach to the relationship between nature and culture "in which mind and nature, heart and reason, join forces to transform the systems of domination, internal and external, that threaten the existence of life on Earth."[82]

One critical area in which King suggests women employ this ecofeminist approach is that of "body consciousness." Cultural and political liberation depend upon accepting and knowing our bodies as well as learning how to work with them in order to become healthier. To view our flesh as the enemy is to participate in the domination of nature.[83]

Survivors often internalize systems of domination and perpetuate these oppressions against the body. Eating disorders, substance abuse, revictimization, and other self-destructive behaviors reenact the assault of patriarchal culture on nature and sexuality; at the same time, the deeply ingrained—and violently reinforced—split between the sacred and the natural is echoed in the survivor's guilt over feelings of sexual pleasure. Alienation between sexuality and spirituality is reenacted on the bodies of women, just as the culture / nature split activates assaults upon the earth. Sexual violence is sacrilege, and ecofeminism's emphasis on reuniting the natural world with the sacred provides a vision *to restore the survivor's experience of her body, her sexuality, and her life as sacred.*

Giselle (a pseudonym) suggests a direction for balancing love and anger, compassion and outrage, in the journey toward healing and embracing life:

> Hate cannot be stopped with hate. Abuse cannot be stopped with abuse. That does not mean you don't stop the people who are doing this, or that you stop prosecuting them. But you do it from a place of love. If I didn't feel love for the child in me who had been raped, I would not have this outrage.
>
> Sometimes I sit here and feel such compassion for my father, I weep. Other times I see myself taking a gun and shooting his balls off. I am letting it all come right on through. And the more I allow all of it to come up, the more I find myself moving toward love. The more I block the rage, the more I stay stuck. And so for me they're both right there. I reconcile it by saying I trust the process. I trust the validity of my outrage. The outrage is because I honor and value and love life.[84]

Her account refers to spiritual resources that connect healing directly with earth's sacred power:

> I feel there's a great deal of magic involved in this healing process. And what I mean by magic is that the old ways of healing, that have been

lost, are waking up. I'm awakening in my cells a lot of that old knowledge. It comes from the earth, from the spirit of the earth.... This knowledge connects with the capacity to heal the rift that has the world in crisis, that has us in danger of extinction. It's the healing power of mother earth. It's been taken away and lost. And She's coming back through us now.[85]

These approaches emphasize the concepts of renewal and rebirth that arise from brokenness and suffering. Images of rebirth invoke the power that is released when women confront their painful histories and seek a new understanding of their own lives. For many, this past experience includes the loss, the shattering, of former foundations, both social and psychic. Something new is needed to heal this dismemberment, to render a woman "strong at the broken places."[86]

One of the most powerful accounts of this transformation is that of Kyos Featherdancing:

I sometimes wonder when the work is going to be finished. I don't think it ever really is. It doesn't overwhelm me as much as it used to. I used to cry and cry about it. It felt like everything inside of me was collapsing. I don't feel that way now.... I've let it go and given it to the wind, and let the wind heal it.

I'm excited about my life now. I'm excited about the healing I'm going to do next, because it's going to be the ultimate freedom that I've been wanting—the healing of my spiritual life. I know now that I can truly be a healer and that what I've lived through doesn't have to hold me back. When it does, I can control it. I can tell it to leave me alone. I can spend time with it. Whatever I choose. It doesn't have to hinder my walk with the spirit.[87]

Among the various tools that may be helpful in the process of spiritual recovery, rituals, group healing exercises, and creative imagery are particularly useful because of the combination of new vision and community energy they involve. To fully enter into this transformative process in community with survivors is both a challenge and an opportunity for those who relish the joys of resistance. Survivors are rarely drawn to images of pretty buds opening or sweet little butterflies emerging from cocoons. Theirs is the country of Inanna, scourged and slaughtered by her shadow-sister and hung on a hook to rot. Theirs is Tiamat, silenced, skewered, and split asunder. These are the creation stories, the stories of death, dismemberment, and rebirth, that survivors recognize. This is chaos, coming apart, going to pieces, dying to the old self.

How do we get to renewal? To rebirth? So many healing survivors tell the story: the only way to it is through it. Authentic being can only be achieved by acknowledging the terrors of the past as our own. We experience transformation when we discover our own power on the other side of suffering—the phoenix arising from the ashes. Survivors may know this feeling of recovering flight, but they can also give you details of the fire.

Returning now to hell, I am not complacent or naive. The survivor's journey is perilous, painful, and exhausting. It is accompanied by the profound and persistent feeling of struggling uphill against overwhelming odds. I am not sure there can be complete healing in such a broken world. I am not sure it is even a fruitful goal. In the words of another survivor, "Healing is not a finite thing. You don't graduate."[88]

What are the rhythms and patterns of the dance for survivors? How do authenticity and transformation spiral through these lives? Women who have survived abuse must do more than acknowledge the past. We must affirm it. I am not suggesting that we view our victimization or abuse as a positive experience to "make us better people" or as "learning experiences" or even as that which did not kill us and therefore made us stronger. Such views may serve either recovery or denial, but spiritual renewal does not require them. What is required, I think, is to be able to claim events of one's past, even horrific events, as one's own: That was me. That happened to me. That is part of who I am. We cannot go on to new creations without being able to claim the paths that brought us here, even if they were dangerous roads.

As for transformation, that is what happens in hell. If we emerge, and many of us do, we are not the same on the return journey. When Inanna descends into the underworld, she is stripped naked, destroyed, and hung on a hook. Survivors know the feeling. But what is the dance for Inanna as she returns to the light? Women recovering from sexual abuse seek a new understanding of themselves as sexual beings, free of fear. Celebrating the beauty and power of erotic union is a wondrous ritual indeed if once it was crushed, bruised, and brutalized. Certainly, there is always an element of acknowledgment here, a nod to the past, almost a memorial, for what has been lost. But my own experience assures me that deep, sweet sexual / spiritual celebration may well be part of this transformation process.

Affirming erotic power, as I have noted, means that we learn to live with and accept the ambiguities that accompany complex relationships. Survivors of sexual abuse require nothing less. Even as we swing into the wild rhythms of celebration and renewal, there are times when the music slows, the memories of tragedy or betrayal are affirmed, and our own heartbeats assure us that we are as we are. Nothing less. Ambiguity flutters at the corners of our sexual encounters, our mirror-reflections, our self-images, our day-to-day encounters with celebration and pain.

This much is required if we are to extend our transformations outward to transform that which generated assaults upon us. Audre Lorde summed it up in her journals, as she struggled through the agonies of breast cancer: "I do believe not until every woman traces her weave back strand by bloody self-referenced strand, will we begin to alter the whole pattern."[89]

Sex is never safe. I risk everything here, dancing the shedding dance. Still, even as my skin peels back, just as I brace for the pain of air and light against raw flesh, I can feel the softest brush of lips against this brand-new surface of myself, and I let you in. A sound goes with it—something like the subtle vibration of a brush on cymbals or the sound of footsteps slow-dancing in the next room.

Living with AIDS: Positive Transformation

Awareness of the tragic in eros is at its most pointed in the lives of women with HIV/AIDS. As Linda Singer asserts, the sexual epidemic that reaches its apotheosis in AIDS is "more than a health or medical problematic; it represents a kind of rupture in the sexual / political order of things" involving reconsideration not only of the "politics of the personal" but even of the "politics of pleasure."[90] New forms and techniques of "sexual discipline and management" are brought to bear in order to generate an organized response to epidemic conditions.[91]

Regulating bodies is nothing new. However, the crisis mentality toward sex generated by the AIDS epidemic reinforces a new perspective on pleasure: "Just when post-Freudian discourse seemed to proffer the prospect of pleasure without guilt, epidemic conditions forced the confrontation between pleasure and finitude."[92] Ecstasy is no longer linked with eternity but becomes the gateway to death. AIDS adds a new twist to Christianity's tendency to associate pleasures of the flesh with punishment and condemnation.

> [T]he choice is no longer one of allying oneself with the fate of the body rather than of the soul, but is rather a matter of differing probabilistic corporeal destinies measured against the possibilities not of salvation in the next life, but of deterioration and death in this one. . . . The threat or risk is no longer primarily the threat of disembodied divine judgment, but rather comes to take root in the body of the other.[93]

In the age of AIDS, two forces that have enormous power over the human psyche come into play: fear of death and the need for meaning. By almost unbearably highlighting the already deeply rooted relationship between death and sexuality, "AIDS confronts every facet of human understanding and fear."[94] AIDS tips the scales. This death-fear is intensified by the fact that HIV/AIDS strikes at the heart of life, in the midst of youth and the deepest stirrings of erotic energy. Most of those afflicted with HIV are under forty-five, and more and more are children. John Backe notes our inability to "avoid dealing with the reality of death as it so aggressively positions itself in the path of life."[95]

Eros, which should maintain the equilibrium between life and death, becomes death's ally, and fear of eros deepens in the process. Meanwhile, we still want to know why terrible things happen so we can keep believing that they will not happen to us. This is a setup for projection.

Religion's Response

In the search for meaning and comfort, we may seek help from traditional religion. But too often, mainstream religions do not provide protection for those living with HIV/AIDS against projections of blame, guilt, and fear. Rather, they participate in the process. There is evidence of substantial correlation between participation in mainstream Christian religions and both negative attitudes toward AIDS victims and resistance to community education about sex and HIV/AIDS.[96] As Andrew Greeley points out, these attitudes are exacerbated by religious orientations emphasizing rigid biblical literalism and significantly eased by a more "gracious" concept of God.[97]

In part, this failure is also motivated by the quest for meaning. Religious people who desire to provide care and comfort must face "the hard reality of the plight of the person who is ill and the question of its ultimate meaning. It is impossible to give care and not wonder why people suffer."[98] AIDS extends "a particular temptation to play God and to answer the question in terms of the fault of the

Dancing after the Whirlwind

victim."[99] In the need to avoid the conclusion that life is absurd, the church colludes in projecting blame on the suffering and in distinguishing between "innocent" and "guilty" victims.[100]

Churches and spiritual communities can be vital sources of spiritual and physical help and support for those who are HIV-positive. Some religious institutions have responded by making educational materials about sex and drugs available to their parishioners, encouraging care and compassion for the infected, providing sensitive pastoral care, meals, housing, and program space to people with AIDS, even calling on the government for more research and program funding.[101] Many women living with HIV/AIDS find comfort, solace, and strength through their participation in mainstream religious traditions. Spiritual connectedness is one of the most significant factors in a woman's struggle to transcend denial.

But too many churches remain ineffectual. In part, the problem can be attributed to the failure of clergy members to engage in "genuine pastoral involvement" even with bereaved families. Too often, these attitudes turn churches into forces of judgment and "moralistic condemnation" rather than spiritual resources.[102] Many church leaders "see pastoral care in the AIDS crisis as either one last opportunity for condemnation of the sinful or as one brief occasion for simple kindness toward the soon dead."[103]

While some people with HIV/AIDS have received comfort and care from mainstream religious institutions, others have received condemnation and betrayal. Consideration of the religious dimension of AIDS has been insufficient, and the tendency in cases of sexual abuse to blame the victim is also evident in the theological response to AIDS.

The bizarre equation of AIDS with the wrath of God is alive and thriving in the minds of those most invested in the alienation of sexuality and spirituality. Huddled for shelter behind the chimerical bastion of manufactured meaning, "good" people invoke the will of God to ensure that only "bad" people get AIDS. Since suffering with AIDS is viewed as punishment, and therefore evidence not of chaotic or random dangers but of ordered and systematic judgment, one need only rein in eros in order to avoid suffering the affliction oneself or bearing responsibility for easing the suffering of others.

Positive Women

J B Coles, an HIV-positive Sioux Indian from South Dakota, provides a powerful spiritual response to the voices of condemnation as she responds to death and destruction by remembering why she is alive:

> I Grab for the Gusto
> My Mother gave me life, but God
> gave me Wings, not AIDS.
> To Stand Strong and trust in God,
> Follow the promptings Within, not Without.[104]

Although research on women who are living with HIV/AIDS lags woefully, a few resources reveal the experiences of the women themselves. As HIV-positive women find their voices, and speak and write about their own experiences, they share not only their pain and rage but also their hope, solace, and determination. Here are the voices of body and soul, acknowledging sexual and spiritual pain, affirming sexual and spiritual healing. Lacking educational resources to analyze or express their experience, HIV-positive women have created their own. Andrea Rudd and Darien Taylor, two HIV-positive women, gathered writings, interviews, poetry, photographs, and works of art from HIV-positive women and women with AIDS all over the world. This collection, *Positive Women*, speaks volumes about what hinders and helps spiritual recovery and renewal.[105]

One of the most powerful accounts for me is that of Jae, a bisexual native New Yorker and self-described sexual addict. Her commentary brings together issues of sexuality and spirituality, the pain of silence, and the struggle toward transformation. Jae describes herself as closeted about her HIV status, her addictions, and her bisexuality. Sexual addiction is, for her, "a compulsion that consumes the major part of one's life, devouring time with the surrounding rituals. It is an escape from pain. I also believe it is a search for the spiritual."[106] Finding no home in the usual women's roles, she tried "to live a new sexual freedom and found myself trapped in it."[107] Her insistence on sexual freedom not only served to distract her from developing other aspects of herself but also brought to her "the worst new plague of our times."[108] Discovering her positive status early and remaining asymptomatic, she now finds herself "moving in and out of denial, in and out of anger, in and out of the frustration of what it means to be a woman with AIDS in today's world."[109] She describes herself as always on the opposite side, "overshadowed, outnumbered, a worker without a voice that is heard."[110] As she struggles to "balance awareness and knowledge" without getting lost in denial, she is giving up her addictions, pursuing a graduate degree, and cleaning out the poisons her body has accumulated. "I am moving on with my life while I can."[111] The conclusion of her personal statement moves me beyond words: "My sexual search has been a spiritual longing and this foreign HIV virus is steering me on my path to discover a new self, a new way of partnership. Perhaps a new archetype of women's sexuality will form in my process of discovery and recovery."[112]

In her *Cancer Journals*, Audre Lorde comments that "imposed silence about any area of our lives is a tool for separation and powerlessness."[113] Women living with HIV/AIDS, already isolated by fear and often by betrayal, are made yet more powerless by silence. As fear of discrimination and acts of overt hatred render them silent about their HIV-positive condition, society's failure to acknowledge HIV as a real and growing problem for women negates the reality of their lives. And the almost total cultural silence toward their sexual feelings and needs makes maintenance of a well-developed sexual identity almost impossible. The personal narratives of HIV-positive women and women with AIDS, and the accounts of helping professionals, reinforce the same point: silence hurts.

Women living with HIV/AIDS in secrecy describe the feelings of intense loneliness and alienation from others brought about by keeping a secret: fear of the unknown; fear about whether or when they will become sicker or develop "full-blown" AIDS; fear of losing their jobs, lovers, friends, and family members; fear of losing their homes, security, insurance. These fears are well founded, and they know it. When their HIV-positive status is known, women write of being ostracized; of being refused treatment; of being humiliated, neglected, surrounded by brightly colored Caution signs and suspicious glares, made to feel evil, sinful, and dirty.

The Need to Break Silence

Still, the pain of the silence itself is also terrible. Isabel, from Zimbabwe, writes, "The most horrible aspect of all this for me is not talking to anyone about it.... I think the worst thing about the virus is the feeling of isolation and the fear that accompanies any step toward breaking the isolation."[114]

Writing anonymously, a woman from Switzerland reveals in journal entries the damage of concealed fear:

> Self pity, fear is slowly gnawing at me. AIDS—is it true that a time bomb ticks within me? How long until this new, frightful epidemic breaks out within me? How long until my body has no more resistance and slowly but surely disintegrates? . . .
>
> Oh God, I have lied to everyone in Zurich. I am so afraid of being treated like a pariah, and HIV positive people are being treated that way. What will become of me? I am 25 years old, a grown-up woman, you would think. But look at me, what am I? A nothing, a nobody. It is so terrible.[115]

In spite of the risks, however, breaking silence is often break-through, soul healing, community making, liberation. Lori Ayers, a member of ACT-UP in New York, notes in her own autobiographical account: "At first I told no one I had the dreaded AIDS virus and that made it much harder. Fear grows and breeds when it is not faced. . . . As I told more people I realized how important it was to have honesty in my life about all things."[116]

Women who reveal their HIV/AIDS status write and speak of re-lief, of support, of coming to terms, of finding meaning and reconciliation:

> I didn't tell anyone, except the people I had slept with. Absolutely no-body knew for years. . . . It was very alienating keeping it a secret. But when I thought about what would happen if they knew, keeping it a se-cret seemed less of a stress. . . . The shit hit the fan, so to speak, and everything had to come out. I was in hospital for two days before anybody knew. When they found out, everyone just went bonkers. But for me, it was actually a huge release [Heather, Canada].[117]
>
> Essential for me is to be able to talk openly about being HIV posi-tive. It belongs to me like my feet, my hands. It has become an impor-tant part of me [Nicole Follonier, Switzerland].[118]

As I have noted, however, spiritual healing often requires trans-formation as well as authenticity; for women with HIV/AIDS the transformation process is again deeply encumbered by society's failure to respond to the HIV/AIDS crisis with compassion and care. Our cultural response—like that of religious institutions—too often compounds this tragedy with misery. Society's ignorance about women and HIV/AIDS, the lack of ethnic-, language-, and tradition-specific educational tools,[119] and the inadequacy of social and medical services, especially for women of color and poor women, exacerbate the stress of HIV/AIDS.

Given the horrendous range of obstacles women living with HIV/AIDS must face on a daily basis, and the accompanying fear that available resources will not be adequate to cope with increasing illness and the high cost of medical care, it is not surprising that many of them suffer from depression and despair:

> I want to be allowed to be bitter.
> I want to be allowed to be angry.
> I want to be allowed to feel sorry for myself.
> Without always having to consider that there are those worse off.
> Is that supposed to be a comfort? [Inger M, Denmark].[120]

> I know this disease exists and that I can die of it. But as there was nobody that I could talk with about it, I felt as lonely as a stray man from Mars.... I often thought I would kill myself. Why should a helpless freak survive? Somebody who has no plans to carry out? But I have never done it. When I tried to commit suicide, I thought I had enough good reasons to put an end to all this. When they saved my life, first it left me indifferent. But then I thought many times how good it would have been if I had succeeded. But now it doesn't matter. I'll wait it out [Maria, Hungary].[121]

Authenticity and Spiritual Transformation

The lives of women with HIV/AIDS are not always hopelessly bound in grief and fear. Rather, they sound erotic ambiguities, life and death, tragedy and celebration. I have been repeatedly stunned in my research by the number of women who write positively about their experiences, the women who insist that those of us who are not infected rethink our relationship to their "positive" status. Perhaps the greatest spiritual strength of women living with HIV/AIDS is their ability to absorb their experience authentically, to claim it as their own, and then to find ways through which the HIV-positive experience itself actually empowers erotic transformation:

> It was a momentous occasion and a turning point when I found out I was HIV positive. No one knows how long one has in this world

and it is a gift to realize that each moment is precious.... I know that when I die I will be satisfied with my life as I have lived it, in a way that I might not have if I hadn't had this virus in my life [Lori Lynn Ayers].[122]

I also improved a lot after finding out I was HIV positive.... Now, when I am at home doing nothing, I think: "I don't know how much time I have left. I am going out. I am going to live." I go out more often. I take better care of myself. I know that what counts is today. I have begun to like myself more and to do things that I like [Beatriz of the Grupo Pela Vidda, Brazil].[123]

I cannot come to a standstill in my inner development or even put in a pause. I feel again as though I were sitting on the top of an enormous wave and being thrown and tossed through life. Every single day is filled with so many experiences that bit by bit I am forced to live a richer and deeper life [Dina, Switzerland].[124]

When I was young I kept putting things off. Now with this virus I have no time. I want to live for my son. I want to live so that he'll say one day, "I'm tired of you, you old lady." I want to live for myself. There's a rainbow out there, and I want it. I may not make it, but I am sure going to try for it [Anonymous].[125]

Sex

Among other things, HIV/AIDS has changed and will continue to change sex. As a culture, we are still struggling with the ramifications of this deadly, sexually transmitted disease. As individuals, women with HIV/AIDS sort out their sex lives in intense circumstances. Fear may lead women to choose abstinence, but this may not be the safest route. As Gillian Walker stresses, "attempts at celibacy after being diagnosed with AIDS sometimes backfire" because celibate lifestyles may lead to increased isolation and lack of human touch; "in their starvation for intimacy, some people may launch into reckless sexual indulgence."[126] A reduction in sexual contact between couples when one has been diagnosed with AIDS is extremely common.[127] On the other hand, partners of HIV-infected individuals may engage in frequent, unprotected sex with the infected partner, seeking deeper identification and rejecting death's separation by embracing the risk of death. "The tender intimacy of sex stirs the most profound longings for the eternal union of the lovers, but ecstasy is shrouded with grief."[128]

Again, the weight of love in death's embrace. Often, our response is to fear love, reinforcing the creation of an atmosphere in which sexual contact is directly associated with death: "If you have sex, you will get AIDS and die, so don't have sex." John Backe notes that this response is further complicated by homophobia: "All together, this leaves a formidable tangle of emotions, fears, feelings, and facts for people to sort out."[129] Meanwhile, the cultural response to HIV-positive women either negates them sexually or encourages them to put up as many barriers as possible without acknowledging their need for sexually fulfilling relationships.

As we confront these ambiguities and fears, the rejection of erotic power is our least effective spiritual response. We need its transformative power to overcome denial and to accomplish spiritual healing. Confronting the cancer that eventually took her life, Audre Lorde turned to erotic power to combat fear, understanding herself not only as a casualty in the struggle against the forces of death but also as a warrior.[130]

> Living a self-conscious life, under the pressure of time, I work with the consciousness of death at my shoulder, not constantly, but often enough to leave a mark upon all of my life's decisions and actions.... [T]his consciousness gives my life another breadth. It helps shape the words I speak, the ways I love, my politic of action, the strength of my vision and purpose, the depth of my appreciation of living.[131]

Lorde asks, "What is there possibly left for us to be afraid of, after we have dealt face to face with death and not embraced it? Once I accept

Dancing after the Whirlwind

the existence of dying, as a life process, who can ever have power over me again?"[132]

Enlivening rather than rejecting erotic power in the age of AIDS requires transformations we have not yet begun to imagine. As Linda Singer stresses, traditional attitudes that condemn contemporary society for its single-minded pursuit of pleasure are inadequate to cope with the current situation.[133] What is needed is neither unbridled sexual liberation that ignores or romanticizes sexual risks nor the imposition of negative attitudes and discipline. Rather, Singer calls for the development of new imagery, language, and practice that eroticize safe sex.[134]

There are ironies in this suggestion as well. The disciplinary innovations associated with marketing safe sex carry with them "the implicit assumption . . . that sex was safe before AIDS. Sex was safe, it seems, as long as it was mostly women who died for and from sex in childbirth, illegal abortions, faulty contraception, rape, and murder at the hands of their sexual partners. For men, sexual safety may simply be a matter of wearing a condom. For women, however, sexual safety is not so easily achieved."[135]

Spiritual Healing in Community

AIDS raises the stakes on body / mind / spirit integration. Communication between body and soul, sexuality and spirit, is literally a life and death matter. As their own personal narratives reveal, what helps women living with HIV / AIDS the most is each other. Isolation is a one-way ticket to failing health, failing spirit, and more isolation. Unfortunately, people outside the positive community often "just don't get it," and positive women usually do not have the time to educate those too slow to learn. In addition, support groups that provide real help for certain communities may be alienating or unhelpful for others. Groups constituted primarily of white middle-class gay men, for example, may provide vital services for that community but be of little relevance to a poor Hispanic mother of two who was heterosexually infected by an IV-drug user. Carole Campbell makes the excellent point that "[p]oor women, in comparison to middle class women, are not always able to 'talk it out' endlessly and may not find much relief in this type of therapy."[136]

Repeatedly, women with AIDS report experiencing spiritual transformation when they find and connect with communities who understand and accept them. Enormous growth and strength can also come from engaging in meaningful activity for social and political change. Out of a wide range of experience and need, a variety of organizations emerges: the politically energetic and often controversial ACT-UP (AIDS Coalition to Unleash Power), the People with AIDS Coalition, Positive Women groups in England, Canada, and the United States, organizations serving communities in HIV-stricken areas worldwide, such as the Grupo Pela Vidda in Rio de Janeiro, Brazil, the Mashambanzou AIDS Crisis Centre in Harare, Zimbabwe,[137] the Winnipeg Body Positive group (PLUSS), the Hungarian Society of HIV Positive Persons, AIDS Support Organization Uganda, and many other grass-roots religious and community-support organizations.

I watched my former student, Krista Blake, daily become stronger and more full of life as she became engaged in AIDS education and activism. I watched her family grab hold and hang on to her incredible combination of commitment, spirituality, sarcasm, and hope. Krista had something to do while she was alive. That, too, can be a focus of spiritual transformation, as these witnesses attest:

> Since my condition, my life has become more real and fruitful. I and my husband have helped to form an HIV/AIDS support group in the city of Lusaka.... I am involved in giving educational talks to church women and school children on AIDS and I try to get them involved in the care of the sick and children in distress. I believe that God has given me a message for the church and other organizations, challenging them to confront AIDS positively. I also believe that God has sent me to help

the suffering women in Zambia who are hurting because they have the disease or have lost a relative by it. I have a heart of compassion and empathy, because I identify with them. I always try to comfort them with the same comfort I myself have received from God and from friends [Rosemary Mulenga, Zambia].[138]

I consider that it is very important to do organized work so that HIV positive women have a place to go for help. Not to let them feel that because they are infected everything is finished and they should let themselves die. That was my case. I started selling and giving away my things because I thought I had only two or three months left. I realize now that I'm winning: one year and a bit already.

We visit people who are infected to invite them to participate in our group so they don't feel so lonely. We all have the same problem, and this way we spread the will to live [Rosa Guerrero, Mexico].[139]

Being in contact with other people gets me out of myself. It is like a medicine. Giving out love and getting it back in exchange heals. Working with other people and volunteers and helping others has helped me love myself and understand and heal myself [Yan San Oya, USA, traditional Puerto Rican background].[140]

I went to Vancouver in January and since then my courage has grown to return to my community and speak in public in my language about HIV. . . . I need a lot of support so I will be able to talk about how I feel to the point where I won't have to keep anything to myself. . . . I couldn't accept being a carrier of HIV for a long time, but now I do. I accept it cause I'm stuck with it. . . . I am more happy now. I must live with it. . . . Now I am willing to accept what I am and I am happy that I'm alive today, so I am able to go to communities and settlements and speak and give out messages [Leetia Geetah, Inuit woman from Baffin Island, Northwest Territories].[141]

In their activism, women living with HIV/AIDS celebrate the ability to speak out, not only because it helps to educate but because it helps to heal:

We need to talk. We need to yell and scream rather than just sit and suffer in silence, because it's not doing anybody any good. And if anybody's in a position of power, if they're being quiet about these things, it ain't doing their people any good. . . . I got into trouble a lot when I was growing up because I have a big mouth. But I love my big mouth. I go to communities to talk about my experiences. I see a lot of people sitting in their chairs, listening to what I have to say. I can feel if it's affecting them to hear me talk about sexual abuse. And I'm not going to stop talking about it [Kesia Larkin, Native community, Vancouver, Canada].[142]

Unlike many who write *about* women with HIV/AIDS, positive women write and think a great deal about their spiritual lives. Anger at God; a new commitment to spirituality; explorations in various communities of faith; divine comfort, strength, and reassurance— all combine in their personal visions. There is some evidence that the availability of spiritual resources or communities and their utilization significantly affects the length and quality of life of people with HIV/AIDS. So Dambudzo of Zimbabwe lists becoming a believer as the first helpful hint in how to live with HIV.[143] And Yan San Oya observes: "It is not easy at times. There are days that I don't have any hope, when I am totally overwhelmed. When that happens, I need to get in touch with myself and sit back and reflect. I just need to get in touch within and maintain and nurture that part of me, the spiritual aspect. It is always there."[144]

The ambiguities of hope and despair also coalesce in me as I write. I have wept every day since I began researching this section of the book. I tell my friends that I need to schedule more time for weeping. I do not always weep about the pain. Sometimes, often, I weep over the compassion, the love, the care, the hope, the commitment, the courage, even the savage joy of resistance. These things move me to tears.

I also weep about the pain. In this grieving, as well as in my hope, I am not alone. As Sister Kay Lawlor, pastoral care coordinator at Kitova Hospital, Masaka, Uganda, writes about the eighth station of the cross: "*Jesus meets the women of Jerusalem.* Jane has no land; Mary has no milk for her baby; Scovia's husband sent her away when he learned she had AIDS; Juliet was put out of her rented room; Betty works in a bar to support her children, providing 'favors' for men to get food for the children. The plight of poor women and AIDS. Jesus weeps."[145]

Although they often take up the burden, HIV-positive people are not responsible for transforming our cultural ignorance and brutality. If we—religious institutions, health care providers, individuals—are to develop the sort of compassionate response that will not only serve the suffering but serve as real resistance to the spread of HIV, we must be willing to take up and carry some of the pain. Working from Henri Nouwen's image of the "wounded healer," Newell J. Wirt observes:

> Care givers who are faithful cannot escape the pain, the tragedy, the psychological toll of care giving. They can only be described as "wounded." That may be a much greater risk than getting AIDS. While they cannot heal this particular disease in the physical sense, it is their capacity for care and empathy, their willingness to be "wounded," that brings a special kind of healing to those who are afraid, alone and dying.[146]

I take as my guideline for spiritual support this advice from Jeri Ann Harvey of the Universal Fellowship of Metropolitan Community Churches. I think it works regardless of one's spiritual affiliations: "How can you help persons living with HIV? Love us. Believe in our ability to still LIVE with HIV. Listen to us, we have wisdom we never dreamed we could have. And support us with your touches and your prayers."[147]

And I take as my call to action this bit of poetry from Miranda LaFaye (her chosen name) of Canada:

BLACK CEMENT DEATH GETS SERIOUS AND
STARS START FALLING DOWN FROM HEAVEN.
LIGHTNING STRIKES AND MAKES THE GROUND
ELECTRIC—SO FLOW THROUGH THE RIVERS
OF LIGHT TO WHERE YOUR LOVE IS NEEDED.
THERE IS NO TIME TO WONDER WHY.[148]

I know how to slow or stop the spread of HIV. I think it's simple. Treat every person living with HIV/AIDS with extraordinary care, compassion, and concern. Give them the very best personal and medical care and the best possible education, not only about the mechanics of the disease but about the journey through it. Remind them that their lives have value, that their gifts are appreciated. Eliminate all forms of sex, class, and race discrimination that separate seropositive individuals into categories of innocent and guilty, worthy and unworthy, valuable and dispensable. Acknowledge, affirm, and respond to them as embodied, sexual, spiritual beings. And love them. Love them well.

The results will be amazing. More people will be willing to be tested. Fewer people will engage in dangerous sexual practices out of rage, hopelessness, or desperation. The erotic power of connection will lead us away from hatred and toward healing. These are not platitudes, and I do not offer them simplistically. Any serious intention to change the world will appear naive.

Physical recovery from HIV/AIDS is still, as far as we know, beyond us. Spiritual recovery and renewal is real and evident, as women who know these journeys best relate their adventures in affirmation and transformation. They are our guides at the crossroads, our challenge and promise, the ones who remind us that no moment of deep erotic connection is ever really lost.

I was well into my adulthood before I had to endure the death of anyone very close to me. I remember wondering when it would come, and how I would hold up when it did. Now, nearing fifty, I have lost friends and family members and grieved with others close to me over the deaths of parents, children, lovers. I know something of the emptiness, the lethargy, the exhaustion that accompanies mourning. I know something of the rage that accompanies those deaths we deem "needless." I've lost five close friends to AIDS, and I remember my stunned shock at hearing one of my HIV-positive friends say so very softly: "All of my friends are dead. All of the support group members who were there when I joined are dead. I'm next."

But death is not what I remember most.

I want you to be alive again so that I can touch you. One night back in my life I made love with an old friend in the middle of a lightning storm. If you, farther back in your life, had accepted that same friend's shy offer to you, rather than turning sex aside that time as an unnecessary barrier to your own erotic friendship with him, he might have carried your death through him to me. This does not mean that I should be dead. But now, so oddly, I wish sometimes that I could make love with you—safely, sweetly, in the shelter of that promise we once made that we would care for each other in our old age.

Epilogue

A Poetics of the Wild

What is the dance for the whirlwind's wake? What is the music for the dance that is never the last dance, the phoenix's foxtrot, the tornado's tarantella, the dance we do among the ashes, across the scattered shards? The answer is not esoteric. You've been humming it in the back of your mind forever. It's the rhythm of your own heartbeat, celebrating the breathing in and out; the erotic rock and roll of embodied love.

All things are connected. Even in the midst of his grief, Chief Seattle left us this legacy. Primordial people all over the world know this. Atomic particles know this. This, it would seem, is obvious.

And things come apart. Our bodies know this. Our hearts know this. The whirlwind knows this. This, too, is obvious.

Bearing both at once would be impossible were it not for the complexities of the web. Within the sway and sweep of change, of growth and disintegration, Indra's net holds the array entire in at least five dimensions. So much is going on all the time that we could not bear it if our perception were to take us that far, so we settle for seeing what we can see from here. And from here there is the appearance of beginnings and endings. From here there is the appearance that letting go of even the most worn-out structures is like falling off a cliff. But falling is not dangerous. Only landing is dangerous. Still, it can be hard to trust that the web will hold. Hard to believe that we will be all right as we are. Hard to believe that we will still be able to dance—after the whirlwind.

In northeastern Ohio, there is a place called Center of the World. A furniture store there advertises on the local television station. My lover and I drive through Center of the World when we take the back roads to Cleveland, sometimes commenting upon the reassurance we feel on finding ourselves at the very center. Although there is nothing besides the name to indicate that this particular place is the axis round which the world revolves, whoever named it knew something. Perhaps they knew what mythmakers know: that the place where civilization begins, where order is established, is always the axis mundi, the center of the world.

Every cornerstone, whether of a new building or a new society, is a new center. As we travel away from civilization's centers, we come to boundary lines that define the limits of order. Past these boundary lines, wilderness. This is the realm of the whirlwind. The wild. Here there is no center, no focal point. This is the realm of chaos and undoing, of unknown and unknowable. It has its own music.

From the viewpoint of home, hearth, and center, the response to wildness is terror. But boundary-crossing into the wild shows us another view. This is also the very source of those erotic rhythms that stir us to dance the dance.

What we see when we consider the wild depends upon our perspective and our choices. And as physicists have lately observed, our practice of perception affects not only our response to what we see

Dancing after the Whirlwind

but also what is seen. When we gaze into the wild, we change it. The picture shifts as we shift our gaze.

The place where civilizations meet the wild is the point of contact. If we pass by without altering our behavior or being affected in any way, we have not interrelated—no contact has been made. This is what Buber meant when he said that the relationship is everything. The point of contact is the place of touch.

Growth depends upon contact. Plants require contact with soil and air, people with their environment and one another. Contact, in turn, depends upon distinctions that enable us to integrate otherness and thus to grow. The boundary between order and chaos, civilization and the wild, is not an impenetrable barricade but a point of interchange where experience and growth can occur.

If we are to heal the damage of denial, if we are to renew our own erotic power and return to ourselves, we must become boundary crossers between order and chaos, civilization and the wild. We must focus at the point of contact where we enter into relation: with our own self-images, with our wildest natures, and with all the myriad others to whom we relate.

This is about the healing of the wild. The wild outside, and the wild within. The wild in the mountain, and the wild in your heart. The wild in making love and in attending death. The wild in butterflies and maggots, sunrises and steaming swamps, the elk's mating and the cheetah's kill.

I think of cheetahs, and I hear the drums again. My heart pounds and my breath comes short. Fear and sex generate many of the same embodied responses. These are life and death matters.

I have seen a cheetah complete a kill, although I wasn't meant to see it. I was driving through a wild animal amusement park in Laguna Niguel, California, early one evening when one of the cheetahs escaped from her compound. The ironies were obvious as all those employees who dutifully fed the cheetahs meat on a daily basis went into an absolute panic over the possibility that this particular cheetah might find her own dinner. She did.

As it happened, she ran down and killed a small antelope a few feet from the front of my car. It took her about fifteen seconds to attack and kill the animal and carry it off with her to a nearby tree. It was one of the most beautiful things I have ever seen.

Wild animal parks are oxymoronic. Tourists drive in closed automobiles over carefully laid out roads and through guarded gates in order to observe "wild" animals enclosed within constructed compounds and fed by humans following carefully planned regimens. On this particular day, this particular cheetah turned order into chaos and returned to the wild.

The human response was overwhelming. Jeeps came from everywhere loaded with guards carrying tranquilizer guns, and the tourists were anxiously herded away. We were not meant to see what I had seen. That no matter how carefully we guard the boundaries, the wild is never far away.

There is something else that the cheetah taught me. Once we enter the wild, we cannot choose what to accept and what to reject. We may want the butterflies without the maggots, birth without death, but the wild defies our sensibilities and gives us everything. All of it. Always.

The dance of eros is the wild way, the path into wilderness and away from civilization's center. Those of us whose identities have been denied find ourselves on the fringes, outside the acceptable, and when we look around from this perspective, we sense the erotic power of the wild. That wild power energizes the will. It is a call to the drum and the dance. The wild is neither safe nor reassuring, but it is the fecund source upon which we can draw toward new life.

But where is wilderness? The wild within takes its deepest stirring from wild surroundings, and many of those have been paved and pummeled, boxed, bottled, and brutalized. We go then, for the sake of healing, into untamed places. Or we find some wild thing (in ourselves or elsewhere) unwisely caged and set it free. The deep levels of psyche, like the waters of chaos, are rich sources of creative power into which we enter in order to be reborn. Boundary crossing sparks new creations that could not be achieved in any other way.

Such a crossing is, of course, dangerous. In another paradoxical twist of perspective, the crossing may not only permeate the boundary; it may demolish it. We hover there, aware of the touching point between order and chaos, between the structures of our daily lives and the rhythms of the wild. In order to avoid becoming lost in the underworld, one must know the way in and out.

The paths we choose are reflected in our lovemaking—whether that love is made to beloved human partners, to beautiful ideas, or to the bridge or model car or government we are building. What comes apart in our hands as nature returns the cycle to disintegration will always be a part of something new growing. What is torn apart by violence at our own hands also releases energy, but what's born of it differs. When we hold what we love with care, touching the changes as they move through our fingers without too much shaping and molding, we allow the wild power of eros full creative expression. When we travel wild paths in our lovemaking, without violation or brutality, we allow what we love to change us. This is scary, but it is true.

Such a deepening journey reveals a different picture of the wild. Boundaries can be sealed borders, gated and guarded, built to keep out the "wild things" that constantly threaten to invade. Or they may be points of access to the generative powers of the deep. They may be envisioned as the place to which we "return," dying in order to live again.

Even entering the wild, we find that we cannot stay. Order will prevail. Our consciousness demands it. The act of separation that provides the creative impetus in so many cosmogonic myths is the act of discrimination—of naming. The unformed is formed, the undifferentiated is differentiated, the world is ordered. The conscious mind cannot avoid the act of discrimination. To recognize a thing, to know what it is, is also to know what it is not.

In conscious life, after the advent of language, we cannot return the universe to prima material. Boundaries have been established. And we need these boundaries, these structures, even when we recognize another view. We need to walk as if the earth were flat, to look "up" at the sky, to understand falling objects as moving downward, to distinguish rock from water, ledge from space beyond the ledge, solid ground from thin ice. So we balance form with formlessness, eros with order, seeking the wisdom of the wild.

A common house cat, it is said, is closer to the wild than any other "domesticated" animal. Look into the eyes of the neighborhood tabby, and you can see the fierce reflection of ancient appetites. Lesbians, it is said, keep cats. This may be a stereotype. We have four. Three of them have never been outside, but if I were to open the door, they would, before long, pursue those appetites. I keep them inside because they have no respect for automobiles. In spite of wild animal names like Cougar and Impala, automobiles are not wild.

We seek safety, retreating to routine. We want to live long and practice a dull prosperity. While we experience a measure of success in this and manage some objective thinking along the way, our safe civilizations eventually yield dangers far more final than those of the unbounded.

Recently, I went out by myself into the wild—a three-day retreat on wilderness land in Southern Colorado. I brought many trappings of civilization with me, of course—clothes, sunscreen, tent, and sleeping bag, even a small battery-powered lantern. But only a few miles from camp, the picture changed. More than anything else, what I noticed during my own most recent boundary crossing was fear. How much fear I have, and how much it gets in my way. Over the wilderness border, one cannot count on the deceptions civilizations devise to dupe us into believing we are safe. On the mountain, I also noticed that I had ten times the strength I had assumed. I kept needing a little more—to get down a mountain on a sprained ankle, to cope with fatigue and dehydration, loss of direction and disorientation, and the creatures who assumed quite correctly that the mountain was theirs. And whenever I needed more, it was always there. Since my journey, I have discovered that my hands are much more certain than they used to be, my movements less tentative, jar lids less of a problem. But I never forget the fear and how in the wild I was not just afraid of being lost, of thunderstorms, of bears and cougars. I was afraid of cows.

In her short essay entitled "She Unnames Them," Ursula Le Guin enters the mind of Eve after all the creatures have, at her request, agreed to give up their names. The effect, she notes, is rather more powerful than she had anticipated:

> None were left now to unname, and yet how close I felt to them when I saw one of them swim or fly or trot or crawl across my way or over my skin, or stalk me in the night, or go along beside me for a while in the day. They seemed far closer than when their names had stood between myself and them like a clear barrier: so close that my fear of them and their fear of me became one same fear. And the attraction that many of us felt . . . was now all one with the fear, and the hunter could not be told from the hunted, or the eater from the food.[1]

All things are connected.
>   Wildlife
>   wild sex, wild death
>   wilderness.

Human beings probably don't make love. Very likely, it was there first. We find it or gather it or share it or destroy it, but we can't manufacture it, not even by having sex with one another. Still, the contact boundary between my lover's body and mine is the sacred space where eros and spirit most fully meet, and that union is among the sweetest and most holy places of my life. The primordial state, the wonder of the wild, is not something we once were. It is something we have always been. Only we forget.

I still think orgasm is the best metaphor we have for God. That place where letting go brings life and death together and transforms all that into ecstasy. And if that is not divinity, then why not? What else is more than that?

So come again into the wild. Set the compass spinning and let go. It's true that boundary crossing into the unbounded will always bounce us back to bordered space eventually—only the landscape will be transformed. Even the dance of disintegration and renewal has a pattern. Even fractals fracture into rhythms. Even as the old forms fade, new structures emerge and establish themselves. This is not some promise God fulfills for the faithful or some chance outcome. This is the works. There will always be new life.

So, for now, let go and dance.

Notes

Introduction

1. Joan Timmerman, *Sexuality and Spiritual Growth* (New York: Crossroad, 1992), 7.

2. John Hick, *An Interpretation of Religion: Human Responses to the Transcendent* (New Haven: Yale University Press, 1989), 4.

3. Joyce Trebilcot, *Taking Responsibility for Sexuality* (Berkeley: Acacia Books, 1983), 2.

4. James Nelson, *Embodiment: An Approach to Sexuality and Christian Theology* (Minneapolis: Augsburg Publishing House, 1978), 17.

5. Ibid.

6. Joan Timmerman, *Sexuality and Spiritual Growth*, 9.

7. Andre Guindon, *The Sexual Language: An Essay in Moral Theology* (Ottawa: University of Ottawa Press, 1976), 68.

8. Lucy Goodison, *Moving Heaven and Earth: Sexuality, Spirituality and Social Change* (London: Women's Press, 1990), 2.

9. *Out Look* 14 (1991).

10. Kelly Gabriel Lee and Rudiger Busto, "When the Spirit Moves Us," *Out Look* 14 (1991): 83–85.

11. Ellen Bass and Laura Davis, *The Courage to Heal: A Guide for Women Survivors of Child Sexual Abuse* (New York: Harper & Row, 1988), 156.

12. Joan Timmerman, *Sexuality and Spiritual Growth*, 15.

13. When the Caterpillar inquires, "Who are you?," Alice responds: "I—I hardly know, Sir, just at present—at least I know who I was when I got up this morning, but I think I must have been changed several times since then." Lewis Carroll, *The Annotated Alice: Alice's Adventures in Wonderland and Through the Looking Glass*, introduction and notes by Martin Gardner (New York: Clarkson N. Potter, 1960), 67.

14. Vincent Genovesi, *In Pursuit of Love: Catholic Morality and Human Sexuality* (Wilmington, Del.: Michael Glazer, 1987), 134.

15. Steven F. Morin, "Heterosexual Bias in Psychological Research on Lesbianism and Male Homosexuality," *American Psychologist* 32 (1977): 636.

16. Thanks to Christine Downing for this observation.

17. As an illustration, total deaths for women in states with heavy AIDS concentrations increased between 1981 and 1986 at tremendous rates (e.g., 30 percent in Connecticut and 21 percent in New York). Where states were hard hit by AIDS, deaths rose significantly among women 15 to 44 during this period from diseases such as tuberculosis, chronic obstructive pulmonary disease, and other respiratory and infectious disease thought to be AIDS related. These deaths were almost never attributed to AIDS. Gena Corea, *The Invisible Epidemic* (New York: HarperCollins, 1992), 127, citing the observations of journalist Chris Norwood.

18. Marilyn Frye, "To See and Be Seen: The Politics of Reality," in *The Politics of Reality: Essays in Feminist Theory* (Freedom, Calif.: Crossing Press, 1983), 153.

19. Ibid., 156–158.

20. Contrary to this tendency, Catharine Stimpson defines the term in strictly sexual terms: A lesbian is a woman who engages in sexual activity with another woman. See Catharine Stimpson, "Zero Degree Deviancy: The Lesbian Novel in English," in *Writing and Sexual Difference*, ed. Elizabeth Abel (Chicago: University of Chicago Press, 1982).

Chapter One

1. W. B. Yeats, "The Second Coming," *The Poems of W. B. Yeats* (New York: Macmillan, 1983).

2. Lucy Goodison, *Moving Heaven and Earth*, 1.

3. Carter Heyward, *Touching Our Strength: The Erotic as Power and the Love of God* (San Francisco: Harper & Row, 1989), 3. Also see Carter Heyward, *The Redemption of*

God: A Theology of Mutual Relation (Washington, D.C.: University Press of America, 1982).

4. Joan Timmerman, *Sexuality and Spiritual Growth*, 94–95.

5. This very disturbing and powerful film is entitled *Closetland.*

6. Carter Heyward, *Touching Our Strength*, 12.

7. Winifred Milius Lubell, *The Metamophosis of Baubo: Myths of Woman's Sexual Energy* (Nashville: Vanderbilt University Press, 1994), 180.

8. Narrations of the Japanese cosmogony are compiled with reference to the following editions: *Kojiki,* trans. W. G. Aston (Kobe, Japan: J. L. Thompson, 1932); *Kojiki,* trans. Donald L. Philippi (Princeton: Princeton University Press and University of Tokyo Press, 1969); *Nihongi,* trans. W. G. Aston (London: Kegan, Paul, Trench, Trubner, 1896). An expanded interpretation can be found in L. J. Tessier, "Boundary Crossing: The Chaos-Cosmos Dynamic in Cosmogonic Myth" (Ph.D. diss., Claremont Graduate School, 1987), available through University of Microfilms International, Ann Arbor, Mich.

9. Winifred Milius Lubell, *The Metamorphosis of Baubo*, 179.

10. Winifred Milius Lubell, *The Metamorphosis of Baubo.*

11. Christine Downing, *Myths and Mysteries of Same-Sex Love* (New York: Continuum, 1990), 201–202.

12. Ibid., 202.

13. Sherry B. Ortner, "Is Female to Male as Nature Is to Culture?," in *Women, Culture, and Society,* ed. Michele Z. Rosaldo and Louise Lamphere (Stanford: Stanford University Press, 1984), 67–87. Other interesting analyses of this dichotomy may be found in Susan Griffin, *Woman and Nature: The Roaring inside Her* (New York: Harper & Row, 1978), and Lucy Goodison, *Moving Heaven and Earth.*

14. Christine Downing, *Women's Mysteries: Toward a Poetics of Gender* (New York: Crossroad, 1992), 69–70.

15. Ibid., 78.

16. Rollo May, *Love and Will* (New York: W.W. Norton, 1969), 74.

17. Audre Lorde, "Uses of the Erotic: The Erotic as Power," in *Weaving the Visions: Patterns in Feminist Spirituality,* ed. Judith Plaskow and Carol P. Christ (San Francisco: Harper & Row, 1989), 208.

18. Ibid.

19. Nelle Morton, "The Rising Woman Consciousness in a Male Language Structure," in *The Journey Is Home* (Boston: Beacon Press, 1985), 30.

20. Joan Timmerman, *Sexuality and Spiritual Growth*, 87.

21. Joseph Campbell, *The Masks of God: Oriental Mythology* (New York: Viking Press, 1962), 234.

22. Ibid.

23. Rollo May, *Love and Will*, 72.

24. Joseph Campbell, *The Masks of God: Oriental Mythology*, 235.

25. Catherine Keller, *From a Broken Web: Separation, Sexism, and Self* (Boston: Beacon Press, 1986), 218.

26. Lisa Cahill, *Women and Sexuality* (New York: Paulist Press, 1992), 47. Also see Vincent Genovesi, *In Pursuit of Love*, 140, and Andre Guindon, *The Sexual Language*.

27. Rollo May, *Love and Will*, 73.

28. Ibid., 74.

29. Ibid.

30. Ibid., 75.

31. Plato, *The Symposium*, trans. W. Hamilton (Middlesex, England: Penguin Books, 1970).

32. Ibid., 59.

33. Ibid., 61.

34. Ibid., 62.

35. Ibid.

36. Ibid.

37. Ibid., 63.

38. Ibid., 64.

39. As when his poet describes the earliest means of human locomotion: "These people could walk upright ..., but when they wanted to run quickly they used all their eight limbs, and turned rapidly over and over in a circle, like tumblers who perform a cart-wheel and return to an upright position." Ibid., 59.

40. Audre Lorde, "Uses of the Erotic: The Erotic as Power," 210.

41. Ibid., 211.

42. Catherine Keller, *From a Broken Web*, 8.

43. Ibid., 9.

44. Ibid., 114.

45. Rollo May, *Love and Will*, 65.

46. W. Hamilton, introduction to Plato, *The Symposium*, 22.

47. Ibid., 23.

48. Plato, *The Symposium*, 95.

49. It is also significant to note the tendency in earlier Greek poetry to attribute to women "the destructive power of sexuality and the responsibility for bringing all ills on to humankind" (Lucy Goodison, *Moving Heaven and Earth*, 162). Hesiod, writing in the eighth century B.C.E., depicts the establishment of civilization in terms of the conquest of women's reproductive power by principles of justice and the power of the male. Goodison cites Hesiod's description of Pandora as "the founder of the race of women ... who live among mortal men as a source of misery to them" and his claim that Zeus "set women among mortal men as a source of problems, a confederacy of

troublemakers" (163, citing *Hesiod: The Homeric Hymns and Homerica*, trans. H. G. Eve-lyn-White, Loeb Classical Library [Cambridge: Harvard University Press, and London: Heinemann, 1982], 121–23, ll. 561ff.).

50. W. Hamilton, introduction to Plato, *The Symposium*, 26.

51. Friedrich Nietzsche, *Beyond Good and Evil*, trans. Marianne Cowan (Chicago: Gateway Editions, 1955), 87.

52. Beverly Harrison, "Misogyny and Homophobia: The Unexplored Connections," in *Making the Connections: Essays in Feminist Social Ethics* by Beverly Wildung Harrison, ed. Carol S. Robb (Boston: Beacon Press, 1985), 135.

53. Audre Lorde, "Uses of the Erotic: The Erotic as Power," 209.

54. Ibid.

55. Susan Griffin, *Pornography and Silence: Culture's Revenge against Nature* (New York: Harper & Row, 1992), 1.

56. Ibid., 2.

57. For example, Lucy Goodison (*Moving Heaven and Earth*) analyzes developments from the prehistoric period in Crete (3000 B.C.E. to 1600 B.C.E.), through the Mycenaean age, to the culture of classical Greece. She describes the earlier period as one in which "heaven seems to have been no more holy than earth, when spirituality was not divorced from the sexual body; when the symbols of power were female" (125). Beginning in the Mycenaean period, a power shift takes place "towards a society in which one half of the population, the women, are politically inferior to the other half" (150). Not only do male gods in this period become divided from female deities, but there is also separation of "sky from earth, of mind from body, of spirituality from sexuality" (150).

58. Rollo May, *Love and Will*, 70.

59. Ibid., 72.

60. Karen Horney, "The Dread of Woman: Observations on a Specific Difference in the Dread Felt by Men and by Women Respectively for the Opposite Sex," in *Feminine Psychology*, ed. Harold Kelman, M.D. (New York: W. W. Norton, 1967), 134.

61. Ibid., 135.

62. Ibid., 141.

63. Judith Hoch-Smith and Anita Spring, introduction to *Women in Ritual and Symbolic Roles*, ed. Judith Hoch-Smith and Anita Spring (New York: Plenum Press, 1978), 4–6.

64. Ibid., 6–7.

65. Ibid., 7.

66. Susan Griffin, *Pornography and Silence*, 19.

67. Ibid.

68. Ibid.

69. Ibid., 255.

70. See, for example, Diane Wolkstein and Samuel Noah Kramer, *Inanna, Queen of Heaven and Earth: Her Stories and Hymns from Sumer* (New York: Harper and Row, 1983), 52–89, 127–135.

Chapter Two

1. See, for example, the work of Carol P. Christ, Christine Downing, Riane Eisler, Elinor Gadon, and Patricia Reis.

2. Patricia Reis, *Through the Goddess: A Woman's Way of Healing* (New York: Continuum, 1991), 125.

3. Emily Culpepper, "The Spiritual, Political Journey of a Feminist Freethinker," in *After Patriarchy: Feminist Transformations of the World Religions*, ed. Paula M. Cooey, William R. Eakin, and Jay B. McDaniel (Maryknoll, N.Y.: Orbis Books, 1991), 153.

4. Nelle Morton, "The Goddess as Metaphoric Image," in *The Journey Is Home* (Boston: Beacon Press, 1985), 150.

5. Ibid., 151–158.

6. Ibid., 166.

7. Carol P. Christ, "A Spirituality for Women," in *The Laughter of Aphrodite: Reflections on a Journey to the Goddess* (San Francisco: Harper & Row, 1987), 67.

8. Christine Downing, *The Goddess: Mythological Images of the Feminine* (New York: Crossroad, 1981), 9. She specifically mentions Demeter, Ceres, Ninbu, and Isis.

9. David Kinsley, *The Goddesses' Mirror: Visions of the Divine from East and West* (Albany: State University of New York, 1989), 22. Also see Mircea Eliade, *Patterns in Comparative Religion* (Cleveland: World, 1958), 314–316, 332–334.

10. Christine Downing, *The Goddess*, 11.

11. David Kinsley, *The Goddesses' Mirror*.

12. Ibid., 94.

13. Ibid., 58–61.

14. Ibid., 62.

15. *Kojiki* (1969), 50.

16. David Kinsley, *The Goddesses' Mirror*, 113.

17. Diane Wolkstein and Samuel Noah Kramer, *Inanna, Queen of Heaven and Earth*, 37.

18. Ibid., 44.

19. David Kinsley, *The Goddesses' Mirror*, 165.

20. Ibid., 170.

21. Marija Gimbutas, *The Language of the Goddess* (San Francisco: Harper & Row, 1989), 316.

22. Ibid.

23. Ibid., 318.

24. Starhawk, *The Spiral Dance: A Rebirth of the Ancient Religion of the Great Goddess* (San Francisco: Harper & Row, 1979), 17.

25. Ibid.

26. Christine Downing, *Myths and Mysteries of Same-Sex Love*, 200–210.

27. Ibid., 210–212.

28. Ibid., 212.

29. Ibid.

30. David Kinsley, *The Goddesses' Mirror*, 189–190.

31. Ibid., 212.

32. Patricia Reis, *Through the Goddess*, 135.

33. Carol P. Christ, *The Laughter of Aphrodite*, 109.

34. Marija Gimbutas, *The Language of the Goddess*, 316.

35. David Kinsley, *The Goddesses' Mirror*, 75.

36. Ibid., 24.

37. Ibid., 210.

38. Ibid., 120; Patricia Reis, *Through the Goddess*, 126–127.

39. Elaine Pagels, *Adam, Eve, and the Serpent* (New York: Random House, 1988), viii–ix.

40. Ibid., xviii.

41. Ibid., 11.

42. Andre Guindon, *The Sexual Language*, 44.

43. Elaine Pagels, *Adam, Eve, and the Serpent*, 14.

44. Ibid., 17.

45. Ibid., 28.

46. Ibid.

47. Ibid., 96.

48. Ibid., xxvi.

49. Ibid.

50. Walter M. Spink, *The Axis of Eros* (New York: Schocken Books, 1973), 18, 20.

51. There are several sources for this view. Gregory of Nyssa, John Chrysostom, and Jerome wrote that God, foreseeing the sin of Adam and Eve, equipped humans with the reproductive organs of the animals they would become. Ambrose, mentor to Augustine, taught that even sexual intercourse during marriage was a defilement. This view persisted. Two hundred years after Augustine, Gregory the Great considered the experience of pleasure during intercourse to be extremely sinful, although less serious if committed within marriage for procreative purposes. In 1679, Pope Innocent XI decreed that anyone who claimed that intercourse for pleasure was not sinful was guilty of heresy (John C. Dwyer, *Human Sexuality: A Christian View* [Kansas City: Sheed and Ward, 1987], 9–11). Church law reflects and supports this view, e.g., the explicitly antisexual code made law by the Council of Elvira (Spain) (See Carter Heyward, *Touching Our Strength*, 42–44) and the Council of Trent's rulings, which simultaneously

lifted marriage to the status of a sacrament and determined that one must refrain from any sexual activity for at least three days before receiving Holy Communion (Demosthenes Savramis, *The Satanizing of Woman: Religion versus Sexuality* [Garden City, N.Y.: Doubleday, 1974], 85).

52. Elaine Pagels, *Adam, Eve, and the Serpent*, xix.

53. Ibid., 110.

54. St. Augustine, *The City of God*, trans. Marcus Dods (New York: Random House, 1950), Book XIV, Chapter 15.

55. Ibid., Chapter 16.

56. Ibid., Chapter 17.

57. Margaret R. Miles, *Fullness of Life: Historical Foundations for a New Asceticism* (Philadelphia: Westminister, 1981), 77, and Evelyn Eaton and James D. Whitehead, *A Sense of Sexuality: Christian Love and Intimacy* (New York: Doubleday, 1989), 99–103.

58. St. Augustine, *The City of God*, Book XIV, Chapter 21.

59. Ibid., Chapter 24.

60. Ibid.

61. Ibid.

62. Ibid., Chapter 26.

63. Ibid.

64. Elaine Pagels, *Adam, Eve, and the Serpent*, 120.

65. Ibid., 141.

66. Andre Guindon, *The Sexual Language*, 61.

67. Vincent Genovesi, *In Pursuit of Love*, 133.

68. Andre Guindon, *The Sexual Creators: An Ethical Proposal for Concerned Christians* (Lanham, Md.: University Press of America, 1986), 24.

69. Elaine Pagels, *Adam, Eve, and the Serpent*, 146.

70. Ibid., 147.

71. James Nelson, *Embodiment*, 104.

72. Ibid., 105.

73. Andre Guindon, *The Sexual Language*; John C. Dwyer, *Human Sexuality*; Vincent Genovesi, *In Pursuit of Love*; Evelyn Eaton and James D. Whitehead, *A Sense of Sexuality.*

74. Evelyn Eaton and James D. Whitehead, *A Sense of Sexuality*, 108; Vincent Genovesi, *In Pursuit of Love*, 135.

75. Vincent Genovesi, *In Pursuit of Love*, 141.

76. Evelyn Eaton and James D. Whitehead, *A Sense of Sexuality*, 23.

77. Andre Guindon, *The Sexual Creators*, 23.

78. Ibid.

79. Ibid.

80. Ibid., 24.

81. Ibid.

82. Ibid., 26.

83. Ibid., 27.

84. Ibid., 26.

85. Ibid., 27.

86. Ibid., 30.

87. Andre Guindon, *The Sexual Language*, 86.

88. Andre Guindon, *The Sexual Creators*, 30.

89. Ibid., 32.

90. Ibid.

91. Ibid.

92. John C. Dwyer, *Human Sexuality*, 48.

93. A good summary of the history and viewpoints of feminist theology is included in Mary Hunt's *Fierce Tenderness: A Feminist Theology of Friendship* (New York: Crossroad, 1991). Although her orientation is female friendships, she also includes a good general discussion of the field as a whole. See especially pp. 63–73.

94. Carter Heyward, "Sexual Ethics and the Church: A Response," in *Women, Religion and Sexuality: Studies on the Impact of Religious Teachings on Women*, ed. Jeanne Becher (Philadelphia: Trinity Press International, 1990), 26.

95. See, for example, Elisabeth Schüssler Fiorenza, *Bread Not Stone: The Challenge of Feminist Biblical Interpretation* (Boston: Beacon Press, 1984).

96. Christine Downing, *The Goddess*, 11.

97. Phyllis Trible, *God and the Rhetoric of Sexuality* (Philadelphia: Fortress Press, 1978), 100–101.

98. Ibid., 102.

99. Ibid., 139.

100. Rosemary Radford Ruether, *Sexism and God-Talk: Toward a Feminist Theology* (Boston: Beacon Press, 1983), 19.

101. Beverly Harrison, "The Power of Anger in the Work of Love: Christian Ethics for Women and Other Strangers," in *Making the Connections: Essays in Feminist Social Ethics* by Beverly Wildung Harrison, ed. Carol S. Robb (Boston: Beacon Press, 1985), 13.

102. Ibid.

103. Carter Heyward, *Touching Our Strength*, 96.

104. Ibid., 99.

105. Ibid., 81–82.

106. Ibid., 92.

107. Ibid., 93.

108. Ibid., 95.

109. Ibid., 98.

110. For an excellent philosophical consideration of female-female friendships, one that is very much in harmony with Hunt's approach, see Janice C. Raymond's *A Passion for Friends: Toward a Philosophy of Female Affection* (Boston: Beacon Press, 1986).

111. Mary Hunt, *Fierce Tenderness*, 91–92.

112. Ibid., 21.

113. Ibid., 99.

114. Ibid., 102.

115. Ibid., 100–101.

116. Rita Nakashima Brock, *Journeys by Heart: A Christology of Erotic Power* (New York: Crossroad, 1991), 10.

117. Ibid., 10–11.

118. Ibid., 21.

119. Ibid., 25.

120. Ibid., 69.

121. K. Roberts Skerrett, "When No Means Yes: The Passion of Carter Heyward," *Journal of Feminist Studies in Religion* 12:1 (1996): 71–92.

122. Carter Heyward, *When Boundaries Betray Us: Beyond Illusions of What Is Ethical in Therapy and Life* (San Francisco: HarperSanFrancisco, 1993), 166.

123. Ibid., 167.

124. Ibid.

125. Rita Nakashima Brock, *Journeys by Heart*, xv.

126. Ibid.

127. Ibid.

128. Kwok Pui-lan, "The Future of Feminist Theology: An Asian Perspective," in *Feminist Theology from the Third World*, ed. Ursula King (Maryknoll, N.Y.: SPCK / Orbis Press, 1994), 72.

129. Ibid.

130. Ynestra King, "Healing the Wounds: Feminism, Ecology, and the Nature / Culture Dualism," in *Reweaving the World: The Emergence of Ecofeminism*, ed. Irene Diamond and Gloria Feman Orenstein (San Francisco: Sierra Club Books, 1990), 106–121.

131. Cheryl Townsend Gilkes, "The 'Loves' and 'Troubles' of African-American Women's Bodies: The Womanist Challenge to Cultural Humiliation and Community Ambivalence," in *A Troubling in My Soul: Womanist Perspectives on Evil and Suffering*, ed. Emilie M. Townes (Maryknoll, N.Y.: Orbis Books, 1993), 232–249.

132. For example, within Judaism, the works of Judith Plaskow, Susannah Heschel, Esther Broner, Naomi Goldenberg, Norma Joseph, Susannah Ostriker, Tamar Frankiel, Alice Shalvi, and Lynn Gottlieb; within Islam, the works of Riffat Hassan, Ghazala Anwar, Margot Badran, Sondra Hale, Leila Ahmed, Nawal El Saadawi, and Leila Ahmed.

133. Mary Daly, *Beyond God the Father* (Boston: Beacon Press, 1973).

134. Mary Daly, *The Church and the Second Sex, with a New Feminist Postchristian Introduction by the Author* (New York: Harper & Row, 1975).

135. Mary Daly, *Outercourse: The Be-Dazzling Voyage* (San Francisco: HarperSanFrancisco, 1992), 137–140.

136. Mary Daly (in cahoots with Jane Caputi), *Websters' First New Intergalactic Wickedary of the English Language* (Boston: Beacon Press, 1987), 89.

137. Ibid.

138. Ibid.

139. Ibid.

140. Ibid., 90.

141. Mary Daly, *Beyond God the Father*, 19.

142. Emily Culpepper, "The Spiritual, Political Journey of a Feminist Freethinker," in *After Patriarchy: Feminist Transformations of the World Religions*, 146.

143. Ibid.

144. Ibid.

145. Ibid., 151.

146. Nelle Morton, *The Journey Is Home*, 127.

147. Mulk Raj Anand, *Kama Kala: Some Notes on the Philosophical Basis of Hindu Erotic Sculpture* (Geneva: Nagel Publishers, 1963), 5.

148. Ibid.

149. Ibid.

150. Walter M. Spink, *The Axis of Eros*, 74.

151. Ibid., 76.

152. Ibid., 69.

153. Ibid., 134.

154. Joseph Campbell, *The Masks of God: Oriental Mythology*, 344.

155. Ibid., 346.

156. Benoy Kumar Sarkar, *Love in Hindu Literature* (Tokyo: Maruzen Company, 1916), 67.

157. Ibid.

158. Joseph Campbell, *Masks of God: Oriental Mythology*, 352.

159. Ibid., 356.

160. Ibid., 357–358.

161. Benoy Kumar Sarkar, *Love in Hindu Literature*, 69–70.

162. Ibid., 70.

163. Ibid., 84.

164. Mulk Raj Anand, *Kama Kala*, 32.

165. Walter M. Spink, *The Axis of Eros*, 100.

166. Ibid., 105.

167. Ibid., 101. This contrast may be acceptable in terms of traditional Western monotheistic theologies, but absolute transcendence is obviously not the only option in Western theology. Furthermore, an autoerotic concept of divine creative activity may also have roots in Western cultures, for example, in the Old European understanding of the parthenogenetic power of the Great Goddess.

168. Mulk Raj Anand, *Kama Kala*, 25.

169. Ibid., 26.

170. Ibid.

171. Ibid., 38.

172. Ibid., 42.

173. Ibid.

174. Judith Hoch-Smith and Anita Spring view Hindu creation myths as paradigmatic of those mythic themes in patriarchal cultures that blame women for the loss of contact with the gods and the whole range of human troubles. They point out Kali's association with "the all devouring maw of the abyss" and Shiva's loss of favor with the gods because he became absorbed in sexual union with Kali and therefore "mired in 'female illusion.'" Introduction to *Women in Ritual and Symbolic Roles*, 4.

175. Lorna Rhodes AmaraSingham, "The Misery of the Embodied: Representations of Women in Sinhalese Myth," in *Women in Ritual and Symbolic Roles*, ed. Judith Hoch-Smith and Anita Spring (New York: Plenum Press, 1978), 103.

176. Ibid.

177. Ibid., 104.

178. Junko Minamato, "Buddhist Attitudes: A Woman's Perspective," in *Women, Religion and Sexuality*, ed. Jeanne Becher, 158.

179. Ibid., 158–159.

180. Ibid., 159.

181. Rita M. Gross, "Buddhism after Patriarchy?" in *After Patriarchy: Feminist Transformations of the World Religions*, 66. Also see Rita M. Gross, *Buddhism after Patriarchy: A Feminist History, Analysis, and Reconstruction of Buddhism* (Albany: State University of New York Press, 1993).

182. Ibid.

183. Ibid., 75.

184. Ibid., 76.

185. Ibid., 80.

186. Miranda Shaw, *Passionate Enlightenment: Women in Tantric Buddhism* (Princeton: Princeton University Press, 1994), 27.

187. Ibid.

188. Walter M. Spink, *Axis of Eros*, 125.

189. Miranda Shaw, *Passionate Enlightenment*, 32.

190. Ibid.

191. Ibid.

192. Ibid., 44.

193. Ibid., 21.

194. Ibid.

195. Ibid.

196. Ibid., 22.

197. Ibid., 67.
198. Ibid., 27.
199. Ibid., 26.
200. Ibid., 27.
201. Ibid., 7.
202. Ibid., 34.
203. Ibid.
204. Ibid., 40.
205. Ibid., 41.
206. Ibid., 45.
207. Ibid., 69.
208. Ibid.
209. Ibid.
210. Ibid., 70.
211. Ibid., 71.

Chapter Three

1. Maurice Friedman, introduction to *The Knowledge of Man*, by Martin Buber (New York: Harper & Row, 1965), 27.

2. Martin Buber, *The Knowledge of Man*, 76.

3. Ibid.

4. Ibid., 77.

5. Martin Buber, *I and Thou*, trans. Walter Kaufman (New York: Charles Scribner's Sons, 1970), 69. Also see Carter Heyward, *Touching Our Strength*, 23.

6. Martin Buber, *The Knowledge of Man*, 78.

7. Thanks to Christine Downing for this insight.

8. Carter Heyward, *Touching Our Strength*, 26.

9. Among others, see Vivienne C. Cass, "Homosexual Identity Formation: A Theoretical Model," *Journal of Homosexuality* 4 (1979): 219–235; Beata E. Chapman and JoAnn C. Brannock, "Proposed Model of Lesbian Identity Development: An Empirical Examination," *Journal of Homosexuality* 14 (1987): 69–80; Eli Coleman, "Developmental Stages of the Coming-Out Process," in *Homosexuality and Psychotherapy*, ed. John C. Gonsiorek (New York: Haworth Press, 1982), 31–43; Barry M. Dank, "Coming Out in the Gay World," *Psychiatry* 34 (1971): 180–197; J. D. Hencken and W. T. O'Dowd, "Coming Out as an Aspect of Identity Formation," *Gay Academic Union Journal* 1 (1977): 18–26; Lou Ann Lewis, "The Coming-Out Process for Lesbians: Integrating a Stable Identity," *Social Work* [September / October] (1984): 464–469; G. J. McDonald, "Individual Differences in the Coming Out Process for Gay Men: Implications for Theoretical Models," *Journal of Homosexuality* 8 (1982): 47–60; K. Plummer, *Sexual Stigma:*

An *Interactionist Account* (London: Routledge & Kegan Paul, 1975); Richard Troiden, "Becoming Homosexual: A Model of Gay Identity Acquisition," *Psychiatry* 42 (1979): 367–371.

10. Vivienne C. Cass, "Homosexual Identity Formation," 220.

11. Ibid.

12. Ibid., 222.

13. Adrienne Rich, "Compulsory Heterosexuality and Lesbian Existence," in *Feminist Frameworks*, 3rd ed., ed. Alison M. Jaggar and Paula S. Rothenberg (New York: McGraw-Hill, 1993), 489.

14. Ibid.

15. Vivienne C. Cass, "Homosexual Identity Formation," 222. Many stage theorists overlook this aspect of establishing a gay or lesbian sexual identity, emphasizing personal realization but not the crisis of incongruence. The various terms for this stage reflect this emphasis: *signification* (Plummer), *awareness* (Hencken and O'Dowd), or *identification* (Dank).

16. Cass, "Homosexual Identity Formation," 225.

17. Ibid., 222.

18. Joan Sophie, "Internalized Homophobia and Lesbian Identity," *Journal of Homosexuality* 14 (1987): 57.

19. Eli Coleman, "Developmental Stages of the Coming-Out Process," 33.

20. Lou Ann Lewis, "The Coming-Out Process for Lesbians," 465.

21. Beata G. Chapman and JoAnn C. Brannock, for example, propose a five-step Model of Lesbian Identity Awareness and Self-Labeling ("Proposed Model of Lesbian Identity Development: An Empirical Examination") that includes a stage called "incongruence." This process involves recognizing that one's feelings toward girls and women are different from heterosexual or nonlesbian others. Lou Ann Lewis ("The Coming Out Process for Lesbians") discusses "being different" and "dissonance."

22. Joan Sophie, "A Critical Examination of Stage Theories of Lesbian Identity Development," *Journal of Homosexuality* 14 (1987).

23. Caryl B. Bentley, "My Third Coming Out at Last Has My Own Name," in *The Coming Out Stories*, ed. Susan J. Wolfe and Julia Penelope Stanley (Watertown, Mass.: Persephone Press, 1980), 79.

24. If our understanding of sexual identity is too rigid, we fail to recognize and affirm the dynamic nature of this process. For example, women who adopt a lesbian identity but later change to a bisexual or heterosexual self-understanding may be ostracized by the gay and lesbian community as "traitors." They may also be accused of denial. One woman who had self-identified as a lesbian for a number of years and who later chose to marry a man and have children spoke to me about her feeling of not belonging anywhere. The struggle to accept a lesbian identity is difficult; I have also known women who chose a heterosexual lifestyle later in life but still identified themselves as lesbians.

25. These techniques are set out in some detail in Vivienne C. Cass, "Homosexual Identity Formation," 226–227.

26. Joel W. Wells and William B. Kline, "Self-Disclosure of Homosexual Orientation," *Journal of Social Psychology* 127 (1986): 196.

27. Carter Heyward, *Touching Our Strength*, 24.

28. Eli Coleman, "Developmental Stages of the Coming Out Process," 33–34.

29. Nancy Wilson, *Our Tribe*, 32.

30. Ibid., 26.

31. Emery S. Hetrick, M.D., and A. Damien Martin, M.D., "Developmental Issues and Their Resolution for Gay and Lesbian Adolescents," *Journal of Homosexuality* 14 (1987): 27.

32. Ibid.

33. Queer theory has developed some interesting challenges to this position.

34. Mary Hunt, *Fierce Tenderness*, 45.

35. Christine Browning, "Therapeutic Issues and Intervention Strategies with Young Adult Lesbian Clients: A Developmental Approach," *Journal of Homosexuality* 14 (1987): 47.

36. Carmen De Monteflores and Stephen J. Schultz, "Coming Out: Similarities and Differences for Lesbians and Gay Men," 64. My own personal experience bears this out. Regardless of their chronological age, women who are "coming out" as lesbians often reenter adolescence and may feel confused (or alarmed) about the associated tumultuous emotions, desires, and urges they are experiencing.

37. Christine Browning, "Therapeutic Issues and Intervention Strategies with Young Adult Lesbian Clients"; J. H. Hedblom, "Dimensions of Lesbian Sexual Experience," *Archives of Sexual Behavior* 2 (1973): 329–341; D. I. Riddle and S. F. Morin, "Removing the Stigma: Data from Individuals," *APA Monitor* (1977): 16, 28.

38. Carmen de Monteflores and Stephen J. Schultz, "Coming Out: Similarities and Differences for Lesbians and Gay Men," 68.

39. Caryl B. Bentley, "My Third Coming Out at Last Has My Own Name," 79–80.

40. Christine Browning, "Therapeutic Issues and Intervention Strategies with Young Adult Lesbian Clients," 46.

41. Jo-Ann Krestan and Claudia S. Bepko, "The Problem of Fusion in the Lesbian Relationship," *Family Process* 19 (1980): 277–289; Christine Browning, "Therapeutic Issues and Intervention Strategies with Young Adult Lesbian Clients," 51–52; B. Burch, "Psychological Merger in Lesbian Couples: A Joint Ego Psychological and Systems Approach," *Family Therapy* 9 (1982): 201–208; M. Karpel, "Individualization: From Fusion to Dialogue," *Family Process* 15 (1976): 65–82; Phyllis A. Kaufman, Elizabeth Harrison, and Mary Lou Hyde, "Distancing for Intimacy in Lesbian Relationships," *American Journal of Psychiatry* 141 (1984): 530–533; Letitia Anne Peplau, Susan Cochran, Karen Rook, and Christine Padesky, "Loving Women: Attachment and Autonomy in Lesbian Relationships," *Journal of Social Issues* 34 (1978): 7–27; Sallyann Roth, "Psychotherapy

with Lesbian Couples: Individual Issues, Female Socialization, and the Social Context," *Journal of Marital and Family Therapy* 11 (1985): 273–286; Sondra Smalley, "Dependency Issues in Lesbian Relationships," *Journal of Homosexuality* 14 (1987): 125–135.

42. For more on this perspective, see Marilyn Frye, "Some Reflections on Separatism and Power," in *The Politics of Reality*, 95–109, and Sarah Lucia Hoagland, "Some Thoughts About Heterosexualism," *Journal of Social Philosophy* 21 (1990): 98–107.

43. Lesbian leisure cruise lines sought to advertise on the sitcom *Ellen* hoping to benefit from the extensive media coverage of Ellen DeGeneres's plan to come out on her show. Network executives have rejected this advertising, however, indicating that they believe exposure to such advertisements would not be appropriate for children. These executives evidently have no such qualms over ads that associate leisure cruises with heterosexual romance. The episode in which Ellen came out was scheduled to air at a later time than usual, presumably because of the "adult content."

44. Nancy Wilson, *Our Tribe*, 26–28.

45. Ibid., 28.

46. Ibid.

47. Emery S. Hetrick and A. Damien Martin, "Developmental Issues and Their Resolution for Gay and Lesbian Adolescents," 28.

48. Alice Walker, *Possessing the Secret of Joy* (New York: Harcourt Brace Jovanovich, 1992), 279.

49. Nancy Wilson, *Our Tribe*, 25.

50. Ibid.

51. In this sense, certain factions of the lesbian and gay political establishment may be reenacting the political folly of certain early feminist leaders, who incorporated virulent racism into their political agendas in order to appeal to the racist agendas of men with political clout. The same motivations undoubtedly contributed to the tendency of early "second-wave" feminism to dissociate itself from lesbian issues.

52. Nancy Wilson, *Our Tribe*, 25.

53. Richard R. Troiden, "Self, Self-Concept, Identity, and Homosexual Identity: Constructs in Need of Definition and Differentiation," *Journal of Homosexuality* 10 (1984): 106.

54. Carter Heyward, *Touching Our Strength*, 27.

55. Joan Sophie, "Internalized Homophobia and Lesbian Identity," 57.

56. Nancy Wilson, *Our Tribe*, 43.

57. Ibid.

58. Audre Lorde, "The Transformation of Silence into Language and Action," in *Issues in Feminism: An Introduction to Women's Studies*, ed. Sheila Ruth (Mountain View, Calif.: Mayfield Publishing, 1990), 139.

59. Nancy Wilson, *Our Tribe*, 49.

60. Corinne Squire, introduction to *Women and AIDS: Psychological Perspectives*, ed. Corinne Squire (London: Sage Publications, 1993), 10.

61. The most spectacular recent example of this tendency is probably Elaine Showalter's *Hystories: Hysterical Epidemics and Modern Culture* (New York, Columbia University Press, 1997). Showalter lumps recovered memories of childhood sexual abuse with Chronic Fatigue Syndrome, Gulf War Syndrome, and reports of alien abduction—generalizing that they are all contemporary hysterias brought on by millennial anxiety.

62. I remain uncomfortable with the term *survivor* but employ it here for lack of a better alternative. Although it is certainly a better choice than *victim*, there are drawbacks that disturb me. On the one hand, because it implies that the trauma is in the past, it diminishes the significance of ongoing suffering. On the other, it projects an image of "hanging on by one's fingernails" and thus fails to acknowledge the strength, healing, and growth toward thriving that are present in the lives of many women with histories of abuse.

63. L. J. "Tess" Tessier, "Women Sexually Abused as Children: The Spiritual Consequences," *Second Opinion* 17 (1992): 15.

64. My thanks to Carol Fitzpatrick for this and many other insights.

65. This poem was written by Terri Johnson and first appeared in L. J. Tessier, "Spiritual Consequences of Child Sexual Abuse," *Second Opinion* 13. Terri has since changed her name to Tara McKibben and asks that her true name be included.

66. E. Sue Blume, *Secret Survivors: Uncovering Incest and Its Aftereffects in Women* (New York: John Wiley and Sons, 1990); Sandra Butler, *Conspiracy of Silence: The Trauma of Incest* (San Francisco: New Glide Publications, 1978); Mary deYoung, "Self-Injurious Behavior in Incest Victims: A Research Note," *Child Welfare* 61 (1982): 577–84; David Finkelhor, *Child Sexual Abuse: New Theory and Research* (New York: Free Press, 1984); David Finkelhor, "The Trauma of Child Sexual Abuse: Two Models," *Journal of Interpersonal Violence* 2 (1987): 348–366; Pat Gilmartin, *Rape, Incest, and Child Sexual Abuse: Consequences and Recovery* (New York: Garland Publishing, 1994); M. Gorcey, J. M. Santiago, and F. McCall-Perez, "Psychological Consequences for Women Sexually Abused in Childhood," *Social Psychiatry* 21 (1986): 129–133; Shane M. Murphy et al., "Current Psychological Functioning of Child Sexual Assault Survivors: A Community Study," *Journal of Interpersonal Violence* 3 (1988): 55–79; Leonard Shengold, *Soul Murder: The Effects of Childhood Abuse and Deprivation* (New Haven: Yale University Press, 1989).

67. Pat Gilmartin, *Rape, Incest, and Child Sexual Abuse*, 71.

68. Bennet G. Braun, "Psychotherapy of the Survivor of Incest with a Dissociative Disorder," *Psychiatric Clinics of North America* 12 (1989): 307–324; L. J. "Tess" Tessier, "Women Sexually Abused as Children," 15.

69. Helen Vanderbilt, "Incest: A Chilling Report," *Lear's*, February 1992, 52.

70. Ibid.

71. Roland Summit, "The Child Sexual Abuse Accommodation Syndrome," *Child Abuse & Neglect* 7 (1983): 183.

72. Roland C. Summit, "The Centrality of Victimization: Regaining the Focal Point of Recovery for Survivors of Child Sexual Abuse," *Psychiatric Clinics of North America* 12 (1989): 413.

73. Ibid., 414.

74. Ibid., 422.

75. Ibid., 415.

76. Kathy Steele, "Sitting with the Shattered Soul," *Journal of Personal Exploration and Psychotherapy* 17 (1987): 19. Some recent publications contest the validity of these memories. Critics cite lack of corroborating evidence and blame therapists and the media for generating a witch hunt. These positions do not account for the significant number of survivors who experienced flashback memories of severe abuse prior to seeking therapy or hearing media accounts.

77. Ibid.

78. Ibid., 21.

79. Ibid.

80. Ibid.

81. Ibid., 22.

82. Ibid.

83. Christine Courtois, quoted by Mary Sykes Wylie in "The Shadow of a Doubt," *Family Therapy Networker*, September / October 1993, 28.

84. Roland Summit, "The Centrality of Victimization," 416.

85. L. J. Tessier, "Spiritual Consequences of Child Sexual Abuse," 15–16.

86. A network news television program recently aired a story featuring a woman who claims to have been manipulated into falsely believing she had been raped by her father. Whether or not the reported circumstances of the case are factual, the media, responding to the culture's enormous desire to deny, is much more likely to cover stories like this than to focus on the many documented and undisputed cases of child sexual abuse.

87. Judith Lewis Herman, "Presuming to Know the Truth," *Moving Forward* 3 (1994): 12.

88. Ibid., 22.

89. Mary Sykes Wylie, "The Shadow of a Doubt," *Family Therapy Networker*, 70.

90. Ibid., 22. Wylie is citing an interview with Harold Lief, a psychiatrist on the board of the False Memory Syndrome Foundation.

91. Linda Meyer Williams, "Adult Memories of Childhood Abuse: Preliminary Findings from a Longitudinal Study," *APSAC Advisor* (1992): 19–21.

92. Ibid., 20.

93. Mary Sykes Wylie, "The Shadow of a Doubt," 28.

94. Ibid., 27.

95. Judith Lewis Herman, "The Abuses of Memory," *Mother Jones*, March / April 1993, 4.

96. Kathy Steele, "Sitting with the Shattered Soul," 22.

97. Ibid.

98. Quoted by Mary Sykes Wylie in "The Shadow of a Doubt," 28.

99. Ibid., 29.

100. Keith Russell Ablow, "Recovered Memories: Fact or Fantasy?," *Washington Post Health*, June 22, 1993, 7.

101. Judith Lewis Herman and Emily Schatzow, "Recovery and Verification of Memories of Childhood Sexual Trauma," *Psychoanalytic Psychology* 4 (1987): 10–11. In *Making Monsters: False Memories, Psychotherapy, and Sexual Hysteria* (New York: Scribner's, 1994), Richard Ofshe and Ethan Watters critique this study as well as the one conducted by Linda Meyer Williams (cited above). Although they do raise some relevant concerns, they offer no evidence that invalidates the findings in either study. In fact, recent critics of recovered memory offer little or no evidence that recovered memories of child sexual abuse are *not* true. Rather, they stress evidence that memory is unreliable and may be subject to suggestion or distortion. Again, these claims do not address the many cases in which recovered memories precede therapeutic treatment. Neither therapists nor the media made these memories.

102. Ibid., 4.

103. Judith Lewis Herman, "Presuming to Know the Truth," 13.

104. Ibid.

105. Mary Daly defines "dis-ease" as the complex of emotions such as guilt, anxiety, depression, and frustration that are embedded in women who are separated from their Selves by the "separaters / fracturers / batterers / flatterers who control their lives." See Mary Daly, *Websters' First New Intergalactic Wickedary of the English Language*, 194, 219.

106. Carter Heyward, *Touching Our Strength*, 122.

107. Cheryl Townsend Gilkes, "The 'Loves' and 'Troubles' of African-American Women's Bodies: The Womanist Challenge to Cultural Humiliation and Community Ambivalence," 235.

108. Mary Hunt, *Fierce Tenderness*, 45.

109. Alexandra Juhasz, "Knowing AIDS through the Televised Science Documentary," in *Women and AIDS: Psychological Perspectives*, ed. Corinne Squire (London: Sage Publications, 1993), 150.

110. Gena Corea, *The Invisible Epidemic: The Story of Women and AIDS* (New York: HarperCollins, 1992), 4.

111. Ibid., 5.

112. Ibid., 40.

113. Ibid., 17.

114. Ibid., 210.

115. Ibid., 76. This change in the surveillance definition also resulted in many newly diagnosed AIDS cases among blacks, Latinos, and IV-drug users as well as a significant overall increase in reported AIDS cases. Prior to the 1987 revision, homosexual and bisexual men represented 67 percent of AIDS cases meeting the CDC definition. In the first year following the change in the definition, IV-drug users rose from 24 to 36 percent of such cases, Hispanics from 13 to 16 percent and women from 2.6 to 3.6 percent. Still, many conditions appearing in women and drug users were left out of the definition (p. 77).

116. Patricia Kloser and Jane Maclean Craig, *The Women's HIV Sourcebook: A Guide to Better Health and Well-being* (Dallas: Taylor Publishing, 1994), 15, 331.

117. Gena Corea, *The Invisible Epidemic*, 253.

118. Ibid., 41.

119. Corrine Squire, introduction to *Women and AIDS: Psychological Perspectives*, 1, citing J. Chin, "Global Estimates of AIDS Cases and HIV Infections: 1990," *AIDS* 4 (1990): S277–283.

120. Corinne Squire, introduction, 4, citing Centers for Disease Control, "The Second 100,000 Cases of Acquired Immunodeficiency Syndrome—United States, June 1981–December 1991," *Morbidity and Mortality Weekly Reports* 41, 28–29, January 17, 1992; Public Health Laboratory Service (1992); *Communicable Disease Report* 2 (1992).

121. Corinne Squire, introduction, 4, citing M. Merson, "Foreword," *AIDS Supplement* 1, *AIDS in Africa* 5 (1991): i–ii.

122. Corinne Squire, introduction, 1, citing J. Chin, "Global Estimates of AIDS Cases and HIV Infections."

123. Centers for Disease Control, *HIV/AIDS Surveillance* (Atlanta: U.S. Department of Health and Human Services, 1992).

124. Corinne Squire, introduction, 4.

125. In the early years of awareness, the disease was sometimes called GRID—Gay Related Immune Deficiency.

126. Centers for Disease Control, 1991; Hortensia Amaro, "Reproductive Choice in the Age of AIDS: Policy and Counselling Issues," in *Women and AIDS: Psychological Perspectives*, ed. Corinne Squire, 25.

127. Tamsin Wilton, *Antibody Politic: AIDS and Society* (Cheltenham, England: New Clarion Press, 1992), 65; Corinne Squire, introduction, 6. The reason for this seems fairly straightforward: while both semen and vaginal fluid contain infectious quantities of the virus, the means of transmission from male to female is much more direct and involves a much higher quantity.

128. Mary Hunt, *Fierce Tenderness*, 45.

129. Corinne Squire, introduction, 8.

130. Gena Corea, *The Invisible Epidemic*, 42; Tamsin Wilton, *Antibody Politic*, 58.

131. Tamsin Wilton, *Antibody Politic*, 58.

132. Corinne Squire, introduction, 1–2.

133. Ibid., 2.

134. Tamsin Wilton, *Antibody Politic*, 49.

135. Hortensia Amaro, "Reproductive Choice in the Age of AIDS," 22.

136. Tamsin Wilton, *Antibody Politic*, 49.

137. Ibid., 50. Wilton also makes the interesting point that healthy low-fat foods are marketed to women by focusing on their concern for the health of their family members. However, when women are themselves targeted as consumers of low-fat foods, the marketing is based on the claim that these foods will make women more attractive to men.

138. Ibid., 51. The medical establishment has been notoriously unresponsive on medical concerns particular to women, including increasing levels of heart disease and breast cancer. The traditional focus on the male body inhibits deeper understanding of female physiology; at the same time, medical practitioners frequently assume that the basis for women's physical illness is psychological.

139. Ibid.

140. Ibid., 52. The medical establishment regulates the entire process of giving birth, from conception to delivery, while actively resisting alternatives such as home delivery and midwifery.

141. Gena Corea, *The Invisible Epidemic*, 131.

142. Of course, this ill-treatment was not limited to women. I know firsthand of a situation in which a young man hospitalized with serious HIV-related disease in a large, metropolitan-area hospital was neither bathed nor fed for three days. As a recent arrival in a large city, he had no one to intervene. Had he not received a visit from an out-of-town friend, he would simply have been left to die.

143. Tamsin Wilton, *Antibody Politic*, 57.

144. Gena Corea, *The Invisible Epidemic*, 26.

145. Corinne Squire, introduction, 5.

146. Ibid.

147. Tamsin Wilton, *Antibody Politic*, 63.

148. Gena Corea, *The Invisible Epidemic*, 128.

149. For a thorough discussion of the scope of the problem see Rita Nakashima Brock and Susan Brooks Thistlethwaite, *Casting Stones: Prostitution and Liberation in Asia and the United States* (Minneapolis: Fortress Press, 1996).

150. Tamsin Wilton, *Antibody Politic*, 56.

151. Gena Corea, *The Invisible Epidemic*, 44.

152. Tamsin Wilton, *Antibody Politic*, 61.

153. Ibid., 60–61.

154. Gena Corea, *The Invisible Epidemic*, 87.

155. Ibid., 87.

156. Tamsin Wilton, *Antibody Politic*, 61.

157. Ibid., 62.

158. Ibid.; also see Lorraine Sherr, "Testing in Pregnancy," in *Women and AIDS: Psychological Perspectives*, ed. Corinne Squire, 58.

159. Gena Corea, *The Invisible Epidemic*, 149.

160. Corinne Squire, introduction, 6.

161. Tamsin Wilton, *Antibody Politic*, 67.

162. JoAnn Loulan is one author who does specifically discuss the use of dental dams and other techniques for safe lesbian sex.

163. Tamsin Wilton, *Antibody Politic*, 68.

164. Mary Hunt, *Fierce Tenderness*, 45.

165. Corinne Squire, introduction, 67.

166. Ibid., 68.

167. Ibid., 69.

168. Hortensia Amaro, "Reproductive Choice in the Age of AIDS," 28.

169. Ibid., 34.

170. Tamsin Wilton, "Antibody Politic," 71.

171. Hortensia Amaro, "Reproductive Choice in the Age of AIDS," 23.

172. Gena Corea, *The Invisible Epidemic*, 113.

173. Ibid., 109–110.

174. Hortensia Amaro, "Reproductive Choice in the Age of AIDS," 23.

175. Gena Corea, *The Invisible Epidemic*, 111.

176. E. Anne Lown, Karen Winkler, Robert E. Fullilove, and Mindy Thompson Fullilove, "'Tossin' and 'Tweakin': Women's Consciousness in the Crack Culture," in *Women and AIDS: Psychological Perspectives*, ed. Corinne Squire, 90.

177. Gena Corea, *The Invisible Epidemic*, 65.

178. The deputy chief of the Community Research Branch of the National Institute on Drug Abuse estimates that 80 percent of female drug addicts have been sexually abused (Corea, *The Invisible Epidemic*, 65). There is also a high correlation between HIV-positive status and histories of sexual abuse. Corea cities research indicating that women sexually abused as children are twice as likely to be HIV infected and that sexual assault survivors show a 40 percent frequency rate for HIV (217).

179. Gena Corea, *The Invisible Epidemic*, 68–69.

180. Ibid., 67.

181. E. Anne Lown et al., "'Tossin' and 'Tweakin,'" 91.

182. Ibid., 95.

183. Ibid., 97.

184. Alexandra Juhasz, "Knowing AIDS through the Televised Science Documentary," 151.

185. Patricia Kloser and Jane Maclean Craig, *The Woman's HIV Sourcebook: A Guide to Better Health and Well-being*.

1. Mark 14:66–72, Luke 22:56–62, John 18:15–18, 25–27.

2. Matt. 26:72.

3. Matt. 26:73.

4. Carter Heyward, *Touching Our Strength*, 32.

5. In *Perfect Enemies: The Religious Right, the Gay Movement, and the Politics of the 1990s* (New York: Crown Publishers, 1996), John Gallagher and Chris Bull chronicle the massive resistance to gay rights orchestrated by the religious right in the 1990s. See also Gary F. Kelly, *Sexuality Today: The Human Perspective* (Guilford: Dushkin Publishing Group, 1988). A number of contemporary evangelical organizations actively oppose any level of tolerance of gay and lesbian lifestyles within their religious institutions. One particularly dangerous trend is evangelical outreach to African American religious institutions, which encourages the view that homosexuals are threatening the legitimate rights of people of color by claiming the status of a minority group and asking for "special rights."

6. It is important to acknowledge and honor the exceptions to these trends. For example, the January 1992, "Report of the Reconstructionist Commission on Homosexuality" called for "complete equality of gay and lesbian Jews in all aspects of Jewish life." The controversial report entitled "The Church and Human Sexuality: A Lutheran Perspective" by the Division for Church in Society, Department for Studies of the Evangelical Lutheran Church in America, called for compassion and understanding toward gay and lesbian persons and even supported a position of "open affirmation of gay and lesbian persons and their mutually loving, just, committed relationships of fidelity." In addition, the Unitarian Universalist Association demonstrates an active concern for fostering acceptance, inclusion, understanding, and equality for all gay, lesbian, transgender, and bisexual individuals, as well as confronting homophobia, through its Office of Bisexual, Gay, Lesbian, and Transgender Concerns.

7. Andre Guindon, *The Sexual Creators*, 159.

8. Ibid.

9. Ibid.

10. Ibid., 186.

11. This relationship between loss and transformation is explored in some detail in Craig O'Neill and Kathleen Ritter, *Coming Out Within: Stages of Spiritual Awakening for Lesbians and Gay Men* (San Francisco: HarperSanFrancisco, 1992).

12. Ibid.

13. Ibid., 180.

14. Betty Berzon, "Developing a Positive Gay Identity," *Positively Gay* (Los Angeles: Mediamix Associates, 1979).

15. Ibid., 2.

16. Ibid., 3.

17. See, for example, the writings of Carter Heyward, Nancy Wilson, and Mary Daly. There are also some interesting perspectives set out in *Que(e)rying Religion: A Critical Anthology*, ed. Gary David Comstock and Susan E. Henking (New York: Continuum, 1997).

18. Andre Guindon, *The Sexual Creators*.

19. Ibid., 160.

20. Ibid., 163.

21. Ibid., 165.

22. Ibid.

23. Ibid.

24. Ibid.

25. Ibid., 165–166.

26. Ibid., 167.

27. Carol Gilligan, *In a Different Voice: Psychological Theory and Women's Development* (Cambridge: Harvard University Press, 1982).

28. For early feminist theories on the possible origin of women's tendencies in this direction, see, for example, Nancy Chodorow, *The Reproduction of Mothering: Psychoanalysis and the Sociology of Gender* (Berkeley: University of California Press, 1978) and Dorothy Dinnerstein, *The Mermaid and the Minotaur: Sexual Arrangements and Human Malaise* (New York: Harper & Row, 1976).

29. See Chapter 3, note 41.

30. Christine Downing reminds me, however, that this tendency may be even more common among gay men, perhaps because separations are often less painful.

31. Some may contend that this happens because the relationship was basically always a friendship rather than a passionate love affair. This theory is related to the contention that women are really not that interested in sex. My experience, and that of lesbians I know, does not bear this out.

32. Adrienne Rich, XIII of "Twenty-One Love Poems" from "Dream of a Common Language" in *The Fact of a Doorframe: Poems Selected and New 1950–1984* (New York: W. W. Norton, 1984). Elsewhere, Rich writes:

> An honorable human relationship . . . is a process, delicate,
> violent, often terrifying to both persons involved, a process
> of refining the truths they can tell each other.
>
> It is important to do this because it breaks down
> self-delusion and isolation.
>
> It is important to do this because in so doing we do justice
> to our own complexity.

It is important to do this because we can count on so few
people to go that hard way with us.

"Women and Honor: Some Notes on Lying,"
On Lies, Secrets, and Silence: Selected Prose 1966–1978.

33. Hall Carpenter Archives Lesbian Oral History Group, *Inventing Ourselves: Lesbian Life Stories* (London: Routledge, 1989).

34. Susan J. Wolfe and Julia Penelope Stanley, eds., *The Coming Out Stories* (Watertown, Mass.: Persephone Press, 1980), 202.

35. The term is "misappropriated" because Kierkegaard uses it in a different sense. See, for example, *The Concept of Anxiety*, ed. and trans. Reidar Thomte in collaboration with Albert B. Anderson (Princeton: Princeton University Press, 1980), 46.

36. Nancy Wilson, *Our Tribe*, 11.

37. Ibid., 23.

38. Judith McDaniel, "Coming Out: Ten Years of Change," in *The Coming Out Stories*, ed. Susan J. Wolfe and Julia Penelope Stanley, 94.

39. Betsy Petersen, *Dancing with Daddy: A Childhood Lost and a Life Regained* (New York: Bantam Books), 177.

40. Ellen Bass and Laura Davis, *The Courage to Heal* (New York: Harper & Row, 1988), 404.

41. From act 3 ("Don Juan in Hell") of *Man and Superman* by George Bernard Shaw (New York, Penguin Books, [1903] 1977), 133.

42. Joan Timmerman, *Sexuality and Spiritual Growth*, 61.

43. "Discovering Existential Comfort," paper presented at Southeast regional meeting of the American Academy of Religion, March 20, 1994.

44. Ellen Bass and Laura Davis, *The Courage to Heal*, 413.

45. Kathy Steele, "Discovering Existential Comfort."

46. L. J. "Tess" Tessier, "Women Sexually Abused as Children," 17.

47. Tara McKibben. She has given permission to use this quote, which first appeared in L. J. "Tess" Tessier, "Women Sexually Abused as Children," 16, and requested that her true name be cited.

48. Kathy Steele, "Sitting with the Shattered Soul." It is important to note, however, that not all survivors report this shattering. Another survivor states, "They got everything else, but they never got my soul. They couldn't touch my soul."

49. L. J. "Tess" Tessier, "Women Sexually Abused as Children," 17.

50. Leonard Shengold, *Soul Murder: The Effects of Childhood Abuse and Deprivation* (New Haven: Yale University Press, 1989). See L. J. "Tess" Tessier, "Women Sexually Abused as Children," 17.

51. L. J. "Tess" Tessier, "Women Sexually Abused as Children," 20.

52. Ibid., 16.

53. Sam Kirschner, Diana Adile Kirschner, and Richard L. Rappaport, *Working with Adult Incest Survivors / The Healing Journey* (New York: Brunner / Mazel, 1993), 59.

54. Ibid., 60.

55. Ibid., 57.

56. Ibid., 58.

57. Ibid.

58. L. J. "Tess" Tessier, "Women Sexually Abused as Children," 15.

59. Ibid., 21.

60. Marie Marshall Fortune, *Sexual Violence: The Unmentionable Sin* (Cleveland: Pilgrim Press, 1983), 195.

61. Ibid., 197.

62. Ibid., 196–198.

63. Ibid., 198. Several Christian feminist theologians have challenged traditional applications of resurrection theology to sexual violence, suggesting, for example, that the emphasis on the redemptive power of suffering perpetuates cycles of abuse (see Joanne Carlson Brown and Carole R. Bohn, eds., *Christianity, Patriarchy and Abuse: A Feminist Critique* [New York: Pilgrim Press, 1989]).

64. Marie Marshall Fortune, *Sexual Violence,* 209.

65. Ibid.

66. Ibid., 210.

67. Sheila Redmond, "Christian 'Virtues' and Recovery from Child Sexual Abuse" in *Christianity, Patriarchy and Abuse,* ed. Joanne Carlson Brown and Carole R. Bohn, 75.

68. Ellen Bass and Laura Davis, *The Courage to Heal,* 398.

69. David R. Blumenthal, *Facing the Abusing God: A Theology of Protest* (Louisville, Ky.: Westminster / John Knox Press, 1993), 251.

70. Ibid., 249.

71. Ibid.

72. Ibid., 258.

73. Ibid.

74. Patricia Reis, *Through the Goddess,* 113.

75. Ibid., 117.

76. Ibid.

77. Ibid., 118.

78. Ibid., 119.

79. Irene Diamond and Gloria Feman Orenstein, *Reweaving the World.* Also see Judith Plant, ed., *Healing the Wounds: The Promise of Ecofeminism* (Philadelphia: New Society Publishers, 1989) and Carol Adams, ed., *Ecofeminism and the Sacred* (New York: Continuum, 1993).

80. Ellen Bass and Laura Davis, *The Courage to Heal,* 379–380.

81. Ynestra King, "Healing the Wounds: Feminism, Ecology, and the Nature / Culture Dualism," 117.

82. Ibid., 118–119.

83. Ibid., 119.

84. Ellen Bass and Laura Davis, *The Courage to Heal*, 455.

85. Ibid., 457.

86. Linda T. Sanford, *Strong at the Broken Places: Overcoming the Trauma of Childhood Abuse* (New York: Random House, 1990).

87. Ellen Bass and Laura Davis, *The Courage to Heal*, 399.

88. Ibid., 393.

89. Audre Lorde, *The Cancer Journals* (New York: Spinsters Ink, 1980), 11.

90. Linda Singer, *Erotic Welfare: Sexual Theory and Politics in the Age of Epidemic*, ed. Judith Butler and Maureen MacGrogan (New York: Routledge, 1993), 62.

91. Ibid., 63.

92. Ibid.

93. Ibid., 65.

94. John Backe, "A Serious and Special Opportunity for Ministry," in *AIDS, Ethics and Religion: Embracing a World of Suffering*, ed. Kenneth R. Overberg (Maryknoll, N.Y.: Orbis Books, 1994), 251.

95. Ibid., 252.

96. Andrew M. Greeley, "Religion and Attitudes toward AIDS Policy," in *AIDS, Ethics and Religion: Embracing a World of Suffering*, 126–130.

97. Ibid.

98. Newell J. Wert, "The Biblical and Theological Basis for Risking Compassion and Care for AIDS Patients," in *AIDS, Ethics and Religion: Embracing a World of Suffering*, 238.

99. Ibid.

100. Ibid.

101. William A. Doubleday and Suki Terada Ports, "Fighting AIDS and HIV Together," in *Envisioning the New City: A Reader on Urban Ministry*, ed. Eleanor Scott Meyers (Louisville, Ky.: Westminster / John Knox Press, 1992), 282–283.

102. Ibid.

103. Ibid., 282.

104. Andrea Rudd and Darien Taylor, eds., *Positive Women* (Toronto: Second Story Press, 1992), 79–80.

105. Ibid.

106. Ibid., 102–103.

107. Ibid., 104.

108. Ibid., 103.

109. Ibid., 104.

110. Ibid., 105.

111. Ibid., 104.

112. Ibid., 105–106.

113. Audre Lorde, *Cancer Journals*, 9.

114. Andrea Rudd and Darien Taylor, eds., *Positive Women*, 129.

115. Ibid., 91.

116. Ibid., 22–23.

117. Ibid., 69–70.

118. Ibid., 206.

119. William A. Doubleday and Suki Terada Ports, "Fighting AIDS and HIV Together," 280.

120. Ibid., 156.

121. Ibid., 212, 214.

122. Ibid., 24.

123. Ibid., 36–37.

124. Ibid., 86.

125. An anonymous woman quoted by Gillian Walker, "An AIDS Journal," in *The Evolving Therapist: Ten Years of the Family Therapy Networker*, ed. Richard Simon et al. (Washington, D.C.: Family Therapy Network; New York: Guilford Press, 1992), 52.

126. Ibid., 46.

127. Ibid., 48.

128. Ibid., 49.

129. John Backe, "AIDS: A Serious and Special Opportunity for Ministry," 253.

130. Audre Lorde, *The Cancer Journals*, 21.

131. Ibid., 16.

132. Ibid., 25.

133. Linda Singer, *Erotic Welfare*, 65.

134. Ibid., 82.

135. Ibid., 67.

136. Carole Campbell, "Women and AIDS," in *AIDS, Ethics and Religion*, 93.

137. *Mashambanzou* is a Shona word meaning, literally, "the time of day when elephants wash themselves"; less literally, it is translated as "dawn of a new day" (frontispiece of *Positive Women*).

138. Andrea Rudd and Darien Taylor, eds., *Positive Women*, 28.

139. Ibid., 166.

140. Ibid., 188–189.

141. Ibid., 194.

142. Ibid., 59.

143. Ibid., 171.

144. Ibid., 188.

145. Kenneth R. Overberg, ed., *AIDS, Ethics and Religion*, 274.

146. Newell J. Wirt, "The Biblical and Theological Basis for Risking Compassion and Care for AIDS Patients," in *AIDS, Ethics and Religion*, 240.

147. Quoted by Mary Elizabeth O'Brien in *Living with HIV: Experiment in Courage* (New York: Auburn House, 1992), 50.

148. Andrea Rudd and Darien Taylor, eds., *Positive Women*, 199.

Epilogue

1. Ursula Le Guin, "She Unnames Them," in *Hear the Silence: Stories by Women of Myth, Magic and Renewal*, ed. Irene Zahava (Trumansburg, N.Y.: Crossing Press, 1986), 193–194.

Index

Campbell, Joseph, 30

Cass, Vivian, 97–100, 102

Chaos, 3, 25, 41, 42, 55, 189; chaotic, 16, 40; control of, 20; and the wild, 19, 210, 211, 212, 213

Children, 113–15; and AIDS, 192; and sexual abuse, 123, 124, 181

Child sexual abuse, 118, 128, 155, 176, 177, 180; denial of, 119, 120–36; perpetrators of, 124, 128, 133–34, 181, 183, 184; power dynamics of, 132–34, 135; as sacrilege, 18, 67; severe, 125, 180; "sex abuse industry," 128; spiritual consequences, 182. *See also* Survivors of child sexual abuse; Women sexually abused as children

Christ, Carol, 48, 54

Christianity, 37, 41, 45, 57, 158; on AIDS, 191, 192–94; feminist, 68–75, 76; and homosexuality, 161, 165, 166; and sex-spirit relationship, 78; on sex, 58–59, 60, 62, 63–68. *See also* Augustine; Christian theologians; Feminism; Jesus

Christian theologians, 45; sex-positive views, 63–68

Coming out, 104–11, 116, 160, 162, 164, 172, 174

Congruence, 98; and sexual identity, 99, 100, 117, 160, 162, 168

Corea, Gena, 140, 141, 145

Courage to Heal, The, 7

Courtois, Christine, 131

Culpepper, Emily, 76–77

Daly, Mary, 75–76

Demeter, 25–26, 52, 53

Denial, 1, 3, 18, 34, 85, 118–19, 158, 162; of child sexual abuse, 2, 13, 18, 120–36; consequences of, 10, 11, 13, 22, 93–94, 96, 131, 158; culturally imposed, 2, 12, 17, 19; definition of, 9–10, 41, 93–94; of eros, 16, 36, 41, 90, 91, 96, 145; forms of, 11, 106–7, 137; of HIV-positive women, 2, 13, 18, 139–55; and identity, 97, 98; of lesbians, 2, 13, 18, 99, 101, 103, 106–8, 110, 112, 113, 115, 116–17, 164; overcoming, 8, 40, 47, 63, 103, 175, 176; and projection, 41–42, 85, 100. *See also* Lesbians; Seeming; Survivors of child sexual abuse; Women positive for HIV/AIDS; Women sexually abused as children

Dissociation, 13, 120, 123, 178, 180

Dissociative Identity Disorder (DID), 123, 180

Downing, Christine, 26, 28, 49, 53, 54

Dwyer, John, 64, 67

Eastern religious traditions, 45, 78–79, 81–82, 85–86, 87, 89, 90. *See also* Buddhism; Hinduism; Tantrism

Embodiment, 42, 65, 66, 70–71, 72–73, 135; embodied, 17, 20, 65; and women, 28–29, 38, 48, 87

Eros, 37, 38–41, 90, 155, 212; characteristics of, 29–31; and death, 69–70, 191, 192; definition of, 29; as deity, 15, 30, 36; in Eastern religions, 79, 80, 83–86; erotic bond, 169; in feminist theology, 68–74, 77; Greek, 32–35, 36–37, 78; and incarnation, 65; and joy, 25, 84, 116; in spiritual life, 21, 29, 46, 116; theoretical views of, 29–30, 31–32, 34, 36, 38, 41–42, 76. *See also* Erotic power

Erotic power, 6, 17, 154, 165, 192; fear of, 17, 39, 40, 42, 62, 63, 90; of goddesses, 23, 25, 26, 46, 48, 53, 185; and love, 32–

Troiden, Richard, 116

Underworld, 19, 42, 55. *See also* Hell

Walker, Alice, 115
Whirlwind, 2, 15, 16, 17, 19, 22, 25, 43,
 100, 117, 135, 157, 158, 159, 209, 210
Whitehead, Evelyn Eaton and John, 64
Wild, the, 2, 16, 17, 18, 210–16
Williams, Linda Meyer, 129
Wilson, Nancy, 113–14, 115–17, 118, 174
Wilton, Tamsin, 147
Woman, 57; fear of, 40–41; as "other,"
 140
Womanist theology, 68, 77
Women: African American, 74, 75, 76;
 of color, 134, 138; fear of, 40–41; third
 world, 75, 134
Women positive for HIV/AIDS, 2, 3, 10,
 11, 13, 18, 38, 89, 118–19; defined,
 12, 135–54; and drug use, 138, 151–
 53; invisibility of, 140–44; ironies of,
 138, 145–44, 145; and lesbians, 148–
 49; and prostitution, 145, 146–47;
 reproductive issues, 149–50; sexual
 identity of, 195–96, 199–201; spirituality of, 138, 153–55, 194–207; statistics regarding, 141–43. *See also*
 Denial; Identity; Sexuality;
 Spirituality
Women sexually abused as children, 2,
 3, 10, 11, 13, 18, 38, 89, 118, 135, 155,
 175; defined, 12; and forgiveness,
 182–84; identity of, 123, 131, 133, 134,
 135, 179, 180; spirituality of, 175–90;
 symptoms, 122. *See also* Denial; Identity; Sexuality; Spirituality; Survivors
 of child sexual abuse